RTKL LIBRARY

Syntax of Landscape
The Landscape Architecture
of Peter Latz and Partners

Udo Weilacher

Syntax of Landscape
The Landscape Architecture
of Peter Latz and Partners

Birkhäuser
Basel · Boston · Berlin

Layout and cover design: Peter Willberg, London
Translation: Michael Robinson, London
Translation of Preface: Julian Reisenberger, Weimar
Copyediting of the English edition: Jessica Read, Lindenberg

This book is also available in a German edition:
ISBN 978-3-7643-7614-7

Bibliographic information published by
The Deutsche Nationalbibliothek
The Deutsche Nationalbibliothek lists this publication in the Deutsche Nationalbibliografie; detailed bibliographic data are available in the Internet at http://dnb.ddb.de.

Library of Congress Control Number: 2007932819

This work is subject to copyright. All rights are reserved, whether the whole or part of the material is concerned, specifically the rights of translation, reprinting, re-use of illustrations, recitation, broadcasting, reproduction on microfilms or in other ways, and storage in data banks. For any kind of use, permission of the copyright owner must be obtained.

© 2008 Birkhäuser Verlag AG
Basel · Boston · Berlin
P.O.Box 133, CH-4010 Basel, Switzerland
Part of Springer Science+Business Media

Printed on acid-free paper produced from chlorine-free pulp. TCF ∞

Printed in Germany
ISBN-13 978-3-7643-7615-4

www.birkhauser.ch

9 8 7 6 5 4 3 2 1

Contents

7 Preface

9 **Landscape architecture as cultural valorization**

33 **Layers of information. How does landscape work?**
34 University of Marburg on Lahnberge
46 Ulm Science City on Eselsberg
56 Plateau de Kirchberg, Luxembourg

79 **Dealing with "bad places"**
82 Saarbrücken Harbour Island
102 Duisburg-Nord Landscape Park
134 Parco Dora, Turin
148 Hiriya Mountain, Tel Aviv

167 **Design as experimental invention**

186 Notes
188 Project data
191 Illustration credits
192 Further selected projects and competitions
195 Selected publications
197 Exhitions and catalogues
198 On Peter Latz and Partners

Preface

The right degree of closeness is the right amount of detachment...

... this is what one repeats to oneself as an author when trying to establish the best possible relation to one's subject, whilst in actual fact oscillating between that enthusiastic curiosity that fuels writing, and the necessary critical reflection. In the end, the hope is to infect the reader with the same joy of discovery and understanding of gardens and of landscapes that ultimately moved me to put pen to paper. I say "ultimately" because, more so than ever before, in this book it has been particularly difficult to find the right degree of closeness through the right amount of detachment – this is not just a book on contemporary landscape architecture written by a teacher, but also a book written by a student about his teacher.

For almost seven years, from 1986 to 1993, I studied landscape architecture at the Technische Universität München-Weihenstephan in Freising and I was inevitably influenced in my professional thinking and actions by Peter Latz's conceptual approaches. The search for critical distance, for an individual standpoint and new perspectives in landscape architecture was already prevalent some 20 years ago, as I wanted to push beyond the know-how I had been invested with. That said, it would be wrong to deny that my studies at Weihenstephan, and Peter Latz in particular, have had a lasting influence on my work.

The awareness of one's own partiality and the knowledge of how difficult it would be to bring together the richness of Peter Latz's work and the complexity of his thinking in a single publication has for years held me back from responding to Anneliese and Peter Latz's willingness for me to write this book. Why then now, just when Peter Latz is preparing to relinquish his teaching and research at the TU München in spring 2008, and at a time when a new generation, in particular Tilman Latz, is gaining influence in the office of Latz + Partner?

To this day I have no truly plausible answers to these questions. It seems that, over the years, so much of the aforementioned 'fuel' has accumulated that it would no longer be prudent to delay ignition any longer, to stick with the metaphor. New generations of landscape architecture students (not only at the TU München and the Leibniz Universität Hannover) have discovered the work of Peter Latz and bemoan, quite rightly, and just as we did 20 years earlier, the lack of a comprehensive publication on the work of Latz + Partner from which one can learn more of their visionary design and planning approaches, and of the theoretical and conceptual background to the projects undertaken at the office in Ampertshausen.

The *Syntax of Landscape* aims to contribute to an understanding of important developments in international landscape architecture. The objective was not to compile a comprehensive, annotated and illustrated catalogue of projects but to discuss some of Peter Latz's work and theoretical approaches with respect to their manifold interrelationships with other positions in landscape and architectural design. As such, the reader will also find works by the landscape architects Bernard Lassus and Richard Haag or the artist Lois Weinberger in this book, as well as short discussions of important principles of landscape and design theory from Lucius Burckhardt, Horst Rittel or the Structuralists from the realm of architecture. I am most grateful to all those who so willingly provided me with information and image material in this respect, in particular Richard Haag, Bernard Lassus, Mary Randlett, Franziska and Lois Weinberger as well as Dr. Martin Weyl.

From the very beginning Anneliese and Peter Latz have trusted and supported me in this broader thematic approach. With great patience and concentration, Peter Latz assisted me in long and detailed interviews. Many passages, short in comparison to the full-length discussions, are drawn from these, the "voice of the designer" speaking directly, printed in italics.

In addition, Latz + Partner supported me with great organisational assistance, in particular their colleague Karin Graßl. This cooperation also clearly showed the immense contribution made over decades by Anneliese Latz to the international success of the office in her role as an experienced and meticulous project partner. This book cannot fully reflect the extent and importance of her input.

For decades, the landscape architect Dr. Gunter Bartholmai, Peter Latz's colleague at the TU München, has accompanied Peter's teaching and research activities with extraordinary dedication. I am thankful to him not only for his valuable information on the conceptual thought behind Peter Latz's work, but also for a whole series of essential images which he provided for this book, as I am to many others who provided illustrations including Manfred Balg, Michael Latz, Peter Liedtke, Sara Cedar Miller, Monika Nikolic, Christa Panick, Jane Sebire, Susanne Wamsler, André Weisgerber and Harf Zimmermann. To Hanno Dutt I am grateful for the insights he provided into Peter Latz's biographical background.

Last but not least, I would like to thank the book's designer Peter Willberg and the translator of the English edition, Michael Robinson, for their excellent work, and – once again – "my" long-standing editor and friend Andreas Müller, who over many years has contributed with level-headedness and great personal commitment to the *Syntax of Landscape*. Without the ever loving and patient professional as well as organisational support of my wife, the landscape architect Rita Weilacher, I would not have been able to realise this extraordinary project. How can I thank her enough?

Udo Weilacher, August 2007

Landscape architecture as cultural valorization

Central Park in New York is an ideal symbol for the new type of open space that had been invented, adapting to a changing social background. It is a model of flexibility and usefulness, but does the same apply to its images of nature?

GIVEN THE MASSIVE inner city planning problems he had had to struggle with for over two decades, he didn't think it was appropriate to talk about "landscape gardening" or "garden art" any more, but from then on used the term "landscape architecture" for his letterhead, for correspondence and on countless plans: Frederick Law Olmsted was apparently the person who coined the term "landscape architecture" in the mid 19th century while working on the 340 hectare site of New York's Central Park. This democratic "Volkspark" (people's park), created as a result of profound changes in the social structure of metropolitan life, was one of the most progressive and farsighted concepts in the world in its day. It is still cited as a model for modern landscape architecture. The creation of the park marked a radical change in the way landscape architecture perceived itself. Until then, it had been defined more as a discipline relating to arts and crafts than to engineering, social science and environmental science.

It was not until just under a hundred years after Olmsted's epoch-making work was completed, as technical progress and industrialized civilization started to re-shape the Central European landscape more vigorously, that the term landscape architecture also gradually started to be accepted in the German-speaking countries as the term for a profession that some people still now classify as art and others as science. Over the last five decades the word "landscape" has been greatly extended both conceptually and in scope, but few people have fully understood how to respond appropriately to the considerable increase in complex problems that landscape architecture faces, or indeed how to develop – as Olmsted did in his day – new expressive forms of contemporary environmental design that suit the prevailing social conditions.

Peter Latz is one of the few people who obviously succeeded in making this cultural breakthrough with his skilful transformation and cultural revaluation of post-industrial landscapes. He is now one of the internationally significant landscape architects acclaimed for his expertise both as a professional practitioner and also for his university research and teaching at institutions including the Technical University in Munich and the Universities of Harvard and Pennsylvania. There is no template for his work. His projects are many and various, and all steeped in his commitment to crafted precision and a sound theoretical and scientific basis drawn from his awareness of the complex range of effects likely to be triggered and characterizing the reality of each project as he finds it.

In order to understand how he works and his almost stubborn determination to face up to complex problems, it is helpful to know that Peter Latz grew up during the period when Germany was rebuilding, in the Saarland on the French border, one of Germany's most important industrial regions and an area soon to be shaken by dramatic structural crises. The post-war period confronted the architect's son with a whole series of responsibilities and challenges that still affect his work noticeably today. Central to all this was not least the question of using available resources efficiently and sustainably – with a large family to be fed and clothed at that time as well. Striving for self-sufficiency was an important factor, whether in his own garden or developing creative self-build techniques, using apparently useless builders' rubble.

Driven by a longing for independence and productive work with nature and landscape, Peter Latz initially wanted to be a farmer with his own farm. As he did not have one, he started to grow vegetables for his family in his parent's garden. "I planted an orchard of several hundred trees at the age of fifteen, and also started to grow strawberries, so that I'd have something I could sell quickly. In the end, I was able to keep my parents and their many relatives supplied with fresh fruit and vegetables for a few years. I used the money I got from selling the orchard to finance my studies. This explains my interest in fruit-growing, and the fruit-tree motif still appears in my projects today."[1] Anyone who has experienced the fruit trees in blossom among the blast furnaces at the former smelting plant in Duisburg – Meiderich, will know what he is talking about.

Anneliese and Peter Latz in their private garden in Ampertshausen near Freising, their personal tribute to the Renaissance garden at the Villa Ruspoli in Vignanello. Between box hedges and roses, a childhood dream was fulfilled.

About three decades after planting his first orchard the dream of his own farm actually became reality under happier circumstances than in the post-war period: Peter and his wife Anneliese Latz acquired a hectare of land and a little old farmhouse near the Bavarian cathedral and university city of Freising. On the outskirts of the little village of Ampertshausen, the site was an idyllic, south-facing slope. Within two years the building had expanded around four sides of a central yard – but not with the intention of growing crops and breeding cattle. Two thirds of the buildings are used for the landscape architecture practice, and the other third as the family home. The landscape architects transformed 3000 square metres of the land into a vegetable and ornamental garden, while the greater part of the estate sloping down to the adjacent valley was developed as a sweep of extensively cultivated meadow parkland.

Anyone looking for the Latz + Partner offices who is not familiar with the place could well end up in the neighbouring farmyard on the north side and think they had got lost. But a few metres further on, having arrived outside the eastern office wing of the atrium-like office complex, they will immediately sense the different spirit of the place. Trimmed hedges provide a protective surround for the orchard on the eastern boundary of the plot, framing the view over the landscaped meadows. Immediately adjacent to this, the new office building, a low timber-frame construc-

The atrium-like new building and a very varied run of hedges are set around the old farmhouse sited in the middle of the slope. The plan reveals that the elaborate sequence of internal and external spaces is a logically designed spatial structure.

LANDSCAPE ARCHITECTURE AS CULTURAL VALORIZATION

tion with a gable roof, thrusts into the valley, facing the sun at its southern end. The entrance on the east side of the house looks very firmly closed, but once you get into the atrium of the building you can enjoy a pleasant sense of seclusion and openness at the same time. A glazed access area provides additional protection against the weather and runs round three sides of the yard. A single cherry tree, oleander and agapanthus in large tubs, the splashing fountain in the gravelled inner courtyard and the luxuriant creepers all around generate an almost Mediterranean, pleasantly relaxed atmosphere – visitors are now in the right mood to discover the private garden on the west side and the water garden to the south.

The water garden, fed by collected rain water, is set at a lower level on the site. From the inner courtyard, you use one of the two flights of stairs in the south section of the atrium to go down one floor into the large conservatory, which opens directly outdoors. Peter Latz did not just design the conservatory, he was responsible for all the new buildings in Ampertshausen. A high proportion of self-build was involved when constructing the Latz family home in Saarlouis, conceived in the fifties as part of a co-operative model, and Peter Latz did his fair share of the building as a teenager. He benefited above all from his early professional contacts with architecture – as early as the mid-sixties he worked free-lance in the urban planning

Water plays a major part in the Latz garden, both aesthetically and ecologically, whether in the form of a little fountain in the inner courtyard or a large pool in the water garden, deep enough for swimming.

office run by professor Erich Kühn and Franz Karl Meurer in Aachen – and from his wide-ranging experience when building his first home in Kassel: in the early eighties, Peter Latz, working with the architects Thomas Herzog and Rudi Baumann, successfully converted an older building into a passive solar house with a large conservatory. "Pullover" was the apposite title for this conversion project, which also had a research angle.

His specialist architectural knowledge and sound grounding in material recycling and roof and façade planting also played a major part while planning and building the new Institute for Landscape Management and Botany at the Technische Universität München-Weihenstephan in 1987/88, where Peter Latz has worked since 1983. A whole series of research projects later initiated by the professor of landscape architecture and planning were set in motion by an interdisciplinary search for possible passive and active solar energy use. His self-build experiences made him increasingly aware of the necessity to understand house, garden and landscape as closely linked components within a tissue of living conditions whose regulatory mechanisms had to be explored very carefully. Here principles are applied in both architecture and landscape architecture that can be seen as fundamentally typical of Peter Latz's work. Anneliese Latz has good reason to call the garden in Amperts-

As early as the eighties, Peter Latz converted an old building in Kassel into an ecological family home with a conservatory, working with his architect friends Thomas Herzog and Rudi Baumann.

LANDSCAPE ARCHITECTURE AS CULTURAL VALORIZATION

The landscape artist sought to link house, garden and landscape closely in all the new Ampertshausen buildings, not just in design terms, but also in relation to their form and structure.

Precisely trimmed mixed hornbeam and privet hedges surround the Latz house like a living protective wall, creating a pleasant, sheltered garden climate where even kiwi fruit flourish.

LANDSCAPE ARCHITECTURE AS CULTURAL VALORIZATION

hausen "Peter's experimental field", and that definitely does not apply to landscape architecture alone.

One feature that applies to concepts in both architecture and garden design – not just in Ampertshausen – is the highly informed treatment of materials. *"I must say at the outset that I work with all materials. But if we have opted for a particular material, we try to take that as far as we can. For example, the exterior façade of my own house is made of the same birch plywood multiplex panels as the bookcase in my office and our bedroom cupboards,"* explains Peter Latz. *"I think it is possible to achieve a great deal of calm and naturalness by using this method, and also to built up rational approaches. One has a repertoire that is rationally restricted, and really can develop. Of course that applies to any material that can be used for such a variety of purposes – and particularly to builders' rubble, for example."*

Reducing the variety of materials plays a very positive part in strengthening the structural framework in all Latz + Partner's work. In Ampertshausen it is the trimmed box and beech hedges that give the garden such a powerful character of its own. Seen from a nearby hill, a richly structured belt of precisely trimmed and shaped hedges, some several metres high, runs around the extended farm buildings like a thick green bulwark. In the background a stand of old tall trees enfolds the farmstead like a sheltering screen. The high hedge wall made up of different plant

A recurrent feature in the houses Peter Latz has converted with an eye to ecology since the eighties is a large, south-facing conservatory, considerably improving both the atmosphere of the house and its energy balance.

The interplay between trimmed and freely growing plants has always been crucial to the way culturally shaped nature has been interpreted in garden design history, and so these typologies are also used in Ampertshausen.

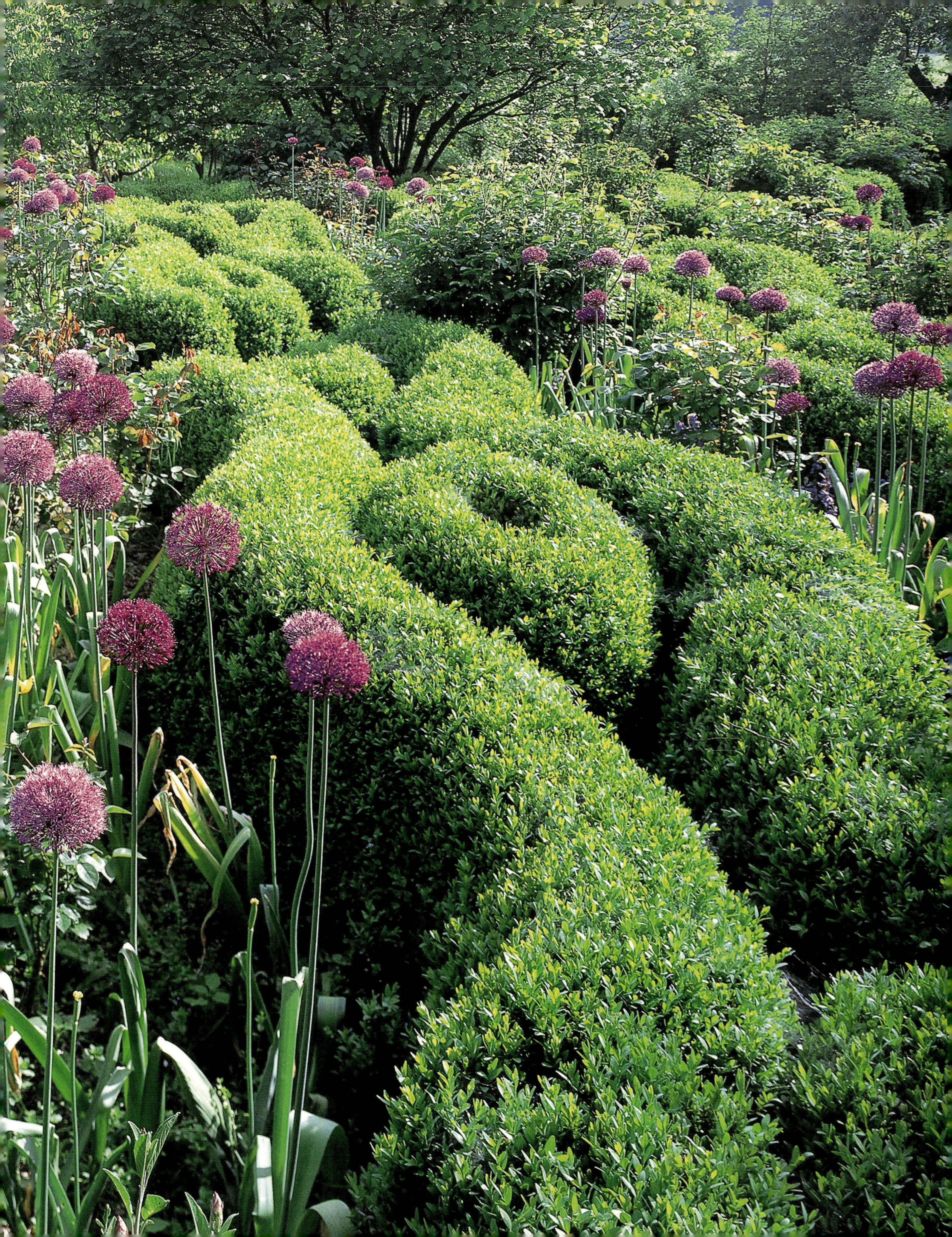

varieties makes it possible to bathe sheltered from the wind and without being overlooked in the simply designed water garden's swimming pool. It also creates a mild micro-climate by the house where kiwi fruit and grapevines can flourish. But protection from the wind and from being overlooked is not a sufficient explanation for the presence of the hedging elements in the Latz garden. A number of other, closely linked aspects are the decisive factors in the virtuoso use of trimmed hedges in the private garden and also in many other of the landscape architects' projects.

Peter Latz identified Italian Mannerism as one of his most important sources of inspiration: *"On the one hand, there are certain items there that have retained the same structure for centuries. I was enormously impressed by the fact that this is possible, and especially that it is possible by horticultural manipulation. This also made me resist a nature ideology that suggests that in nature everything grows as it has to. The second thing that comes from this period is that it is possible to conduct exclusively aesthetic experiments, and they do not even need to make sense. I owe this discovery largely to Herbert Weiermann, the art history professor, who taught us Renaissance horticulture as part of our course. Sometimes he mentioned how 'overloaded', 'excessive' or 'incomprehensible' Mannerist gardens of the Renaissance were, but also pointed out that technical and aesthetic experiments were being carried out. That impressed me, and made me definitely want to try certain experiments – the axes, the waterworks on the hillside, ending in shell-shaped grottoes, tuna fish and scallops as alien elements in the stream and so on. These are all symbols and structures that have been very much transformed, and sometimes they really are not beautiful, at least not in the way we look at things today, but they are aesthetic experiments. [...] These two elements of Mannerism are enormously important to me. [...] The box garden in Ampertshausen is a tribute to the gardens at the Villa Ruspoli in Vignanello, which I rate very highly. Perhaps that is one of the biggest dreams for a landscape architect north of the Alps: creating*

Generations of gardeners at the Castello Ruspoli have tended an impressive hedged parterre laid out in the early 17th century on a striking periphery, affording a sweeping view of the cultural landscape around the building.

A model combination of technology and nature. Inventive water features like the catena d'acqua in Renaissance gardens, here the garden of the Villa Lante, have inspired Peter Latz time and again.

a heightened Mediterranean sense of awareness, a Mediterranean lifestyle, using the resources of design." The gardeners at the Castello Ruspoli have been cultivating an impressive hedge parterre for generations. Marcantonio Marescotti planted it in the early 17th century, and his wife Ottavia Orsini developed it a great deal further. The finely honed work of the hedger's art survived on the sunlit terrace east of the Castello for centuries, underscoring the magnificent view of the countryside, theatrically framed by the trees – in winter as well, when the hedge structures make their presence felt all the more strongly if covered by the occasional fine blanket of snow. *"Trimmed plants, particularly the evergreen box, have an enormous advantage over any other plant typology: they provide a dense structural framework at times when gardens are usually shut up. This typology is always significant if I am aiming for use all the year*

"Perhaps that is one of the biggest dreams for a landscape architect north of the Alps: creating a heightened, Mediterranean sense of awareness, a Mediterranean lifestyle," Peter Latz admits, who has created his own garden paradise.

LANDSCAPE ARCHITECTURE AS CULTURAL VALORIZATION

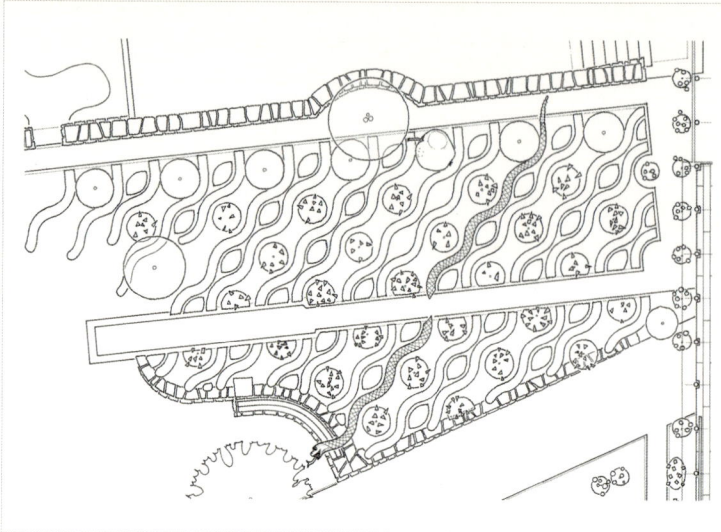

round," explains Peter Latz, and reminds us: *"We do not create picturesque gardens, but they take on picturesque forms from time to time. Our garden with the trimmed box hedges has that too, but it was not developed as a picturesque image, instead as a structure that can be perceived as picturesque from certain sides. And there is a difference."*

Peter and Anneliese Latz, in paying their very personally formulated tribute to Vignanello, are at the same time stressing their fundamental conviction that contemporary landscape architecture can only be carried out sensibly and developed further in awareness of the history of garden art: *"It is possible to work on the assumption that imitation is still one of the soundest design methods. In this respect, it makes sense to study the historical repertoire of a profession that we have an information monopoly on to a certain extent. But of course I do not believe that that is enough. […] One thing is clear in any case: it is not possible to take up any kind of critical position without the historical repertoire and a knowledge of garden art. The only risk you are taking is that you might reinvent the wheel, and sometimes you even do."* Many other projects by Latz + Partner, like for example the Hafeninsel in Saarbrücken or the Duisburg-Nord landscape park, should not really be seen as paying homage to garden art, but draw their conceptual strength from a consciously critical analysis of historical gardening models that Peter Latz feels contemporary landscape architecture cites too often, too arbitrarily and without sufficient thought.

We gain a clear sense of the connection with Renaissance horticulture in the box and rose garden on the west side of Ampertshausen, which can be reached directly from the private living quarters at ground level via the veranda. Something that

At first glance, the green in the box garden west of the house seems to flourish unchecked, but it has geometrical precision, clearly revealed in the drawn plan of the garden.

looks at a first glance like a dense, somewhat random mass of box trees turns out to be a meticulously planned garden ensemble with an undulating pattern of plants when viewed from another angle. The layout of the knee-high box hedges was fixed precisely with a jig-template, and has been kept under control by trimming and shaping ever since. Unlike Baroque garden layouts, marked symmetry and austere geometry or strictly axial arrangement schemes have little part to play in the Latz garden. In the private garden, a single sightline takes the eye directly from the terrace to a landscape window cut in the hedge enclosing the garden, giving a view of the surrounding pastures, meadows and arable land. We inevitably feel reminded of Leon Battista Alberti's central precepts for designing villas and gardens in the 15th century: "A building (close to a town) will be most attractive, if it presents a cheerful overall appearance to anyone leaving the city, as if to attract and expect visitors. I would therefore make it slightly elevated; and I would make the road leading up to it rise so gently that visitors do not realize how high they have climbed until they have a view over the countryside. Meadows full of flowers, sunny lawns, cool and shady groves, limpid springs, streams and pools and whatever else we have described as being essential to a villa – none of these should be missing, for their delight as much as for their utility."[2]

The window in the west garden hedge draws the eye from the living room through the box garden into the surrounding expanse of cultural landscape, its image still largely shaped by farming.

LANDSCAPE ARCHITECTURE AS CULTURAL VALORIZATION

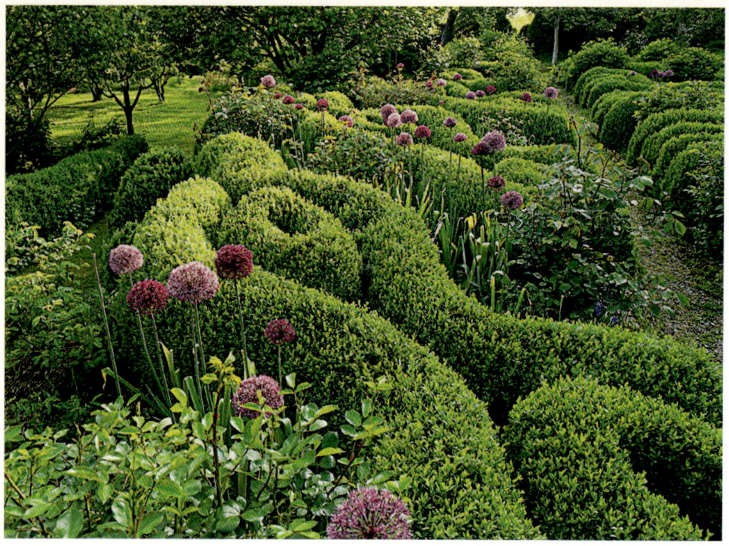
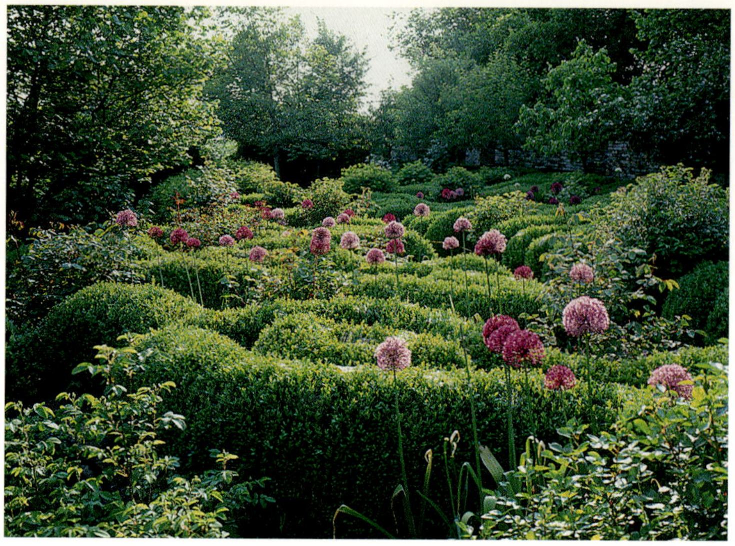
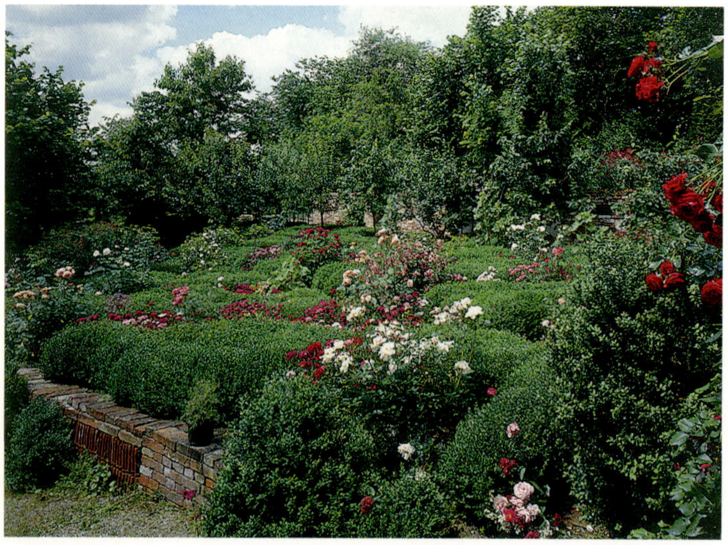
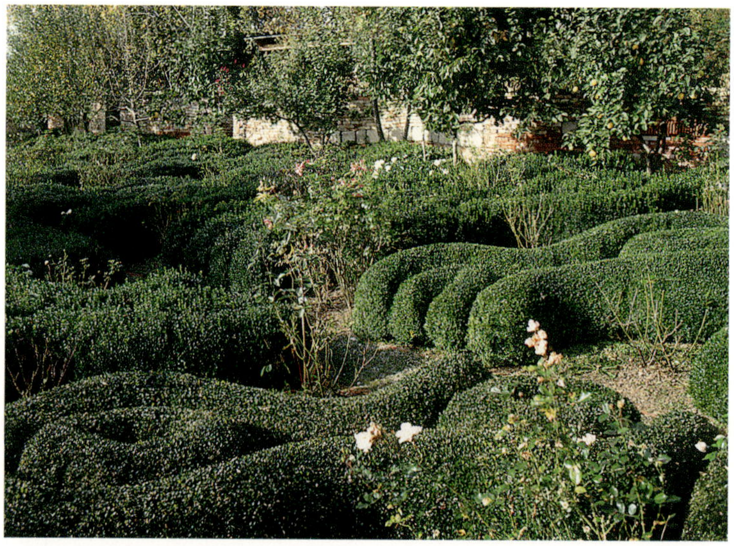
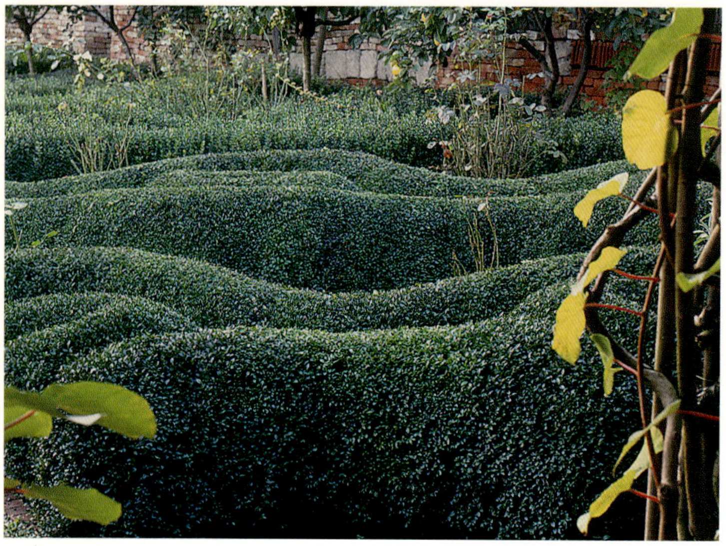
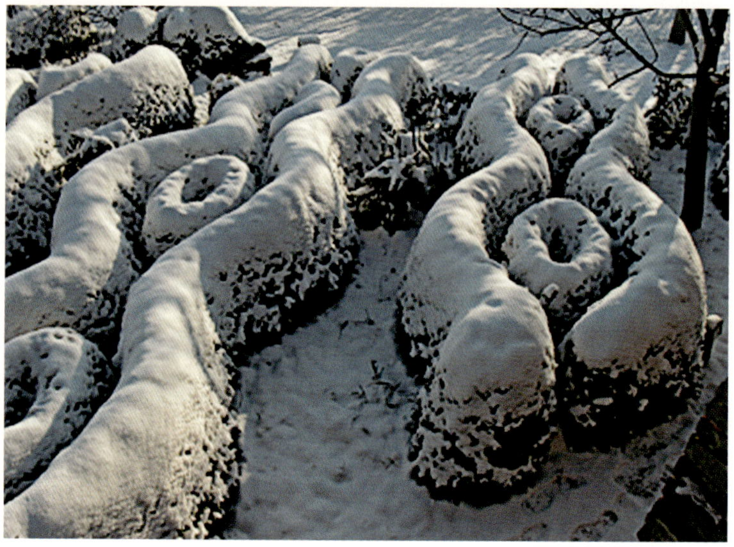

An enchanting, largely monochrome play of colours unfolds throughout the year among the low box hedges in the garden. Thus in the spring countless spherical clusters of flowering onion blossom (Allium aflatunense) appear in their strong purple, while in summer the delicate pink bush roses pour their fragrance out into the garden. Peter Latz explains how important the trimmed hedges are for the structure and year-round appeal of the garden: *"Roses are actually pretty terrible in winter. If you combine them with an evergreen trimmed hedge, never mind how it is arranged – that is a different question – then of course I will always notice whatever is making the greatest effect. This means that in July I have the blooming rose bush in the foreground, and I see the hedges like the green in a bunch of flowers. In winter, suddenly the green structure starts to dominate, and I can't see the roses at all, because they have been pruned back appropriately. That is the pragmatic level.*

Another, very important aspect of trimmed features is that it is possible to control the space they need in a small garden. A trimmed hornbeam is defined, while a hornbeam that is growing freely can turn into a real tree. Trimming makes manipulating dimensions very feasible, and of course I can use the hedge as a substitute for other architectural spatial images. Rather than following the classical method and building a wall round the garden, I can take a trimmed hedge instead, and I can cut a door or a window in the hedge, just as I could with a wall. In other words, it is possible for me to illustrate the architectural language of our everyday world very clearly. Coming in and going out is a very important, archetypal event. I can't do anything about this with a plant that is growing freely. For this reason we are not facing the alternative of the freely growing plant versus a trimmed one. Competition comes from the fence rather than the hedge."

Again and again we come back to the idea of the intelligibility of gardens and landscapes, to the deliberate use of design elements as linguistic elements that the landscape architect deploys to initiate a dialogue with people about their environment and nature. It must always be remembered that visitors come along with their own ideas in their heads, their own associations and connotations, which means that designers have to handle the stylistic resources of garden art and landscape architecture very carefully. Probably one of the most important conceptual approaches is informed treatment of existing or new strands of information that substantially influence whether a place is intelligible and open to interpretation, and thus whether it is usable or not. *"It is indeed very important that from time to time we should revisit pragmatic, scientific and aesthetic planes,"* Peter Latz explains. *"One crucial feature for me is the conviction that open spaces, landscapes, are made up of various layers of information that have first of all to be analyzed. It could always be that there are two or three you don't*

The box garden displays a lively interplay of colours, shapes and scents throughout the year, carefully embedded in an evergreen structural framework that looks particularly impressive in winter.

LANDSCAPE ARCHITECTURE AS CULTURAL VALORIZATION

discover, but you must be able to make out the essential ones. These layers of information can be within the prescribed working area, or frequently they can be outside it as well. […] It is important to be in agreement about these, otherwise there is no point in actually analyzing the information layers."

The French landscape architect and landscape theoretician Bernard Lassus once vividly compared landscape with puff pastry, with the various levels of meaning layered one on top of the other inside it. But Peter Latz knows from experience that it is very rare indeed for the various layers of a landscape to be completely undisturbed. Each new use added to a landscape disturbs what is already there to a certain extent, and brings its own characteristic structures with it. These then manifest themselves as an information layer in their own right. What qualities the historical and contemporary levels have, whether they are still complete or fragmented, whether they can be completed and repaired, or whether it might make more sense to replace them completely with new information layers are questions landscape architects have to address constantly when designing.

The significance of a place, its intelligibility, is influenced to a considerable extent not just by internal but by external factors, such as the surrounding landscape, for example. Thus a walled garden in the middle of a desolate rocky or sandy desert would acquire a very different significance from the same walled garden in the middle of a tropical rain forest or perhaps on the outskirts of a little Bavarian village. *"For example, in my own garden, which has a very particular character, there is a gate in the hedge that you look through at the north slope of the intricate hilly countryside. In summer the farmer puts young, bright red cattle out to graze, and this means that I see the cliché of landscape used for agriculture from my garden, and I can confront it with the garden. That is an enormously important matter. If the farmer suddenly stops doing it, I no longer have this duality between decorative garden and working landscape. Of course I could relate to the edge of the wood behind it, or even cite the forestry experts' research platform, which occupies another of the garden's sightlines. And special events are also suitable for constructing a layer of information or significance, for example, the point at which the sun sets on a particular date can be staged as an effect in the space, even though these are ancient and clichéd ideas. There are a whole series of other possibilities for choosing external reference points, so that they can be included in the textured tissue of information that the garden provides. These can be the mountain, the church tower, the castle and similar landmarks, or also temporary interventions, like for example the mown swathe in a meadow, which not only provides contrasting flowering, but also defines specific directions, and focuses on something quite particular."*

Sun-drenched interiors and sheltered outdoor spaces, decorative Mediterranean fruit in the conservatory and the snowy Bavarian winter landscape beyond the water garden are key features of the Latz house's particular atmosphere.

LANDSCAPE ARCHITECTURE AS CULTURAL VALORIZATION

Many of the design strategies and design elements described above, which take on an almost exemplary quality in Ampertshausen, have long counted as part of Latz + Partner's current standard repertoire, which needs no further explanation as part of their daily planning and design work. These sophisticated methods for dealing with nature in the garden and in the landscape usually aim to create semi-artificial systems in which processes develop that can no longer be defined unambiguously as part of the realm of nature or the realm of technology. It is precisely in re-interpreting post-industrial landscapes, commonly described as "damaged", whether in the Saarland, the Ruhr, in Israel, Italy, France, England or China, that Latz + Partner have proven their internationally outstanding reputation as landscape architects. The skilled use of the mentioned "classical tools" – especially their virtuoso handling of levels of meaning and layers of information as well as their inclusion of the extended context of the man-made landscape – has played a crucial part in founding this reputation. What industrial landscapes have in common the world over, despite the enormous variety of cultural contexts, is the technology of heavy industry. This technology is needed everywhere in the same form for mining and in the iron and steel industries, creating similar landscape structures world-wide. Latz + Partner derive their legitimacy for working in post-industrial landscapes all over the world from this state of affairs.

Uninitiated garden visitors constantly stumble on design elements that attract their attention and raise new questions. Thus for example a whole series of enclosing and retaining walls in Ampertshausen are obviously made of reused

The dark brick-red of the self-built rubble walls radiates a strange warmth over the garden all year round. In winter especially the brick red glows brightly and warmly in the snow-white surrounding.

builders' rubble, old roof tiles, used paving stones, shapeless lumps of concrete, bleached wooden planks and similar things. The broken brick walls using dry-stone technique are reminiscent of part of a landscape of sunken ruins. They provide effective, mainly red colour accents amidst the ensemble of green hedges, and their improvised look makes for an attractive design contrast with the precisely trimmed box hedges. One might even believe that the particular charm of almost forgotten Renaissance gardens with the dignified age of their walls, collapsing in places, provided the inspiration for this motif. In any case, reusing builders' rubble has become one of the trademarks of this landscape architecture practice. Rubble from the conversion of the farm buildings was used in the Latz private garden. The unusual walls look nothing like as dominant as in many large landscape architecture projects, for example on the Hafeninsel in Saarbrücken, but Peter Latz's basic concerns are also in evidence in these almost unassuming approaches to detail.

The use of rubble also adds a new layer of information to the garden, as the old bricks, roof tiles, planks from barns and remains of foundations tell a story of their own that cannot be overlooked – possibly recalling the days when bricks were still hand made, perhaps complaining about the demolition of carefully built barns, commenting on the increasing uselessness of old sheds, reminding us that the landscape is constantly being reconstructed and that material and energy are subject to an enduring cycle. Latz learned early in his childhood that you can make something of everything – even builders' rubble – and indeed you have to. *"I was not able to accept this experience with any ease, but it had something to do with arguments about*

Simple, unadorned and precisely worked materials with the dignity of age, as in the castle garden of Caprarola, lend a mature charm to the Renaissance gardens.

ecology and an ongoing discussion about the fact that every material represents energy processes, and that above all landfill refuse dumps are the worst thing we can do to our countryside. So if we recycle all these materials we save a lot of dumps and a lot of removal points, a lot of clay pits, gravel excavations and so on. So we are researching the recycling field, but not just from the point of view of engineering, for example grading curves or unsatisfactory frost resistance in broken brick concrete, but of course also in terms of social acceptability and aesthetic relevance. What can I actually really do with builders' rubble, or must I hide it away in the foundations? This is what usually happens to recycled materials. But I wanted these materials to make a cultural statement. So I didn't just want them to be hidden in a roadbed, but to make people aware of the high value of these materials."

The fact that the old building materials do not simply look worthless in the Latzs' private garden or seem like an improvised emergency solution is first of all due to how they are included in a way which is completely natural and of exceptional dignity within the overall work of art. The noble art of hedge trimming, of breeding roses, the cultivation of fruit trees and the art of broken brick masonry all acquire an entirely unexpected sense of equality in the garden. Many a detail, such as the curved retaining wall that apparently effortlessly secures the spot occupied by the magnificent solitaire multi-trunk hazelnut tree, cannot possibly be imagined being more effectively constructed in a superior building material. It seems as though the landscape architect wants to help every material to find the dignity inherent within it, whether through skilful craftsmanship in the use of reusable building materials, or by ingeniously combining noble garden plants, framed by carefully deployed

Hazel bushes not only provide shade for the central, semi-circular seating area a little below the box garden. They are planted in a grid, so carry the eye over the surrounding agricultural land before allowing it to linger on the sloping meadow.

building rubble. The specific combination of the cultivated and the rough, certainly consciously based on the philosophical theories of Claude Lévi-Strauss[3], is a constantly recurring feature in the work of Latz + Partner, and lends much of their work a powerfully expressive quality.

Moving from the private garden towards the sloping meadow, you cross the hazelnut grove and almost by chance come across a small, dark quartzite slab in the lawn inscribed "HAZELGROVE O HAZELGROVE HOW BEAUTIFUL IS THY GEAR". This unassuming work of art is by Ian Hamilton Finlay, who was a friend of Anneliese and Peter Latz. The Scottish poet and artist died in 2006. He became aware of Latz + Partner's work in 1996 through a publication on landscape architecture and Land Art, and in particular of their pioneering Duisburg-Nord landscape park project, and tried to make contact in Germany. He was himself interested in revealing invisible levels of meaning in landscape, and he was most impressed by the landscape architects' unusual ways of getting closer to the history of cultural landscape, their careful handling of remembered culture and their sound analysis of destructive forces in the ruins of former industrial landscapes. This interest led to their working together on several projects, and finally developed into a personal friendship. Ian Hamilton Finlay's work, shaded by the hazelnut bushes, fits in with the garden scene very subtly, adding another layer, that of literary information, and changing the intelligibility of the garden unmistakably.

Only a few paces further on, the eye runs over the meadow hillside, which has only a few narrow strips mowed through it. The mown strips lead down to the small

A stone slab by Ian Hamilton Finlay, who admired the Latzs' parks, is set into the meadow in the shade of hazel bushes. The inscription reads: HAZELGROVE O HAZELGROVE HOW BEAUTIFUL IS THY GEAR.

LANDSCAPE ARCHITECTURE AS CULTURAL VALORIZATION

birch wood at the south-west corner and the little oak wood at the southeast corner of the plot. In between, in another round lawn, grows a third group of trees, conveying the transition to the rising stretch of pastureland opposite. The previous owner had already marked the corners of the site with groups of trees, though these had been fast-growing spruce and birch plantations. Latz removed most of the spruce trees and surrounded the remaining birches with a ring of willows, in order to make the grove geometrical. Peter Latz dropped his original, almost provocative intention of planting foreign timber in the landscape, which would have gone against the usual guidelines; the fact is that Latz + Partner are able to break away from such dogma considerably more effectively in other cases, thus making those projects more powerfully expressive.

The mown paths on the grassy slope provide varied displays of blossom and varied patterns of light and shade throughout the year. Only plants that can survive mowing find the carefully tended paths an ideal habitat, and thus accentuate them.

**Layers of information.
How does landscape work?**

University of Marburg on Lahnberge

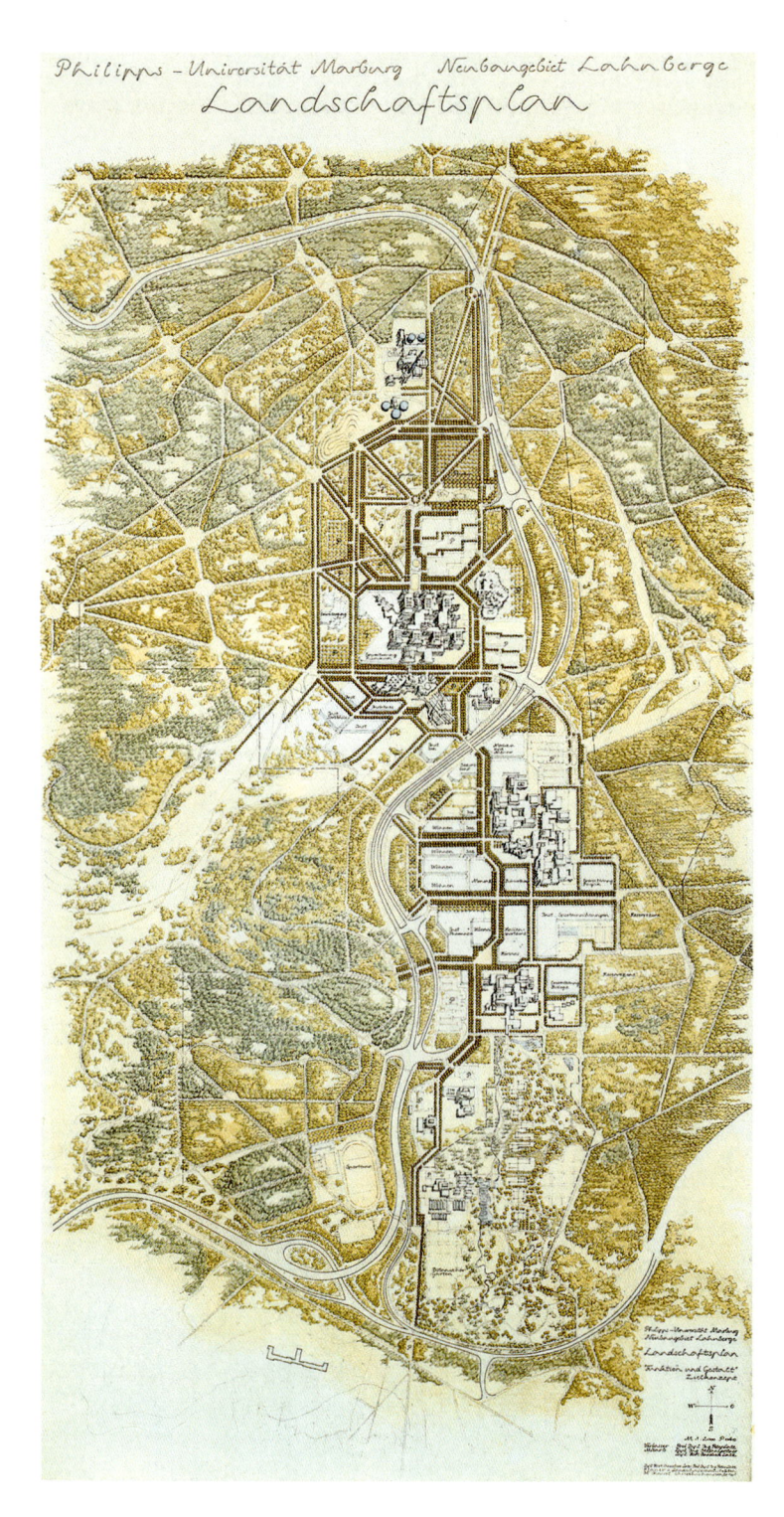

Anneliese Latz drew and watercoloured the landscape plan for Marburg university on the Lahn hills in the seventies. It reveals the close connection between urban design and landscape planning very clearly.

THE ADVANTAGE OF a structuralistic approach in landscape architecture, something that can at best be hinted at in the Latz private garden, comes more into effect in large projects, where the size of the site alone makes it impossible to design each square metre individually. The Marburg University site on Lahnberge covers 170 hectares. It is an extension of the Philipps-Universität, which was planned from 1961 as a completely autonomous complex with its own energy plant and extensive buildings for research, lecture rooms, refectories, large hospital, libraries, large car parks and supply units extending into the extensive Lahnberge woodland east of Marburg. The state university building department in Marburg, and in particular architects Kurt Schneider, Helmut Spieker and Winfried Scholl designed an 'infinite' architectural structure for the entire university. The building complex is capable of continuous expansion using standard, prefabricated structural components intended to guarantee flexible use. The solution lay in developing a table-like building norm on a 60 centimetre grid, the so-called Marburg construction system (7.2 × 7.2 m). The concrete tables formed the basic unit of the reinforced concrete skeleton structure. They piled on top of each other to a height of up to eight storeys, with the intention of ensuring that the columns were equally loaded, and making it possible to construct the building and extension grids independently.

The office of Anneliese and Peter Latz (from 1990 'Latz + Partner') was commissioned in 1976 to draw up an overall development plan for open space and infrastructure as a set of instruments for guiding the building measures as a whole. They were required to look intensively at the primarily technocratic and structural principle of the architecture as well as at the special character of the existing woodland and the campus landscape that was to be created. It was precisely here while planning this large project that their experiences with basic urban development principles and their liking of structural approaches to complex building problems turned out to be extraordinarily helpful. Anneliese and Peter Latz took up the continuous orientation and connection line of the communal areas as designed by the architects into the extendable architectural structure for the entire campus, and continued it actively into the outdoor areas. The analogies between the structurally based Marburg construction system of the architecture and in the landscape architects' planning strategies aimed at flexible use of the outdoor grid are clearly recognizable.

But first of all the archetype of the clearing is the central aspect of the overall concept for the Lahnberge site. The campus is embedded in the surrounding woodland like a little town in its own right, with its own buildings, car parks, paths,

LAYERS OF INFORMATION. HOW DOES LANDSCAPE WORK?

rows of trees, avenues and gardens. The utterly simple idea of placing large building complexes in the middle of spacious woodland clearings inevitably led during construction to damaged woodland peripheries, cut-off connecting pathways, a high level of soil compaction and massive earthworks, and some of this in the immediate vicinity of the nearby recreation areas just outside the town. Consequently it was essential to re-establish the woodland and its periphery in damaged areas, to re-connect the network of broken pathways, restore the recreation areas and integrate the huge building and soil masses into the landscape. This was on one hand to retain the landscape character of the Landberge despite all the building interventions, and on the other to ensure that the clearings occupied by the university buildings were nevertheless able to develop a clear, essentially functional character.

Today there is little sense of damage to the woodland periphery: careful planting created new fringe areas with a rich variety of species, which have developed largely without further intervention. Clearly the landscape architects were able to achieve this only by drawing considerably on the background in forestry they acquired in the early sixties (along with many other course elements) when studying Landscape architecture and planning at the Technische Universität München-Weihenstephan. In Lahnberge in particular, where a key factor was to leave large areas to themselves in the long term, it was essential at the planning stage to devise soundly based woodland planting measures. The experience gained in Marburg in managing existing, spontaneous or newly planted woodland played a key part in many projects in subsequent years, for example in connection with converting extensive industrial areas. Planting trees made it possible to create a strong, spatially effective green structure that had to fulfil a number of functions. It was not just a question of building roads, paths and parking spaces into the wood and its clearings: the primary spatial structure also had to offer all open space users a high level of orientation possibilities and thus make them confident that they are going the right way. To achieve this, not only were rows of trees planted, but swathes were also cut through the woodland to make it easier for users to get their bearings.

The large clearings in the woods are now effectively articulated in spatial terms by the clear tree structures. The overall architectural structure fits into the right-angled base framework with absolute precision. The landscape architects carried out 5 to 15 hectare portions of the outdoor facilities of the University Hospital in two building phases, the first from 1976 to 1985, and then the second from 2000 to 2004. The works included parks and promenades, but also patients' gardens, 30 roof gardens, interior courtyards and terraces. The trimmed hedges acquired the same central importance in the internal structure of the areas framed by trees around the hospital which can be sensed in the Latz private garden – even though the latter was not created until years later. In Marburg too, a precisely planned structure for the hedges articulates the extensive outdoor areas. The hedges create pleasantly proportioned areas for activities and protected outdoor areas, accentuating the imposing, central access areas and making it easier to find one's way around the extensive site. Unlike the curved box hedges in the Latz private garden, the strictly architecturally shaped hedges in Marburg seem like a logical continuation of the architecture by other means, and with equal flexibility of use. This by no means restricts the quality of the time spent in these areas by visitors, employees and patients – on the contrary: people meet in little hedged niches around the hospital where they can sit on benches, chat to each other quietly or simply enjoy the fresh air.

Architecture, gardens and landscape mesh with the surrounding woodland landscape both on the higher structural level, expressed by the rows of trees, and also on the level below, expressed by the clipped hedges. Even the patterning in the street and path surfaces follows strong but simple basic design principles and complements the basic concept, which is like a carefully devised, three-dimensional

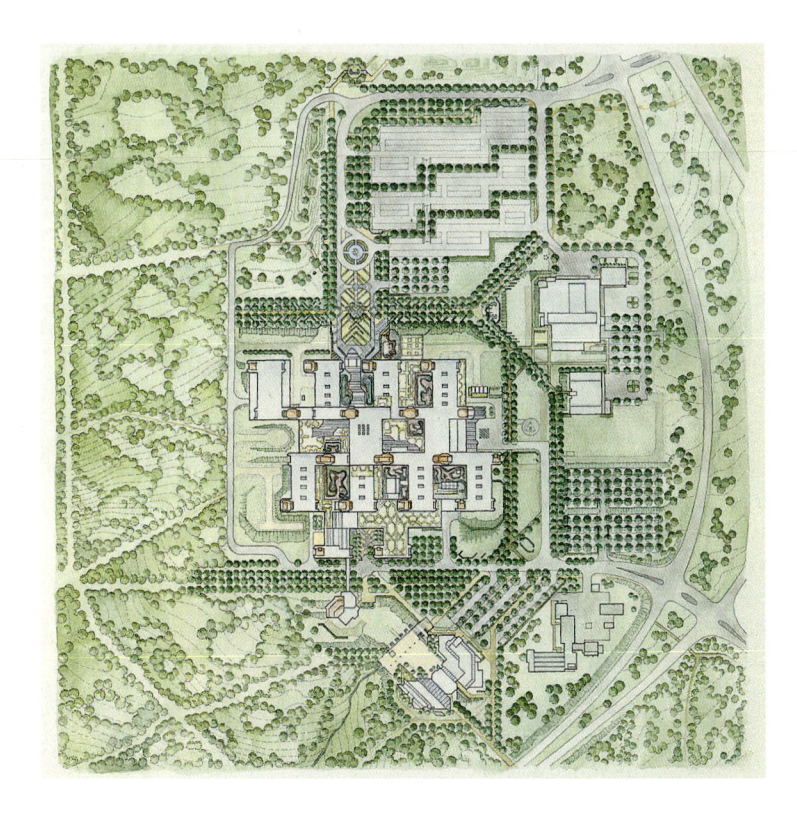

Communal areas forming connecting and orienting lines were part of the endlessly repeating architectural structure from the outset, and Anneliese and Peter Latz extended them logically into the outdoor spaces by planting appropriate trees and hedges.

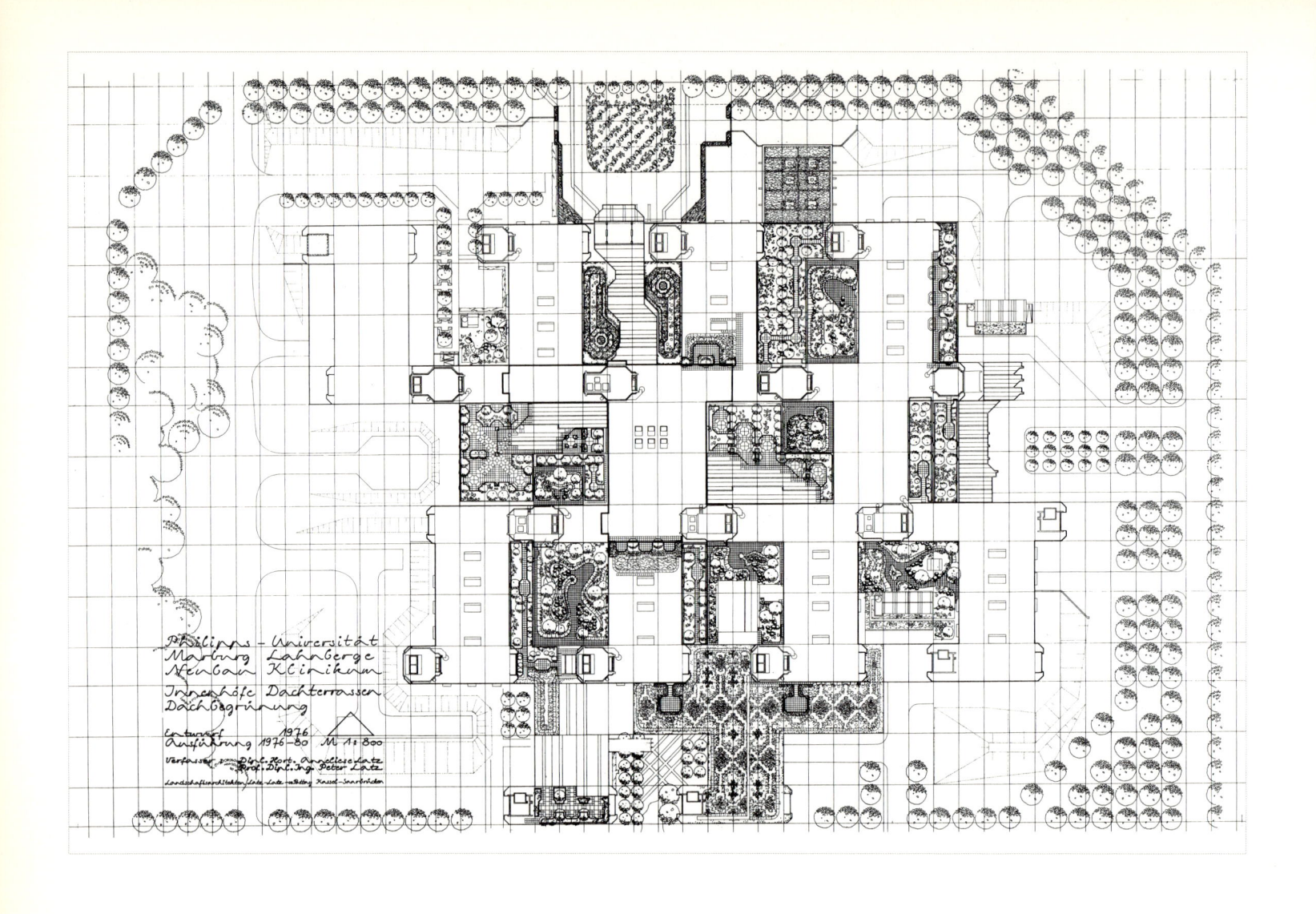

The key when planning the roofs and inner courtyards was not just the ecological aspects, but also the question of how the garden design can help people find their bearings within the building complex.

web pattern. The art objects, furnishings, minor architectural features and lighting sources are also tightly woven into this pattern, and the clear basic structure – like the basic architectural principle of the Marburg grid – supports the integration of new individual elements effortlessly. But any subsequent and often imperfectly considered intervention in the basic green framework sticks out like a sore thumb, and noticeably destabilizes the system of order for the outdoor areas.

The landscape architects followed a different strategy for the numerous internal courtyards in the hospital complex. Here the picture is dominated by the architecture, by buildings constructed in exposed concrete, with glass, steel and opaque glasal façades. The people in the hospital need variety within the network of medical and technical functions, and so the opportunity was taken to develop little individual garden oases, unique objects that seem very unaffected and almost playful in their design. Peter Latz speaks of the courtyards as elements of the sixth information level, always designed naturally at the lowest level in terms of building height, to achieve a kind of "earthing" and offer a contrast with the artificiality of the system as a whole. By contrast, the functional courtyards were designed architecturally, with natural stone slabs as surfacing, setting off the vertical concrete elements in the architecture. While the austere hedge structures around the buildings convey

For Peter Latz, the courtyards are part of an information system. The naturalistic design signals direct contact with the soil, while the architectural design lends the substructural functional courtyards their character.

LAYERS OF INFORMATION. HOW DOES LANDSCAPE WORK?

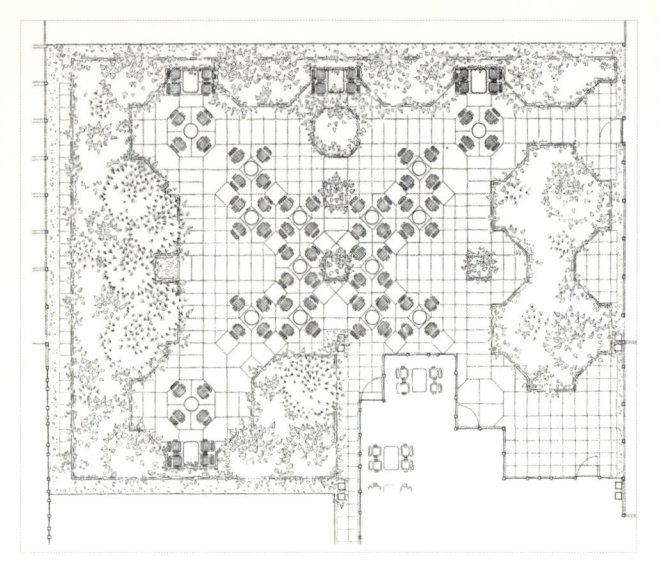

a certain timelessness, as part of another information level of their own, the naturalistic layout of the inner courtyards with their elaborate small stone paving, water sources and brooks speak the typical garden architecture language of the late seventies and early eighties. If Peter Latz is asked whether he ever orientates himself towards the ideas of seventies garden artists like Roberto Burle Marx, he replies by saying *"I have declined to take Burle Marx as my role model"*. But some of the expressive inner courtyard designs in Marburg are not all that far removed from the stylistic qualities shown by the Brazilian Burle Marx, who was an inspiration for generations of European landscape architects in the sixties and seventies.

The timeless impression conveyed by the generous tree and hedge structures in contrast with the inner courtyard did not arise by accident. *"I think that every project has to have timeless qualities,"* explains Latz. *"But now there are projects that do not display these qualities because of investment conditions, because people are aware that after 30 years the building structure will have aged so much that it will have to be pulled down. Nevertheless, it would have been possible to aim to build timeless landscape elements into it, namely as the basic structure of an organization system within complex systems. If I link the most important spatial structural elements, for example backdrops of trees, hedges, or modelled earthworks, with the structure of a university, then I stand a pretty good chance of surviving for two or three generations. But I have to hold myself back a great deal, and can only work with elements that actually can be linked with this function. But if I introduce an information level that is entirely my own next to this, or in a completely different place, there is very little likelihood that it will survive, because one day this might possibly be the space for*

Continuing architecture with the resources of landscape architecture: shaded by the treetops but light, the inner courtyards at the university hospital are transformed into pleasant places in which to spend time in the open air.

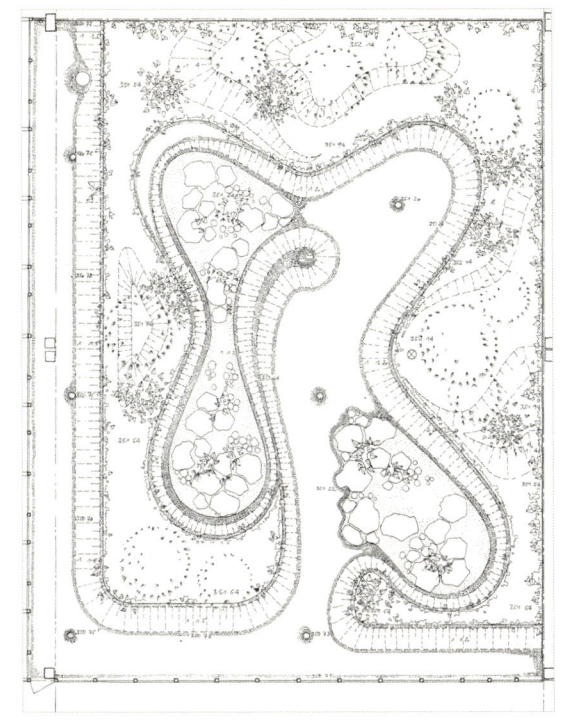

The drive up to the hospital offers trimmed hedge architecture, while the biomorphic designs for the inner courtyards are reminiscent of gardens by the Brazilian Roberto Burle Marx (here for comparison at the Ministery of Education and Health in Rio de Janeiro).

LAYERS OF INFORMATION. HOW DOES LANDSCAPE WORK?   41

new buildings or new programmes, or because they will be neglected on the basis of non-essential function typologies."

"Timelessness is the aim, and the strategy is to link this aim with something that is functionally timeless. If I want a tree canopy one day and interesting trunks beneath it, I can't carve these or cast them in concrete, but I have to plant them in the usual affordable dimensions, for example in the case of pine trees with a trunk circumference of 25 to 35 centimetres. These are not very large trees, and as a landscape architect you will probably not personally experience the time when the trunks and branches form a canopy because of the long time it takes trees to develop. You will probably never personally experience that the designed basic structure actually is effective, and thus fulfils numerous conditions - it symbolizes green, at the same time providing shade in summer and permitting a structure on the ground that is relatively robust and can be used for all sorts of things."

If the hedges and trees planted along the streets and paths in Marburg are seen as information structures in this way, not just as symbolizing urban green, but for example also conveying information about the way the place functions, its artificial character and orientation within the space, then it becomes clear why the most recent extensions to the clinical complex were able to be fitted into the existing situation without any difficulty and why it was possible, naturally and systematically, to extend the green structures, now over 30 years old.

A particular inclination towards technical precision in landscape architecture, which should be comparable with civil engineering and architecture, is a particular characteristic of Latz + Partner that was starting to be noticeable even in the late sixties. In 1968 – Peter Latz had just finished his post-graduate urban development course at the RWTH University in Aachen – he and his wife Anneliese set up a landscape architecture practice in Aachen and Saarbrücken. At the same time, he

The structuralistically inclined concept of architecture and landscape architecture turned out to be helpful in preserving a uniform aesthetic character in the most recent expansion of the Marburg university hospital.

was running a joint practice – SLS – for town planning, and for landscape and system planning, with engineers and architects, including Konny Schmitz. *"We were dealing with real civil engineering, developing steel construction systems for housing and schools, for example. This is why I know so much about building and construction. My ideas about dimensions and the reasons for them come from that as well, and this was just as important to us as systematizing steel construction as a management system. The network plan system and similar approaches also come from those days with SLS. I was working with an architect and two young engineers, who developed the net plan technique, and together we wanted to systematize large-scale construction systems for producing schools, housing and kindergartens rationally. That was my engineering period. Then I got the job in Kassel in 1973 and again worked briefly on developing prefabricated parts. That made great sense on the basis of system technology, but we did not pursue it further because I started hating these prefabricated parts. Nevertheless we developed a lot of them, for example load-bearing elements for roof gardens, troughs and other very well formulated elements, which were intended to cover verges and meet all sorts of other requirements. They weren't bad, but they weren't*

The special feature of the Marburg system is the modular building approach with large stacked concrete tables as basic units. The aim was to realize the construction grid and the finishes and fixtures grid independently of each other.

LAYERS OF INFORMATION. HOW DOES LANDSCAPE WORK?

cheap either. We used them a lot in Marburg. We wanted to achieve the degree of precision in landscape architecture that was available to the building industry."

With the same love of precision, Anneliese and Peter Latz developed not just special-load bearing elements and substrate mixtures for roof-planting at the Lahnberge University Hospital, but also, with the help of the landscape ecologist Friedrich Duhme from Weihenstephan, the entire concept for the roof gardens that not least had to match the exacting structural requirements of the roofs. The gardens offered a whole series of intimate spaces in the roofscape for people to

Anneliese and Peter Latz developed special roof-planting systems in Marburg that had to adapt to the particular features of the building system and the special irrigation requirements and climate conditions of the roofscape.

use, but also broad expanses of extensively planted vegetation that presented an attractive mosaic of colour in every season thanks to the rich variety of species featured. The basic concept is still recognizable after over 30 years, but lack of maintenance and various modifications to the roofscape have put considerable strain on the planting. Unlike the ground environment, the roof gardens were clearly not seen as the central factor creating identity. But for Peter Latz, who at that time in particular was devoting himself particularly intensively to university research in developing efficient roof-planting systems, the Marburg roof gardens were an essential part of the planned mosaic of open space. They also made an essential contribution to increasing the energy efficiency of the entire building project because of their insulating effect.

The whole Marburg University on Lahnberge still looks like a seventies small town quarter in its own right. Its character derives not just from the technocratic and constructional nature of the architecture, but above all from successful integration into the surrounding countryside and the design of an efficient, clearly structured system for the outdoor spaces.

Thanks to vigorous attention to designing roof areas and roof gardens, the extended hospital complex still has a varied mosaic of open spaces that links in with the design of the surrounding area.

LAYERS OF INFORMATION. HOW DOES LANDSCAPE WORK?

Ulm Science City on Eselsberg
University Section West

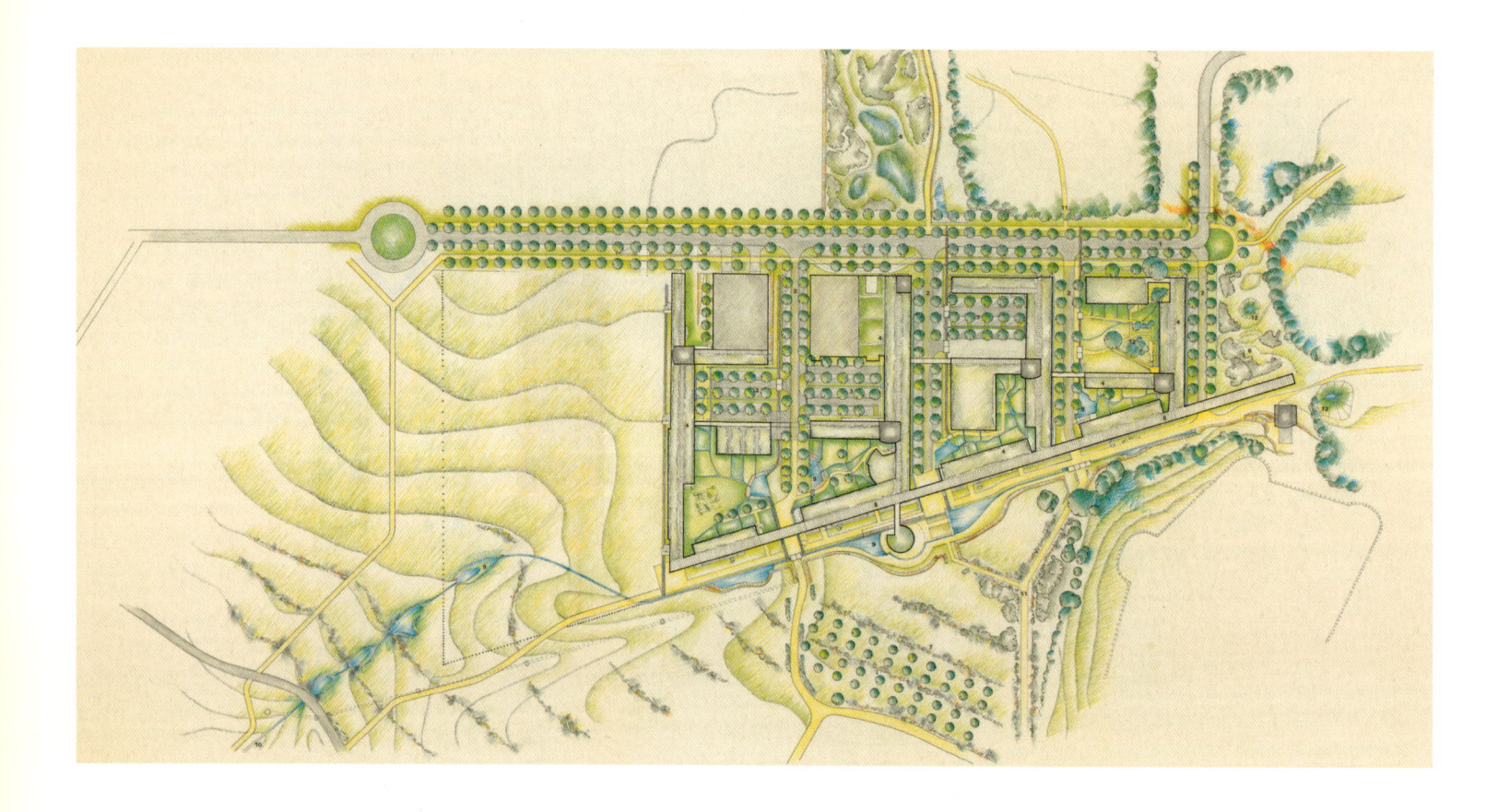

The comb-like structure of Otto Steidle's buildings and the 300 metre long line of buildings facing south-east over the landscape can be made out clearly in the plan of the university campus on the Eselsberg in Ulm.

THE EXPERIENCE GAINED from the large and complex Marburg-Lahnberge project was applied to and further developed for the planning of a new engineering faculty and a central library for Ulm University. In Marburg six design levels were called for, but in Ulm there were only two, the roof areas and the areas surrounding the buildings. Following the same basic idea as in Marburg, an extensive campus was planned in the eighties in Ulm on former agricultural land a few kilometres north of the city on the Eselsberg ridge, to be known as "Wissenschaftsstadt Ulm" (Ulm Science City). The competition for the engineering faculty was announced in 1988 and won by the architects Otto Steidle & Partner, working with Latz + Partner. Peter Latz very much enjoyed working with Otto Steidle, who died in 2004, because his frame construction architecture promised flexibility if extensions were needed, thus clearly reflecting the idea of communication between spaces and people. Over and above the general landscape conditions, the required integration of infrastructure and the difficult geological situation, nature preservation had a considerable part to play in this project, with its strict demands for ecological land use.

The proposed site of the new electro-technical institutions is slightly exposed on the south side. It was originally used for agriculture and forestry, but it also featured dry karstic sinks and bomb craters full of water that had become valuable habitats for special flora and fauna. Latz + Partner had been interested from the outset in preserving the location's landscape character, as in Marburg, and also in ensuring that the natural resources and valuable habitats were protected. The use of locally available building materials and site-appropriate plants, preservation of woodland

The long promenade in front of the south-east façade of the university building connects the shady wooded areas of the campus site to the sunny agricultural landscape in the south-west.

LAYERS OF INFORMATION. HOW DOES LANDSCAPE WORK?

stands and sink-holes, the planting of orchards and hedges in manageable field sizes – these are all incisive attributes of landscape adapted construction. Peter Latz felt it was helpful that the building process was so strongly influenced by ecology and nature conservation, as it made it easier for him to implement a series of important environmental interests that he was pursuing in his work anyway.

One of the architects' and landscape architects' aims that the university botanists and biologists did not accept at first was the highest possible building density in the interest of protecting land as a resource. Something that would be seen as open building development in an urban context seemed dense and stony in an open space at first, but it looks very pleasant today, with well developed planting throughout. The other competing teams in the competition had been in favour of more open building, but they consequently needed much more land to accommodate the amount of building space needed, resulting in much more intrusion into the landscape. A row of timber-framed buildings 300 metres long, running from north-east to south-west, with seminar rooms, computer centre and student workstations, sensuously points its façade south out over the landscape, so that the length of the structure directs the eye into the open fields. Two round buildings containing lecture rooms are attached to the row, and on the north side there are comb-like wings for institutes and laboratories, surrounding a series of courtyards of different sizes. "Steidle was interested in communicating pathways, rooms and junctions in linked study courses," Wolfgang Pehnt explains in his book *Deutsche Architektur seit 1900*[4]. As the 300 metre row is interrupted at the points of connection with the comb

Stormwater management is crucial to protecting the groundwater on the Eselberg's karst topography. Lushly planted retention pools define the image of some of the at times narrow inner courtyards.

structures, the southern and northern activity areas can coalesce. This means that cold air outflow and climatic regeneration are possible without any obstacles. But at the same time the landscape architects had to build all the infrastructure into the linking structures, including a grid gas main, for example, and this had to be planned in with absolute precision from the start of building.

Peter Latz devised a multifunctional access system for the entire complex, and was able to convince the planners as the project proceeded that most of the planned roads in the competition area had too many lanes for the traffic volumes anticipated. So the road widths were reduced, which not only helped to conserve land as a resource, but also achieved cost reductions that could be used for the benefit of the landscape architecture work. This was not the first project in which Peter Latz had effectively contributed himself to securing financing for his landscape architecture plans by skilful proposals for savings on the engineering front. *"It is important not to suffer passively from complex planning and building processes. They have to be addressed actively at an early stage. For example, you must ask to see the right plans at the right time, in order to be able to intervene at the best possible moment. As a rule, the best way to talk to engineers is to tell them what they are responsible for and not to ask how something works, because if you do that, you have lost. Though of course this does not always make you an easy planning partner,"* the landscape architect admits.

The landscape architects took advice from the university biologists and botanists and planted entire wetland habitats, so that all the flora and fauna that had already been on site could have the chance to take the site over again once building was completed. For this reason a whole series of ecological compensation zones, ponds and bog pools were created in the immediate vicinity of the building site, and they still exist today. This produced some authentic landscape corridors which today still guarantee connecting the site to the surrounding landscape. It would seem, and the

An attractive selection of herbaceous and woody plants was employed on the campus to keep the paths and the areas around them pleasant. Attention was also paid to varying path surfaces and to the hedges framing the car parks.

LAYERS OF INFORMATION. HOW DOES LANDSCAPE WORK?

originally sceptical biologists also agree, that this environmental protection strategy was successful, and has meant that the diversity of species on site was maintained.

Of course the building on the upper Eselsberg was not without consequences for the local water regime. Latz + Partner definitely wanted to prevent the collected surface run-off from disappearing into underground rainwater drains as is usually the case. They developed an ingenious rainwater system that extended from the greened roof to rainwater retention reservoirs and out into the open countryside. The basic aim is to keep the water on site for as long as possible, so that it can

The entire intricately branching system of rainwater collection channels finally leads into the rainwater canal, several hundred metres long, running by the south side of the university site. This is how the water is returned to the landscape.

evaporate or be captured in seasonally flooded meadow swales. It was not possible to allow the surface water to infiltrate into the karstic areas to protect the groundwater. The whole slope on the plateau had to be reshaped to accommodate the already enormous scale of the building programme in such a way that rainwater would no longer run northeast into the university campus, but southwest into the open countryside. The faculty grounds are just under 13 hectares. An intricately branching system of open surface channels, swales, reservoirs and ponds was created that contributes significantly to the character of the campus and to the diversity of the natural habitats. Particularly striking is the rainwater canal which, several hundred metres long, runs along the south façade of the specialist buildings. Here all the stormwater is collected, and held long-term in retention basins forming little ponds. Only after heavy rainfall is the water slowly released into the countryside. A string of widely differing wet and dry habitats has formed along the stormwater canal.

Light-coloured limestone, the typical material in the region, governs the aesthetic appearance of all the walls and waterside reinforcements, path surfaces and covering for planted areas. Here too Peter Latz remained true to his usual principle of using as much as possible only those materials that are available locally anyway. He uses brick only for the bottoms of the watercourses, which looks a little off-putting at first because of the contrast in colour and materials. At the time the complex was built, the landscape architects wanted to use an everyday, commonplace material to make the channels watertight. With hindsight, Peter Latz is no longer quite so sure, given the highly individual aesthetic, whether red brick actually was the right

The water channels on the campus provide important lines of communication with the landscape for the local fauna. Many of the now mature expanses of water are also important as habitats for plants and animals.

LAYERS OF INFORMATION. HOW DOES LANDSCAPE WORK?

The combination of locally sourced building materials like limestone, for example, and industrially manufactured building materials like the brick neatly bordering the bottom of the water channels are typical of many of Latz + Partner's projects.

decision. If he could choose, he would use steel channels today – a mass-produced industrial product, deliberately combined with hand-crafted natural stone masonry. This harmony between locally available "authentic" material and industrially mass-produced goods, between "raw and cooked", to quote Claude Lévi-Strauss again[5], runs through the office's work in a variety of combinations. The same natural stone aesthetic crops up again in Kirchberg near Luxembourg, where Latz + Partner also installed an ingenious rainwater system years later, though here combined with steel and exposed concrete.

The rustic-looking dry stone walls and channels on the upper Eselsberg horrified the architects at first, as the landscape was threatening to be too stony for them. But the limestone has lost its light colour over the years, and the vegetation has long

For Peter Latz, adapting building in the landscape context means recognizing and including existing structures of use in the landscape and employing building material that ages well from the immediate vicinity.

LAYERS OF INFORMATION. HOW DOES LANDSCAPE WORK? 53

since grown over large areas of the dry stone walls. Sometimes the rustic stone walls look like sunken remains of ancient ruins, but the landscape architects do not mind that. *"I am relatively content with the outcome. These are not structures intended to last a thousand years, and we are using local material that the flora and fauna of the area are on exceptionally good terms with. And natural stone will also definitely age better than concrete. It would not have been possible to finance enhancing the chunks of limestone with elaborate work by stonemasons."* Any stone cleared from the site was piled up in linear stone walls and field hedges including a variety of species were allowed to grow up out of these. These hedges fit in with the existing image of the countryside almost imperceptibly. *"From then on we had finally got the nature conservation people on our side: they realized we were not working against nature."* The landscape architects planted workable orchards between the hedges in the fields, a reminder of the orchard landscape that is increasingly disappearing around Ulm. Peter Latz also describes these landscape interventions as timeless, because their appearance does not necessarily cut them off from what is already in place.

Different tree species along the paths make it easier to find one's bearings on the university campus and create characteristic profiles for the path areas. The paving at the sides gives a sense that the width of the path has been reduced.

Of course the landscape architects also paid special attention to planting near to and in between the buildings. Different tree species along the various access paths make it easier to get one's bearings. Richly varied, luxuriant shrubs and herbaceous plants create a different atmosphere in each of the garden courts. In the functional courtyards, most of which serve as car parks, trimmed mixed hornbeam and privet hedges and trees ensure that the rows of parked cars do not look endless and desolate, but can also be seen as open spaces within the system as a whole. Fundamentally, Latz + Partner were looking for summery planting with herbaceous and woody plants that would look attractive all the year round. Careful use of very nutrient-poor substrate has made it possible to establish plants 600 metres above sea level that can otherwise only survive in Mediterranean regions. The planting provides very pleasant support for the pleasantly light-coloured, almost maritime-looking architecture of Otto Steidle & Partner's timber frame buildings, with their striking towers reminiscent of ships' bridges, painted in light pastel shades following a colour concept by Erich Wiesner.

Mediterranean plants grow on specially manufactured substrate low in nutrients on the Eselsberg at 600 metres above sea level and support the maritime look of Otto Steidle & Partner's timber skeleton buildings.

LAYERS OF INFORMATION. HOW DOES LANDSCAPE WORK?

Plateau de Kirchberg, Luxembourg

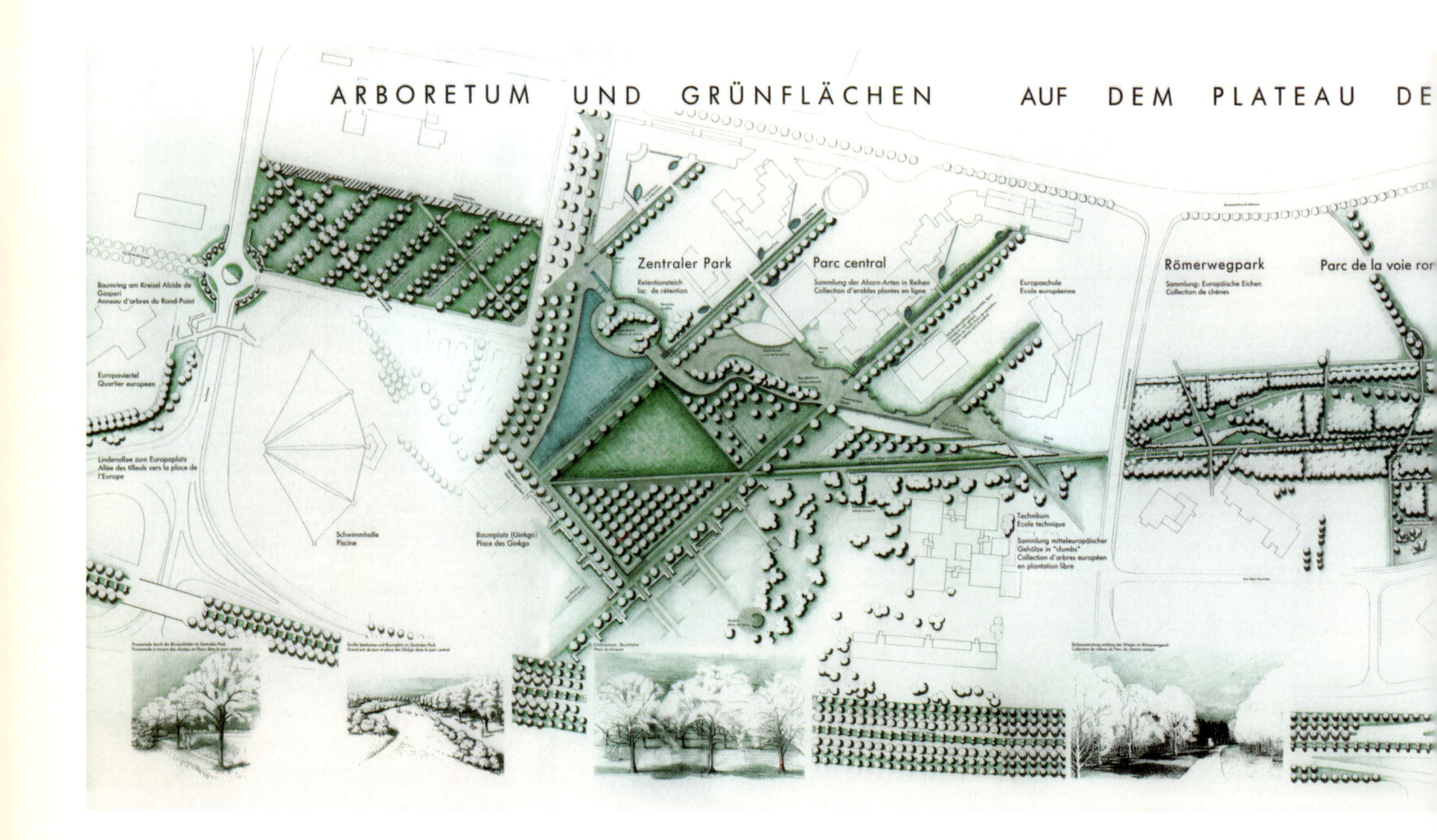

The open space master plan for Kirchberg near Luxembourg city shows (from left to right) the three main open spaces: the Parc Central, the Parc de la Voie Romaine and the Klosegroendchen. The spine, at a length of over three kilometres, is the tree-lined Avenue John F. Kennedy.

KIRCHBERG LUXEMBOURG

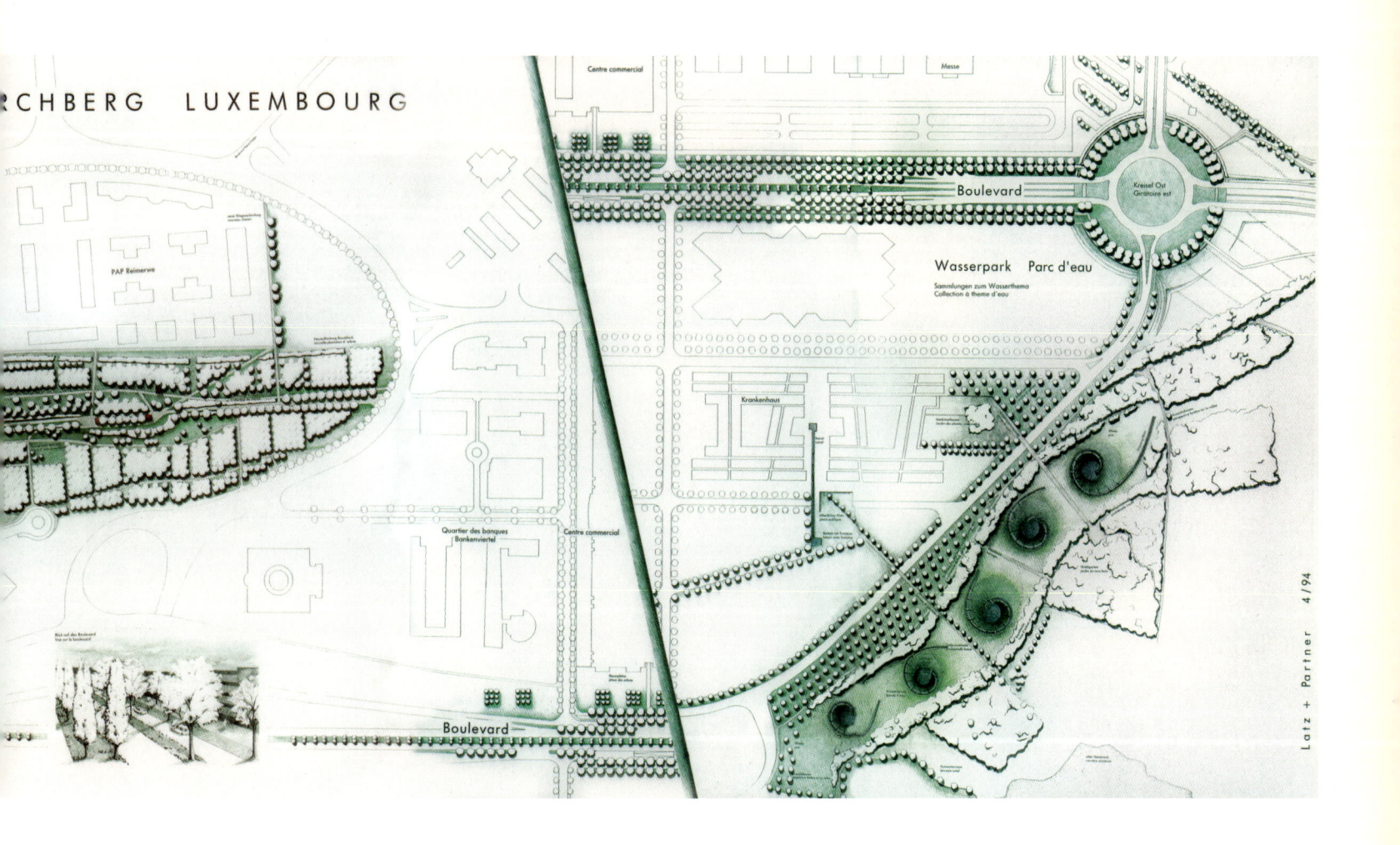

LATZ + PARTNER'S WORK since 1991 on one of the most important urban development projects in Europe on the outskirts of the city of Luxembourg is no less extensive, complex and ambitious than the Marburg-Lahnberge and Ulm projects. "The once essentially rural area of 360 hectares on the Plateau de Kirchberg, with its highly individual topography, fringed by valleys, only half a kilometre east of the capital city centre, experienced its first serious jolt in 1952, when Luxembourg was chosen as the headquarters of the European Coal and Steel Community. Expansion in the European Community attracted additional European institutions in subsequent stages. Some of these were placed in Luxembourg, which ultimately overloaded the office space capacity available within the historic city centre. The state met this emergency by compulsorily purchasing the Kirchberg land and in 1961 passed an act commissioning the 'Fonds d'Urbanisation et d'Aménagement du Plateau de Kirchberg' to plan the new urban district. The 'Pont Grande-Duchesse Charlotte', built in 1963 to plans by Egon Jux, and significantly called the 'Red Bridge' by the local people, boldly spans the Alzette valley and links the centre of

The American artist Richard Serra built his 20 metre high, tower-like sculpture "Exchange" in 1996 from seven slabs of Corten steel weighing just under 38 tons, at the east end of the Avenue John F. Kennedy.

Luxembourg with the plateau, on which a new city district with five quarters developed in the course of a few decades."[6]

The five quarters, Européen Nord, Européen Sud, Quartier du Parc, Quartier du Kiem and Quartier du Grünewald, align themselves with the Kirchberg ridge running along the Avenue John F. Kennedy for a little over three kilometres. Originally conceived as a purely European quarter and developed at first as a strictly functionally structured, car-friendly administrative city with large buildings by internationally distinguished architects in the International Style, the development came under the influence of a remarkable urban development paradigm change in the early eighties. In 1991, an interdisciplinary team including the Luxembourg architect Christian Bauer, the Frankfurt practice Jochem Jourdan and Bernhard Müller PAS, Latz + Partner and Kaspar König, director of the Museum Ludwig in Cologne, drew up an urban development study driven by the idea of looking back at the classical European city. The functionalistic satellite city with its junction-free traffic system along the N51 city motorway was to become a coherent and viable urban neighbourhood with a strong identity and lively links between housing, work, education and leisure functions.

One of the first major rebuilding measures intended to contribute to the Plateau de Kirchberg's new look was the downgrading of the N51 city motorway to an "avenue urbaine", a lively urban boulevard for pedestrians, cyclists, private and public local traffic. The eastern entrance to the city and the start of the Avenue John F. Kennedy is now marked by Richard Serra's highly visible Corten steel sculpture

The circular junction offers pedestrians and cyclists as well as cars a functionally logical and appealingly landscaped street space with trimmed hedges and an avenue of oak trees.

LAYERS OF INFORMATION. HOW DOES LANDSCAPE WORK?

"Exchange", which is a good 20 metres high. The American artist built his tower-like sculpture, made up of seven steel slabs weighing just under 38 tons, in 1996 at Kaspar König's request. It stands in the middle of the junction, setting its monumentality and lack of approachability against the surrounding banks and office buildings. An ensemble of rigorous and architectural trimmed hornbeam hedges and an avenue of oaks enclose this striking junction in a wide radius, ensuring above all a human scale from the point of view of pedestrians and cyclists.

The circular planting provides an introduction to the eightfold avenue that Latz + Partner have used to give the three kilometre long boulevard a new spatial profile. Cypress oaks planted in two rows mark the middle of the 60 metre wide road, flanked on either side by two oak avenues and pear trees, accentuating the footpaths and cycle tracks along the façades of the buildings. The green architecture is not yet fully grown, and can barely hold its own with the proportions of the large building masses. But in future this great green hall will span the boulevard and become Kirchberg's most impressive public "building". Fernand Pesch, president of the Fonds d'Urbanisation et d'Aménagement du Plateau de Kirchberg, was one of the few people who felt from the outset that it would be possible to transform the motorway into a boulevard, and so supported Latz + Partner's plans. "Roads are

One of the greatest challenges in the Kirchberg landscape architecture project was converting the former urban motorway into a boulevard that would make urban life in the street possible again.

modern society's most valuable spaces. Wasted on traffic," says Peter Latz. "So it is necessary to make sure that every aspect of them is working and use this to develop and increase a city's prosperity. There is such a thing as an integrated road: it helps us get our bearings, it is our organizational pattern, probably even on computer chips as well, and probably provides a pattern for data motorways as well. Real roads or streets exist in green areas as an organization model for greenery, for leisure, for pleasure. It organizes leisure, death, children's games, flirting, and is coming into our parks, for which it can provide the organizational pattern for the next century. In pictures it expresses our conflicts and our dreams. I repeat: this integral city-constituting function is the most important asset that culture has handed down. The road is our most important public possession, our collective wealth, and we must cultivate it. The road can be the object for new ideas."[7]

In the eastern section of the Avenue John F. Kennedy in particular, where both the Utopolis multiplex cinema, just under 180 metres long, and the bank buildings restrict the street space, and the traffic noise crashes through the concrete canyons, it becomes clear how ambitious it is to win street space back for people. But the restaurants are already starting to risk setting up their tables and chairs outside. And in the meantime competing outdoor leisure facilities are attracting increasing numbers of people: not far from the place where what is at present the only pedestrian bridge crosses the busy avenue, the new, so-called District Centre branches off to the north, a kind of mall, opened to the public in 1996. This mall was created because no one thought the boulevard had a future, to such an extent that the

Carefully planned tree planting along the office building façades changes the sense of scale of the street and provides shade in the hot summer months, when the restaurants serve their customers in the open air.

LAYERS OF INFORMATION. HOW DOES LANDSCAPE WORK?

original access was from the side that does not abut the Avenue John F. Kennedy. Now that the boulevard really is worth spending time in, the small forecourt rises via a flight of steps, clearly not designed to meet the pressure of today's everyday use, up to the new entrance portal of the 280 metre long shopping mall, flooded with light and fully air-conditioned.

Given the flourishing retail activity in the District Centre, the question arises of whether public life really can be brought back into the street completely, or whether it is not the malls despite everything that present a more attractive and generally effective image of lively public spaces. For Peter Latz, shopping malls of this kind are part of an old model intended to conceal the strict separation of street functions that had developed over the decades entirely in favour of use by traffic. But a glazed shopping mall cannot function in isolation from the actual road system, and has to be on large access roads like the Avenue John F. Kennedy, "from which cars can easily drive into the underground and multi-story car parks. From there people go into the main pedestrian street in the building, which they never leave. The mall becomes a fortress. [...] The pedestrian precinct itself goes into decline, and becomes a social problem area."[8]

It remains to be seen whether the "avenue urbaine" on the Kirchberg will suffer a similar fate despite all the efforts by the landscape architects and the known financial constraints.

The Avenue John F. Kennedy is centrally important to the open space concept that Latz + Partner are responsible for on the Kirchberg, as an infrastructural backbone

The striking dune-like earth formations at the north end of the Kloesegroendchen keep the traffic noise down, offer views into the little valley from their ridges and create extraordinary locations for vegetation, where a wide variety of flower species flourish.

The view west shows the large dimensions of the Kirchberg urban development, and also the Klosegroendchen immediately adjacent to the traffic junction at the east entrance to the city, accentuated in the middle by Richard Serra's large-scale steel sculpture.

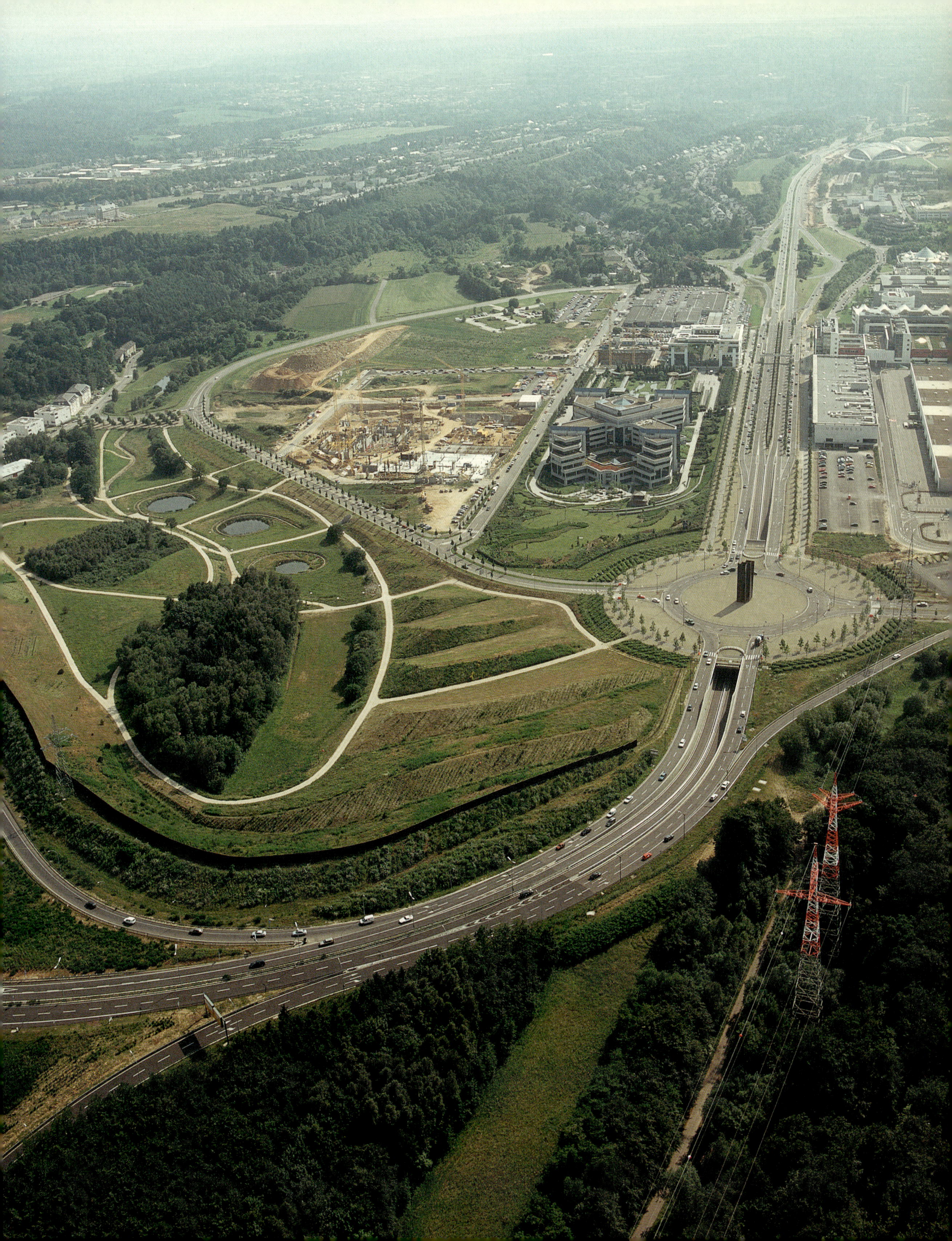

and new urban artery. Ecological and aesthetic rainwater management is also centrally important, embedded in extensive public green spaces designed as landscape architecture in the eastern and central sections of Kirchberg. On the east side, not far from Richard Serra's sculpture, the landscape architects designed the Parc Klosegroendchen, an area of about 30 hectares in a meadow valley. Dealing with excavation spoil from the road building and managing stormwater runoff from the surrounding urban districts play an important part in the project. In comparison with this, the Parc Central in the middle of Kirchberg covers just under 20 hectares and includes the grounds for the adjacent European School and the National Sport and Culture Centre. Befitting its importance in the district, the Parc Central is planned as a prestigious and representative open space. The park fulfils a whole variety of functions, rainwater management being just one of these, albeit an important one. Klosegroendchen for its part is a park with an essentially unpretentious design, offering everyday experience of nature and landscape above all to the residents in the Grünwald quarter and to the patients of the nearby clinic and rehabilitation centre.

The Klosegroendchen is surrounded by busy local streets, main roads and motorways, and so it was no easy task to give the park a peaceful atmosphere. Latz + Partner were determined not to imitate nature or landscape, but wanted to create a sculpturally accentuated park, integrating an efficient rainwater retention system as a visible basic ecological and aesthetic component. In the northern area of the long park they had the road works spoil piled up in the form of a dune-like earth structure, apparently wandering down into the valley. These earth ridges, each several metres high, protect the little valley not just from the traffic noise from the large junction at the northern end of the park, but also make an ideal habitat for many herbaceous plants, grasses and herbs that like dry soil, and blossom luxuriantly in summer. Visitors are inevitably drawn to the highest points on the geometrically shaped ridges, from which it is possible to look down into the valley bottom. On the opposite side of the valley, small woods screen off the view of the acoustic barrier of the adjacent A1 motorway, interrupted by broad, nutrient-poor meadow areas running from the flanks of the ridges into the valley bottom.

In summer, luxuriant banks of iris, cat's-tail and other moisture-loving plants mark the areas along the valley where stormwater is captured in retention ponds and slowly released into the surrounding area. Here too infiltration has to be prevented in order to protect the groundwater, so Latz designed three large, spiralling water channels as the end points of a finely branching rainwater system extending far into

The spiralling, rough masonried rainwater channels reduce the speed at which the water flows, so that larger trash and debris is caught on the way to the retention pond. Finer particles can settle in the pond itself.

the quarter. These not only take the surface water from the roof and traffic areas to the retention ponds, but also are a first water treatment step. Trash and debris in the water is caught in the stone channels and stepped retention system on the way to the retention ponds at the end of spiral outlets. The silt, mud and dust the rain washes off the sealed surfaces can then settle in the still areas of the circular retention pools, before the excess water, once cleaned, flows down the valley and finally into the Alzette in reduced-outflow quantities.

Immediately once the stone spirals were completed, one turning left and two right, their architectural form language along with the earthworks defined the park's sculptural image. The ensemble as a whole was clearly reminiscent of pioneering American Land Art by Michael Heizer and Robert Smithson in the early seventies. Peter Latz is not particularly pleased when his work is occasionally interpreted as landscape art, as he is not so much interested in the aesthetic appeal of individual

objects as in viable structures and functions within a landscape: "If I [...] am seeking specific interpretations of places, space and situations, the whole variety of different cultural languages has to be used. Art is one of these languages. In the history of architecture, there has always been a search for objective criteria of construction technology, the heritage of civilization, the heritage of art, theological meaning and so on. Although our civilization always treats these components separately, I feel that the distinction between art, architecture and landscape architecture possibly does not really make much sense."[9]

Today, some years after the project was completed provisionally in 1999, the stone spirals can only be made out clearly in winter and early spring, when the vegetation around the retention pools is not so luxuriant. From the start, a wide range of habitats for flora and fauna started to establish themselves not just in the ponds, but in the dry stone masonry as well. The aesthetic components now play a minor role.

Illustrations of spiral nebulae and Catherine wheels inspired Peter Latz to use spiral forms for landscape projects from early on.

LAYERS OF INFORMATION. HOW DOES LANDSCAPE WORK?

Wide, curving paths allow visitors to explore the Klosegroendchen, and perhaps it is now only on the earth mounds that they still have a sense that this is an artificial landscape. The Luxembourg sculptor Bertrand Ney added an additional artistic touch. He placed his natural stone sculpture "Coquille" in a niche in the terrain created especially by the landscape architects at the edge of the little valley in 1997. The great bowl is hewn out of a single monolithic block of natural stone and polished. It can almost be interpreted as a symbol of the Klosegroendchen, which collects rainwater like a bowl placed in the landscape and creates new habitats. At the same time, "Coquille", like an elegant piece of furniture in the shade of the little wood nearby, invites visitors to linger. In the future the Klosegroendchen is to be further developed to meet the needs of people living close by to include playgrounds and paved paths – perhaps running the risk that this little valley will to a certain extent lose its casual, almost secretive sense of ordinariness.

The Hôpital de Kirchberg is very close to the Parc Kolsegroendchen, separated from it only by the Boulevard Pierre Werner. Here too Latz + Partner were involved in designing the outdoor spaces, covering about 2.5 hectares, from 1998 to 2003. The fact that a large proportion of this area lay over an underground car park had to be taken into consideration when planning the imposing layout for the hospital's 4000 square metre forecourt. It was, for example, not possible to plant large trees. Other essential background information for the planning was that a number of access functions had to be provided to the inner courtyard. For this reason the landscape architects covered the entire surface of the courtyard with light concrete slabs matching the hospital façade, and created long planting beds scattered over the paved area like islands, leaving enough room for movement where it was needed. As the planting beds had to be slightly raised, the edges were framed in part with

The sculptor Bertrand Ney created the natural stone sculpture "Coquille" in the form of a large shell from a single monolithic stone block for the Klosegroendchen in 1997. The sculpture, rather like an elegant piece of furniture, invites visitors to linger.

light yellow limestone slabs, loosely placed obliquely, which look strangely improvised. Originally all the planting beds were to have been covered loosely with limestone chippings, and thus transformed into dry stone islands with appropriate vegetation. The clients thought this was unduly radical and so had to make do with the hesitant-looking framing. Fountains spring up directly from the surface of the slabs in several areas of the courtyard; the water quickly soaks away through the joints. There is no change of level, pool edge or gutter system to break the even covering. After dark the illuminated fountains look like festive candles. The planting with multi-trunk serviceberries, but above all the preferred use of herbaceous plants and shrubs that like dry soil, with grey foliage and blue flowers, including Russian sage and lavender, interspersed with light-pink roses and smoke bushes, creates a pleasantly light-coloured, relaxed atmosphere in the courtyard. Paul Schneider's monolithic natural stone sculpture in polished blue granite also fits in with the same colour scheme.

This is a different approach from the inner courtyards of the Marburg hospital, where the garden design effectively presented an alternative world to the architecture. The forecourt of the Hôpital de Kirchberg and the architecture, completed in 2003, work together as a carefully matched ensemble. Just as in Lahnberge, the architecture in Kirchberg establishes a clear spatial framework, and the garden design develops a character of its own within this given framework. Material quality,

The Hôpital de Kirchberg receives its visitors in a courtyard filled with the colours and scents of roses and lavender in the summer. At night illuminated fountains like candles accentuate the area.

LAYERS OF INFORMATION. HOW DOES LANDSCAPE WORK?

formal language and airy, open planting match the building. Designed by the architecture practice incopa in Saarbrücken, the building gives the ensemble as a whole a modern look. In comparison with the weighty seventies hospital buildings in Marburg, the architecture in Kirchberg confronts its surroundings more openly and transparently. This means that the indoor and outdoor spaces can be more closely connected, and the architectonic design of the courtyard also ensures a pleasant atmosphere in the hospital consulting rooms.

In just the same way as in the western Quartier du Grünberg, the interplay between nature, architecture and art is a key feature of the central Quartier du Parc, but the imposing character required for the central quarter led to an almost completely different formulation of the basic themes that had already been addressed. The Quartier du Parc is north of the Avenue John F. Kennedy and south of the Boulevard Konrad Adenauer, which runs parallel with it, in the middle of the Plateau de Kirchberg, and features two major building complexes. The southern section of these buildings is immediately adjacent to the Avenue John F. Kennedy. "In 1982 the 'Piscine Olympique' opened under an imposing roof reminiscent of a scallop shell. The Parisian architect Roger Tallibert implemented the conical forms in concrete segments. Roger Tallibert was also responsible for 'd'Coque' – the National Sport and Culture Centre – which was completed immediately adjacent to the swimming pools in 2002. The hilly roofscape of the sports complex corresponds with the formal language of the earlier building, but was given an innovative thrust in the technical sphere by the laminated timber beams spanning a roof area of 4000 square metres."[10]

Latz + Partner designed the hospital's outdoor spaces from 1998 to 2003. Paul Schneider's monolithic stone sculpture in blue polished granite also provides a special touch of colour.

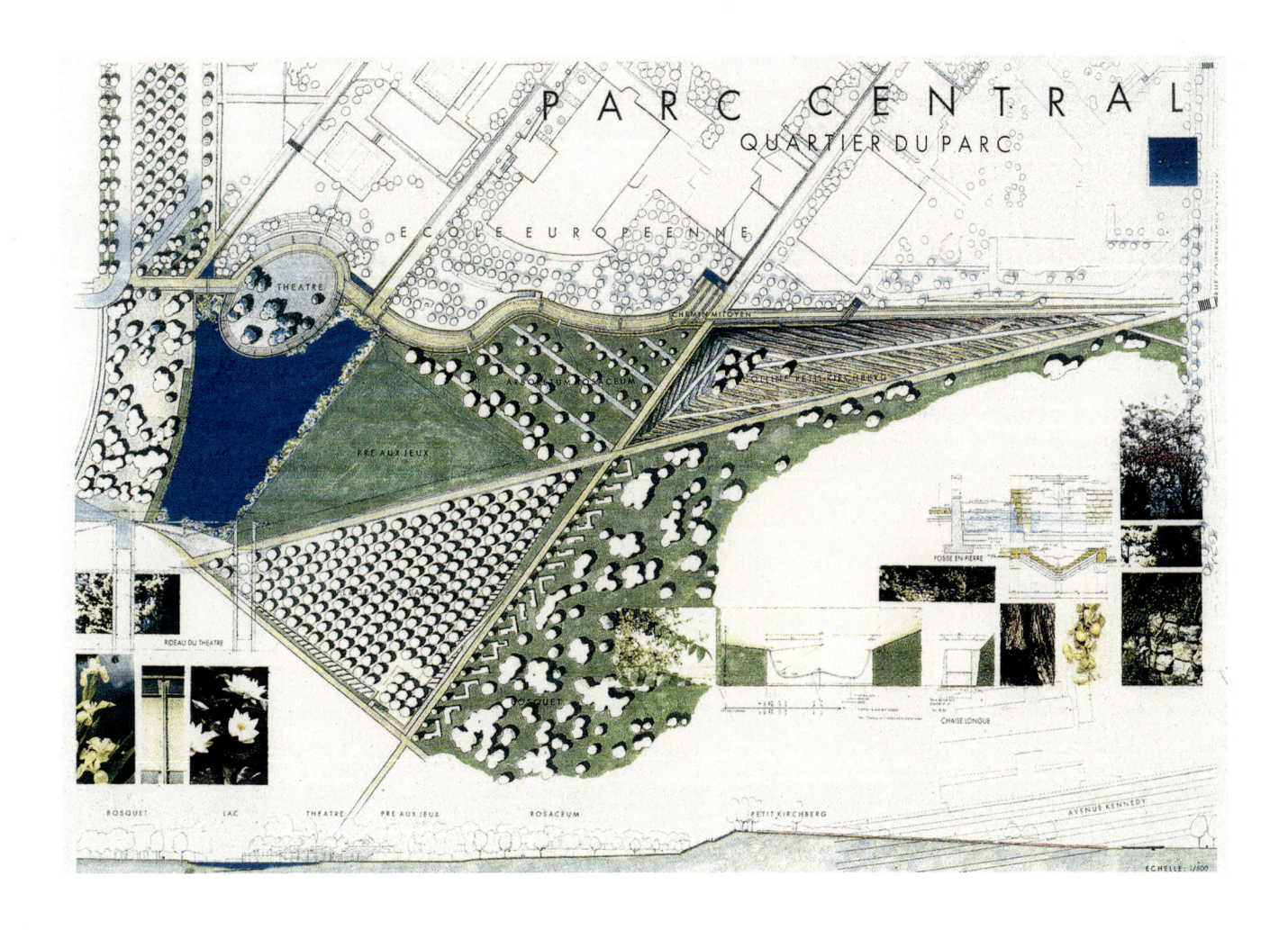

The landscape architects designed the extensive Parc Central, which is sited directly adjacent to the large buildings of the Olympic indoor pools and the National Sport and Culture Centre, as an imposing park that could be used in a number of different ways.

LAYERS OF INFORMATION. HOW DOES LANDSCAPE WORK?

On the northern edge of the quarter is the extensive Ecoles Européennes complex, considerably extended in the year 2000 under the direction of architect Christian Bauer et Associés, in order to make room for more than 3,600 additional pupils at the primary and secondary school levels. The most striking building in the ensemble, clad in red brick and with green roofs throughout, is the oval festival hall. The entrances to the school buildings face the Boulevard Konrad Adenauer on the north side. The school yards face the Parc Central to the south, jointly creating a multi-purpose outdoor space of about 20 hectares.

It is clear from an aerial photograph that the landscape architects wanted to give the whole quarter a clearly intelligible open space structure, varied or interrupted only in specific places, and responding appropriately to the scale of the large buildings. Distinctive lines, running almost exactly north-south and following the most striking edges of the Ecoles Européennes, run through the extensive open spaces in the whole of the Quartier Central. As a rule the lines consist of paths accompanied by rows of trees which appear in the form of incisions into the terrain several metres deep which cut from the lower Parc Central into the higher plateau of the school site. A prominent, wedge-shaped open space extending from the entrance to the Centre National Sportif et Culturel on the park side thrusts north-west on a diagonal to this system of paths running north-south, to the point at which the Parc de la voie romaine, which Latz + Partner also designed, starts on the east side.

The Parc de la voie romaine takes its name from the Roman road that crossed the Plateau de Kirchberg from south-west to north-east over 2000 years ago, linking the cities of Reims and Trier. The landscape north and south of the raised road was planted with dense stands of deciduous and coniferous trees in the sixties, thus obstructing the view of the surrounding area. Peter Latz came up with the idea of establishing a European Arboretum on the entire Plateau de Kirchberg at the very beginning of the project, and the tree stock in the area of the present Parc de la voie romaine was intended to form the heart of this tree collection. Latz + Partner also planted a large number of different tree species and varieties in the Parc Klosegroendchen. Already the stands of trees along the Roman road offered a particular opportunity to develop an existing body of woodland as part of the European Arboretum. First of all, Peter Latz had clearings cut in the existing wood. This was done almost imperceptibly so that the trees, which were originally planted very close together, could grow full crowns. A wide variety of oaks were planted south of the cleared area. Today the Parc de la voie romaine can be experienced as a richly structured stock of trees with varied clearings and views. The sculptor Ulrich Rückriem added four stone sculptures, presenting the theme of the wayside shrine along the road.

Following the route of the old Roman road from northeast to southwest, one finds oneself back at the entrance of the Parc Central, which is identified by a striking earthwork that is visible from a considerable distance. The landscape architects modelled the broader end of the long, wedge-shaped site using existing excavated material to form a large pyramid with unequal sides and a triangular ground plan. Its highest point was designed as a viewing point and planted with cypress oaks. The "little Kirchberg" provides a view of the central area of the park, which unlike the adjacent school site is freely open to the public. Peter Latz had the image of the raised Roman road, from which there were good views originally, in mind when creating this little hill. A wide area of meadowland, divided into sections with a whole variety of characters, opens up to the south-west directly in front of the viewing mound, whose flanks are planted in strips with various different low woody plants. In the foreground, roses, willows and other shrubs and fruit trees are planted

The atmosphere of the Parc de la Voie Romaine, which is part of the European Arboretum, derives mainly from a richly structured stock of large trees, some of which were already there, and some newly planted. They include many different varieties of oak.

LAYERS OF INFORMATION. HOW DOES LANDSCAPE WORK?

in two-row strips in the grass, creating a distant impression of agricultural cultivation. The collection of fruit trees is also part of the European Arboretum, as are all the other large-scale tree plantings and groves in the Parc Central area.

Beyond this strip meadow is a large triangular area of grass available for sport and games, bordered to the southwest by a generous stretch of water. But this is only the visible part of a large volume of retained water extending well under the meadow, fed by the surface run-off and roof water collected from the school site and from the sport and culture centre. If there is particularly heavy rainfall the grassy area for sport and games can be used as a backup rainwater retention reservoir above ground as well. The rainwater channels run through almost the entire Quartier du Parc like a network of fine veins. They are designed in different ways, sometimes as enclosed concrete gutters with protective grates in the school yards, sometimes as open, straight watercourses accompanying the diagonal paths, and sometimes interrupted by simply designed and carefully planted settling ponds on the border between the school site and the public park. These settling ponds ensure that the water can be purified to some extent before it reaches the lake.

The largest collection channel accompanying a path winds in a few curves along the edge of the terrain between the school and park sites, and is lined with coarsely cut, light yellow Luxembourg sandstone. Latz + Partner had all the retaining and terrace walls built from the same material, which was excavated on site when building the school complex, as a reminder of the old vineyard walls by the Moselle. This uniform choice of material gives the parkland a calm and at the same time

The Little Kirchberg, a long earth pyramid with unequal sides, topped with cypress oaks, rises on the north-eastern edge of the Parc Central. There is a good general view of the park from the top.

powerful expressive quality. "I believe," explains Peter Latz, "that we take particular care of the effect made by individual materials. It can be granite slabs, made on a template basis, as in the Melsungen pedestrian precinct, where we wanted to make do without on-site cutting works or paving in unappropriate corners. But it can also be rusty iron elements. The question is always how it can be handled and the extent to which the material in question actually works expressively in the context of a park, a public open space or a private garden. This can differ very considerably, and for this reason the question has to be discussed for different projects." Just as in Ulm, the excavated stone that could not be used, was to be collected in linear residual stone walls to allude to the agricultural history of the location in the park, but the idea did not appeal to the clients as hoped.

An archaic overall impression, reminiscent of the megaliths of early high Mediterranean cultures, is created at the dip in the terrain in the Parc Central where the retaining walls run in a curved line over a length of several hundred metres and at a height of some metres along the border of the school site. We have the skilful combination of industrially produced materials, for example the reinforced concrete door and window lintels or the steel railing construction, to thank for the fact that the open space in general does not slip into rustic monumentalism in design terms. The long straight retaining walls were also built in the same way on the eastern border of the park, along the Rue Erasme, offering sheltered niches for passersby to sit in. Latz + Partner wanted to make spending time in the street more pleasant in the interest of winning the street back as a place where life can be lived.

In the pedestrian zone in Melsungen, old pavement slabs from Berlin were reused in a very precise way.

The fact that the trees and shrubs are planted in parallel rows alludes to the agricultural history of the Kirchberg, while the large retention pond is there mainly to retain stormwater.

LAYERS OF INFORMATION. HOW DOES LANDSCAPE WORK?

The central oval stage thrusting out into the pond is planted with pines that had to make way for building elsewhere. A curtain of water sometimes pours out of the stage's steel frame.

If you follow the large, curved retaining wall inside the park in the direction of the central lake, you reach an oval platform thrusting out into the surface of the water, bordered on its north side by a flight of steps like an open-air theatre. On the water in front of this sits the peaceful "Trois îles" art installation by the artist Martha Pan. It consists of three floating islands, creating fascinating reflections all around themselves. Visitors immediately realize the significance of the amphitheatre-like arrangement, and sometimes use it for little shows and parties. Seen on a plan or from the air, there is an interesting feature corresponding with the open-air theatre by the lake in Christian Bauer's oval festival hall. Architecture and landscape architecture also enter into an interesting dialogue in terms of their functions. On the lake side, the oval platform, which is occupied by single pines, is bounded by a tall tubular steel construction from which a curtain of water pours like a transparent screen at appropriate moments. Effects of this kind, just like the fountains in the southern part of the lake against the backdrop of the National Sport and Culture Centre, are not there solely for design purposes. On the contrary, the fountains enrich the accumulated rainwater with oxygen, and thus prevent it from suddenly reaching its ecological tipping-point.

The basic principle of illustrating functional and even ecological matters while at the same time tying them into the overall concept of the landscape architecture aesthetically is valued highly in all Latz + Partner's work. In Kirchberg, the responsible authorities are not just proud of having an ingenious rainwater management system. The exclusive use of materials obtained from the site for building the natural

Vineyard walls from the Moselle valley inspired the Kirchberg wall constructions by Latz + Partner.

The step in the terrain on the northern edge of the park was built in locally quarried limestone. It is no coincidence that the archaic look of these buildings is similar to that of vineyard walls in the nearby Moselle valley.

LAYERS OF INFORMATION. HOW DOES LANDSCAPE WORK?

stone walls and the viewing mound, and also the replanting and rescue of almost all the existing trees that were in the way of the planned buildings, is seen as additional proof of the high level of environmental awareness shared by everyone involved in the project. For Peter Latz, the special challenge of realizing such enterprises always lies in making the best possible use of available resources and influencing the progress of the building process in such a way that the greatest possible number of required building measures are skilfully matched up with each other to achieve maximum synergy and minimize the overall costs and energy use for the project. This requires a great deal of knowledge about the entire organization sequence of urban development and landscape architecture construction projects.

The consistent preservation of existing large trees, tall oaks and pines partly planted in loosely arranged groves, complements the European Arboretum and gives the Parc Central a "mature" character that could have been achieved only years later by new planting. The landscape architects devised one of the sections immediately adjacent to the central lake as a spacious green hall made up of hundreds of Trees of Heaven. Of course trimmed hedges again play a major role in the park, whether as an imposing setting for the entrance areas to the sport and culture centre, as a maze or as green park furniture made in banks of hornbeam. A 200 metre long piece of hedge architecture was placed along the central north-east axis in the Parc Central, flanked by a row of cypress oaks. Strictly trimmed architectural hedges, all about shoulder high, create a large number of intimate places to spend time in along the path, which the landscape architects fitted out with specially made furniture. Little

Martha Pan's "Trois îles" sail gently on the surface of the water, creating fascinating reflections. The water curtain is not just for aesthetic purposes, but also enriches the pond with oxygen.

Powerful lines, giving a sense of order and structure even in plan, also shape the reality of the Parc Central. The sophisticated design of the different areas creates a variety of habitats within the overall structure.

LAYERS OF INFORMATION. HOW DOES LANDSCAPE WORK?

groups of seats are offered facing the path, while on the other side elegant concrete sofas allow a comfortable rest with views out into the adjacent area of the arboretum. For Peter Latz, parks are first and foremost places to be used by everyone, and every day. He clearly connects back to the key motive of the "Volkspark" movement in the last century, which proclaimed abandoning bourgeois, merely pretentious greenery in favour of open space for general everyday use.

The run of trimmed hedge along one of the main paths in the Parc Central is almost 200 metres long. Small, almost intimate seating niches are built into the hedge, inviting visitors to sit down in a sheltered space.

Dealing with "bad places"

IN RECENT DECADES, Peter Latz has brought off some trend-setting international projects that have won him and his team world-wide acclaim for dealing with damaged landscapes, which he himself calls "bad places". Latz is convinced that landscape architecture's principal concern today should be with such places, and not with decorating and prettifying intact outdoor areas. *"I am concerned with precisely the opposite: deliberately placing gardens in the most horrible places that I can't use at the moment, that I have to visit in protective clothing and so on, and one day making them into places where I can once more say: I want to stay here, this is where I want to be."*

Peter Latz defines "bad places" both tersely and pragmatically: *"Bad places include anywhere I wouldn't allow my four-year-old granddaughter to play,"* but he adds: *"These can be very exciting places."* Remembering that Peter Latz taught at the polytechnic in Kassel in the early seventies, and the extent to which he addressed design teacher Horst Rittel's planning methods and principles at this time, it is immediately clear that "bad" is not to be understood simply in the moral and ethical sense. For Rittel, "wicked" or "tricky" problems are those that in principle cannot be "solved" scientifically, and such problems occur particularly frequently in the design field. Lucius Bruckhardt, who was appointed to the Gesamthochschule Kassel in the same year as Peter Latz, and started his trend-setting teaching as professor of social economics in urban systems, published an article commending problem-oriented, methodical design and called "From academicism in design to the treatment of wicked problems"[11] in the year he was appointed, 1973. Just like his young colleague, Burckhardt mistrusted the idea of design as a purely intuitive activity based on inspiration and art, and was also working on how the planning and design process could be taken out of the realm of purely individual intuition into the zone of greater objectivity and intelligibility. Horst Rittel and Melvin Webber pronounced that "Planning Problems are Wicked Problems"[12], and later explained: "We use the term 'wicked' in a meaning akin to that of 'malignant' (in contrast to 'benign') or 'vicious' (like a circle) or 'tricky' (like a leprechaun) or 'aggressive' (like a lion, in contrast with the docility of a lamb)."[13]

Wicked problems, say Rittel and Webber, are characterized by the fact that in principle they are unique problems that constantly recur. There are no definitive or secure formulations for dealing with them, and they cannot be approached by trial and error, because once something is built – for example, the elaborate restoration of a former industrial site – it cannot be taken back simply or without far-reaching consequences. This vivid exploration of the terms "bad" or "wicked" fits exactly in relation to the vast majority of current planning and design problems in landscape architecture, and quite definitely applies to all the "bad places" that Peter Latz has had to address so far. *"Of course 'bad' has a certain moral implication as well, that cannot be denied. Anyone who is not directly familiar with the specific processes by which bad places come into being will incline entirely towards moral interpretations. For example, if someone makes too much noise, that is not just seen as a measurable quantity that can be scientifically analyzed, but also as a piece of direct aggression that I have to suffer and for which I make someone else morally responsible, for example in the case of aircraft noise, motorway noise or the noise a neighbour makes. That is why there are rules fixing things like not using a lawn-mower at particular times. That is a moral category."*

He addresses the central themes of soil and water in almost all his projects. *"Extremely polluted water-courses. Perhaps that's a moral category as well. Is it possible to expect a people to put up with polluted water-courses on its territory? Extremely lax treatment of something we don't need any more, generally seen as rubbish. But it has to be addressed rather more subtly. There are some very aggressive materials, industrial waste, for example, which is frequently highly toxic and has a direct effect on everything around it. And there is material that the environment fanatics think should all be composted and recycled. The approaches to the solution often lie somewhere in between, and there is a lot of research still to be done in this context. To disapprove of fly-tipping, wherever it happens, is definitely a moral category. A rubbish dump is itself a bad place, I wouldn't let my grandchildren play there. But I have to make an effort and work towards ensuring that I can let them play there one day. They will probably be grown up by then, but perhaps their children could play there."* In the case of obvious problem areas like fly-tipping and polluted waterways one would be able to come up with approaches to solutions quickly: rubbish has to be disposed of and water has to be purified, and so on. *"That is the classical response to such problems, and it's the one I always try first,"* Peter Latz explains. *"But the scale of these problems has become so large and so complex that I can't apply approaches like that any more."*

Saarbrücken Harbour Island

This 1946 oblique aerial view shows the Saar in the foreground and behind it the harbour basin before it was filled in; these features used to form the borders of the Harbour Island in Saarbrücken.

PETER LATZ EMBARKED on his first major and at the same time trend-setting experiment in dealing with a "bad place" in the late seventies on the so-called Hafeninsel (Harbour Island), the site of a former coal harbour on the banks of the Saar in Saarbrücken. In the mid 19th century, when the Saar was canalized to make it more navigable because of increasing industrial growth in the region, the Hafeninsel came into being as an isolated space, bordered to the north by a bend in the river that has now been cut off and in the south by the new canal cut, about 800 metres long. The disused old stretch of water was developed as a harbour basin; its western end was blocked off, and the roads and railway tracks for the harbour area were built across the land gained. Numerous tracks ran through the site, including a north and a south railway line on piers, with elevated tracks. The image of the complex was determined by mobile loading cranes on rails, as well as a large number of utilitarian buildings. The harbour was largely destroyed in air raids in the Second World War, and rendered entirely unusable by sunken ships and gradual silting.

The old arm of the Saar was filled in in the sixties, and a congress hall built at the former mouth of the harbour basin. The rest of the site was used as a coal storage area, car park and building rubble dump in the post-war period. It was not until the late seventies, when planning for the western autobahn bridge over the Saar began, and the Hafeninsel was needed as a seat for the northern end of the cross-strut bridge, that the site, which had become completely overgrown in the meantime, came back into the public eye. The responsible planning authorities were also looking for a concept for revaluing this open space near the city centre, as they wanted to be able to build on its periphery. They thus undertook a planning process in the context of which Peter Latz and his team, including his long standing assistant the landscape architect Gunter Bartholmai, developed three concept variations, based on very different models. Even then, the landscape architects were very well aware that "if the design and formal language for new parks follow the prevailing, tried-and-tested models, they are always accepted, surprising though this may seem, even if they do not meet important conditions for use."[14]

In the first planning stages two design alternatives were created, exactly matching the conventional ideal concepts that quickly find their supporters, then as now. The "landscape garden" concept was based on the classical, historical 18th century landscape park with curved pathways, picturesquely sited groups of trees, meadow valleys and a lake, placed under the bridge like a mirror, was intended to counter the divisive effect of this massive engineering structure. This ideal landscape image could have been given some scenic flavour by using elements from the history of

DEALING WITH "BAD PLACES"

the former harbour, in the form of picturesque ruins or follies. The clients were very taken with this concept from the outset, but Peter Latz and his comrades-in-arms rejected the design on the grounds that the park would not be able to sustain the expected high levels of use in a relatively small area. Also, the mass of the structures that were still in existence could not be adequately hidden with greenery to create a "natural" landscape image, and finally they said that it would not be possible to build the required sound insulation into the project appropriately. "The area is too small in its natural quality as a riverside landscape, and it has too little capacity for coping with the pressure to be placed on it and presents too little scope for regeneration to meet the requirements. The ideal vegetation is not compatible with the rubble subsoils."[15]

The second planning variant also appealed very quickly on the spot, as this image of an architectural park also chimed with familiar precedents. The park with a "geometrical ordering structure" would have taken its direction from 17th century Baroque parks with their imposing sets of trees and hedges, magnificent avenues and clear connections with the urban ground plan. In this design variant, a long channel of water, accompanied by trellises, would have run under the bridge and ensured that the two neoclassical-looking parts of the park were linked. But the landscape architects again disillusioned the supporters of this park variant by pointing out that the proposed elements would not provide sufficient sound insulation and that there was too little "opportunity for expressive forms appropriate to contemporary taste and for allowing free reign to individual developments"[16] – that is to say, the result would have been a complete, immutable picture of cultivated nature, expensive and laborious to maintain and intolerant of those tendencies to change that can never be excluded in public places.

"I have never felt that I wanted to do something new or that what I was doing was new,"[17] Peter Latz pointed out later, but if one bears in mind how carefully the first two design variants had been worked out, presented to the public and then systematically rejected again, it is difficult to avoid the impression that here we are looking at conscious demolition of clichéd notions for ideal urban parks and certain nature images, and equally looking at a search for new expressive forms in landscape architecture. The time was ripe for experiments in this field, as shown by the international competition for the Parc de la Villette in Paris. This had taken place in 1982, i.e. a few years before the Saarbrücken Hafeninsel planning started. It attracted a great deal of attention in the landscape design world: the intention was to convert 55 hectares of former slaughterhouse land into a municipal public park, bearing the

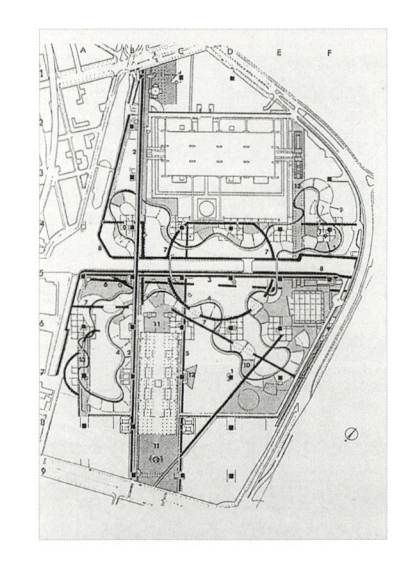

Latz also showed interest in preserving traces of industrial history in his competition design for the Parc de la Villette in Paris.

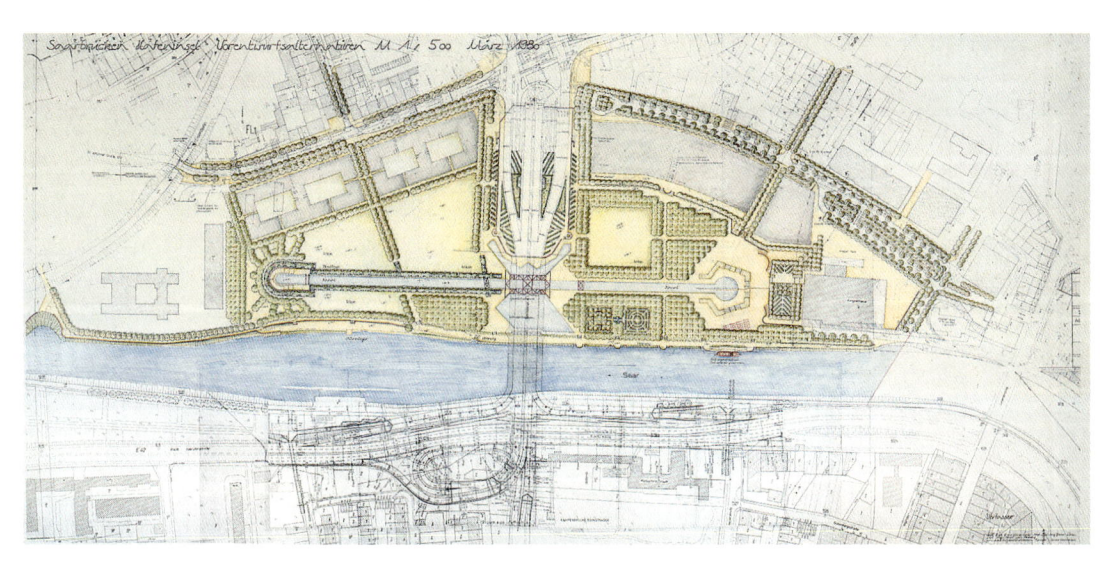

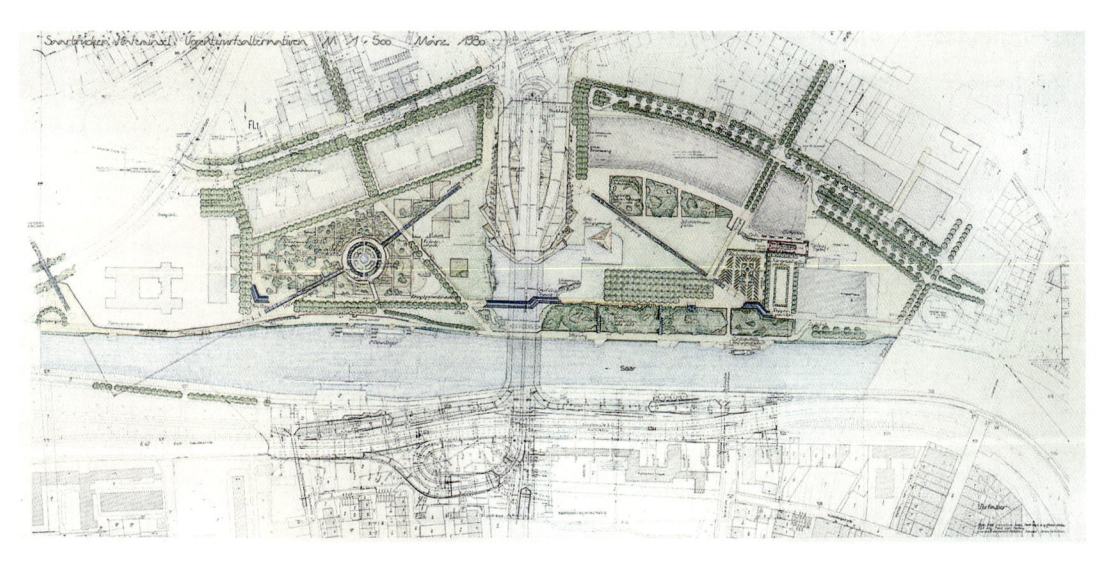

Peter Latz and his team submitted three different design variants to the Saarbrücken clients, here in the form of plans drawn by Gunter Bartholmai and Niki Biegler: the landscape garden concept, the geometrical urban garden and the syntactical design.

DEALING WITH "BAD PLACES"

history of the location in mind. 471 teams entered this competition, and it fuelled more international discussion about aesthetic expressive forms in landscape architecture than scarcely any other comparable project. It was also noticeable there that the aim was not to create a classical park, but to design a "Volkspark", offering full scope to the public's changing needs and requirements.

Radical departures of this kind from traditional ideal concepts and approaches have never been uncontroversial, particularly not in one's own professional field. Peter Latz also sensed this, and therefore insisted at a later stage: "One should not simply denounce everyone who deviates from the rules devised by Lenné and von Sckell about two hundred years ago. It is not possible simply to ignore developments since that time. A lot of alternatives that were never taken any notice of cropped up in the history of garden art. And often, if one looks more closely, it turns out that there's no serious need to pick up Lenné and Sckell, people just do."[18] Instead of giving the Hafeninsel a superficial facelift and transforming it into a neoclassical picture-book park, Latz + Partner finally came up with a third, so-called "syntactical" design concept intended to get by with a minimum of interventions, include the existing ruderal vegetation and deliberately work with the information levels available on site. Sticking an alien aesthetic over the existing surface would have destroyed all the information and traces of history available on the spot. "A new syntax had to be developed for the city centre that would fit the existing urban structure back together again, tie in the varied manifestations on the site but not throw memories away, trying instead to crystallize out of the rubble what had been thrown into

In the first few years after completion, the view from the south bank over the river Saar to the Harbour Island was characterised by the emptiness of the former storage yard and the new ruin buildings.

the rubble, and lost; we produced a syntactical design for an open urban space."¹⁹ Peter Latz's vocabulary identifies him as convinced exponent of structuralism in landscape architecture, and he declares: *"Yes, I am definitely certain at the bottom of me that in case of doubt, structure is more important than form. That is quite certainly correct, and I also try to convey that in discussions at the university, which is not always easy because structures are relatively unattractive at a first glance. They are not very exciting, they are usually neutral, something in the background, essentially, like the percussion in a band. The solo trumpet steals the show, but there is only a rhythm because the bass and drums create it. They both have to be there, however."* But the aim of the syntactical design in Saarbrücken was not just to ensure a viable basic structure and thus the rhythm of the park, but also to give the landscape a voice by linking up what is already there with new design elements. *"The language of things and the way things are combined create information that is linguistic in character,"* Peter Latz explains. *"If they are to acquire this linguistic character, they need everything that language constitutes: they need a diversity of accurate terms and a strong syntax. My soft spot for this approach is certainly also something to do with the fact that I am the product of a language with strong syntax, and I learned Latin."*

And indeed the syntactical design was chosen in 1980, but it was not until 1984, once the autobahn bridge was under construction, that it was possible to start implementing the project. In order to secure the structure of the place, Peter Latz and his team chose three components in addition to the industrial remains from the wide variety of fragmented and covered layers of structure and information: the municipal access network, along with sightlines, the existing flora in the ruins and

On the Harbour Island, the various found items and landscape elements – the ruins of former coal heaps, new planting and important sightlines – into the surrounding area join to form new connections.

DEALING WITH "BAD PLACES"

The Harbour Island park was constructed on the basis of the syntactical design, weaving together four structural layers: the access network with linked sightlines, the public gardens, the rubble flora and the traces of industrial use.

88

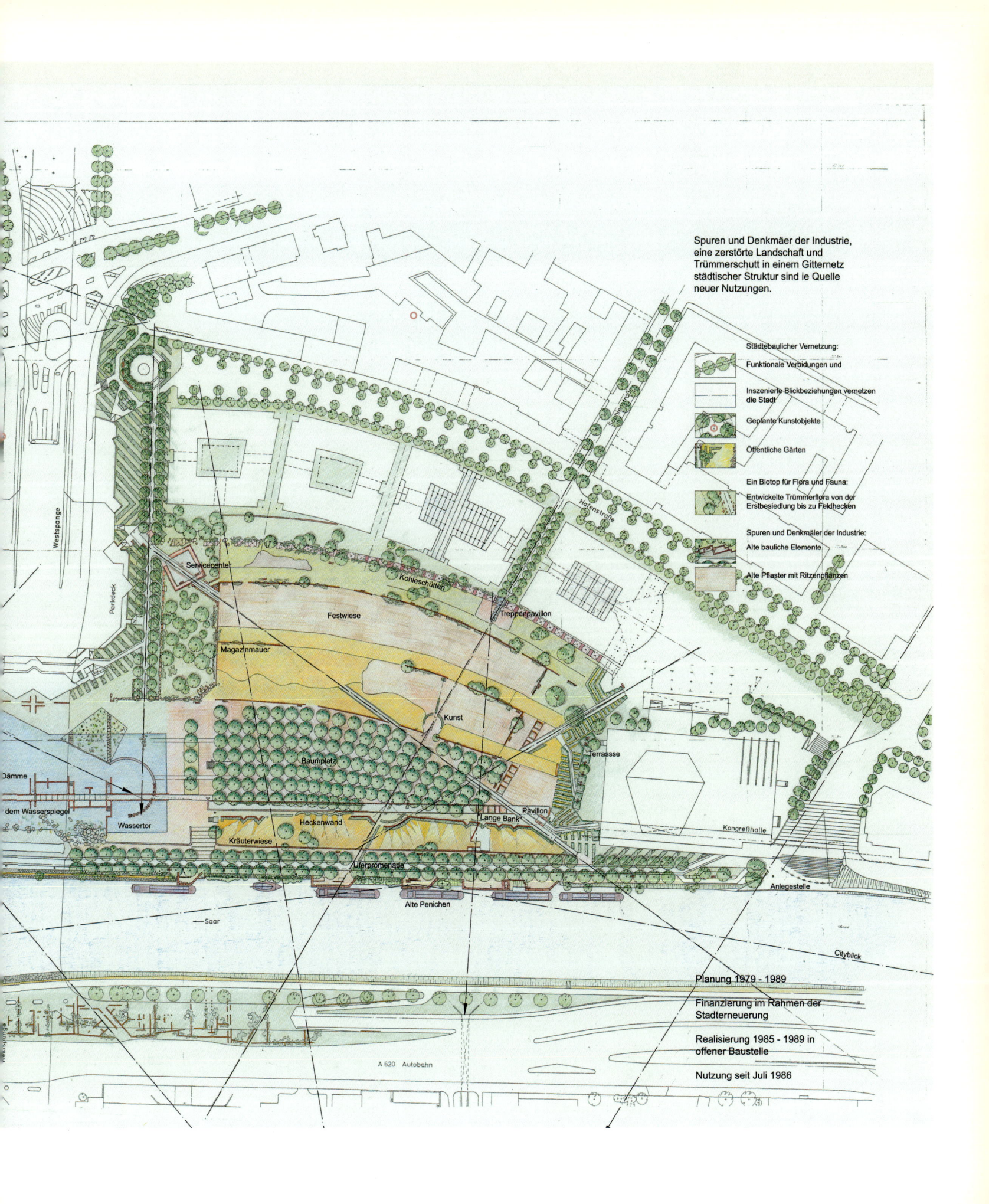

Spuren und Denkmäer der Industrie, eine zerstörte Landschaft und Trümmerschutt in einem Gitternetz städtischer Struktur sind ie Quelle neuer Nutzungen.

Städtebaulicher Vernetzung:
Funktionale Verbidungen und

Inszenierte Blickbeziehungen vernetzen die Stadt

Geplante Kunstobjekte

Öffentliche Gärten

Ein Biotop für Flora und Fauna:
Entwickelte Trümmerflora von der Erstbesiedlung bis zu Feldhecken

Spuren und Denkmäler der Industrie:
Alte bauliche Elemente

Alte Pflaster mit Ritzenpflanzen

Planung 1979 - 1989

Finanzierung im Rahmen der Stadterneuerung

Realisierung 1985 - 1989 in offener Baustelle

Nutzung seit Juli 1986

DEALING WITH "BAD PLACES"

a series of public gardens. Also a rational system was taken up for designing the park that did not have to be invented specially, but already existed on the spot, or at least in the plan: the Gauss-Krüger coordinates. Superimposing these structural levels produced a complex basic framework that still gives the municipal park its character today. It also makes it possible to find one's bearings on site, even if the originally planned sight axes in the surrounding area have now become overgrown with luxuriant greenery.

Some of the connections between the park and the external elements that – rather like the Latz garden in Ampertshausen – were originally important for the intelligibility of the park landscape have now been cut off, but this has meant that other ways of reading the park have become more effective; the fact is that the density of the design interventions in the area was almost too high in the early stages. Within the site, a dense, still intact network of paths and tracks of different kinds runs through the varied park with its areas of meadowland and water, gardens and squares with trees, and an ensemble of various set-pieces from the past and the present, archetypal garden art images and art installations.

Coming from central Saarbrücken via the higher harbour road, visitors descend a wide flight of open-air steps by the congress hall to enter the eastern half of the park, which derives its character from a spacious festival ground and a large square with trees planted on a grid. Around these low-maintenance areas, which survive completely without the usual areas of lawn, trimmed mixed hedges with stone niches, clinker walls and impressive bastions made up of picturesquely overgrown fragments of buildings create a varied spatial framework. Housing was originally

Industrial traces and monuments, a landscape that has been destroyed and rubble within the urban structural grid create places for new uses. These connections are particularly clear in the western part of the park.

In the eastern part of the park are the great festival meadow connecting up with the building development on the north side, the Congress Hall on the east side and the Saar river bank promenade on the south side.

DEALING WITH "BAD PLACES"

planned on the north-western border of the park, and Peter Latz imagined that the people living close by would quickly take these areas over and make great use of them. Instead, a multi-screen cinema flanks this part of the park, though this does not seem to reduce the intensity of use. People find their way into the park from the landing stages on the Saar and along the great avenue of trees on the river promenade. They picnic in the meadows in the shade of the trees, play football in the wide open spaces, use the temporary skater facilities or sit on the green terrace of the restaurant by the Congress Hall and watch people using the park.

The great weight of the bridge crossing the middle of the park creates a division that had to be masked. But the design dominance of the bridge is mitigated by enormous avenues of poplars flanking it on both sides and creating new sightlines,

Many sun-worshippers gather on the sandy beach by the retention lake under the bridge in the hot summer months. Large poplar avenues form a green screen for the motorway bridge in the northern part of the park.

relating to the large water-gate in the eastern part of the park, for example. It is one of the most striking and from the outset most controversial brick structures in the park, and so draws a great deal of attention to itself. The gate derives its name from the fact that all the surface and drainage water from the park is pumped up through pipework in the walls, and falls back to ground level from various heights. The noise of the rushing water cancels out the local traffic noise, and purification and oxygen enrichment are ensured before the water is used to feed the lake under the bridge.

As far as the much discussed aesthetic effect of the wall of water is concerned, Claus Reisinger summed it up very well in his knowledgeable account of the Harbour Island in *Die Gartenkunst*: "One element that should also never be missing in a landscape garden on classical lines is a ruin: Latz placed it in the pool in the form of a 'water-wall' or 'water-gate'. It is both a factory façade and an aqueduct, a gateway to the bridge or the ruins of an ancient arena – the Colosseum in Rome or the arena in Nîmes may have provided the inspiration. Its position in the water is also reminiscent of ancient sites, the Villa Hadriana, for example, or Pozzuoli, sunk in the water with its baths. But the 'Roman Fortress' in Schwetzingen is not so distant either. [...] The 'water-wall' is by no means inferior to any 'classical' water temple."[20]

Claus Reisinger pays no heed to the assertion that is heard in the trade from time to time that Peter Latz based his ideas for the water-gate on the factory wall with water gushing out of it in the Parc de Clot in Barcelona – rightly, as the landscape architects Dani Freixes and Vicente Miranda did not start to construct their brilliant district park on the former workshop site of the Spanish railway company Red Nacional de los Ferrocarriles Españoles (Renfe) until after 1985.[21] But if we remember

The view from the bridge shows the great water-gate in the foreground, with the silhouette of the Congress Hall discernible in the background. A mysterious atmosphere is created under the bridge as the light changes.

DEALING WITH "BAD PLACES"

the enthusiasm for Renaissance gardens that emerges so clearly in the Latz private garden as a tribute to the Ruspoli Garden in Vignanello, then Claus Reisinger's reading is confirmed. But yet another possible interpretation for building new and keeping old ruins suggests itself forcefully. This was provided by Bazon Brock, whose approach was described even in 1981 by the Kassel sociology professor Lucius Burckhardt in a *Bauwelt* article with the programmatic title, "The smallest possible intervention": "If the ruin is particularly a bearer of information that helps us to process the present, then the theory of the smallest possible intervention must address the building of ruins. Something incomplete, already a ruin, is the precise opposite of those 'neat solutions' that destroy our world, always certain they are in the right, and always ending up in disaster."[22]

The ruins that Peter Latz preserves and sometimes builds as new structures reveal several significant design approaches that are important in all his subsequent projects, especially those of post-industrial use: ruins are retained to secure traces, to preserve information and thus to make landscape intelligible. Ruins are not just made safe, but even especially built on occasion, in order to point out the value of things that are open and incomplete in a world that is changing all the time but makes ever increasing demands for marketable finished products, even in situations where they can never exist, in nature and landscape. And finally the ruins are evidence of the delight in technical and aesthetic experiment that particularly fascinates Peter Latz in Renaissance garden creations. This can be seen most clearly in the western half of the island. Visitors reach this via a long, narrow bridge over

The 1985 Parc del Clot (bottom) in Barcelona is one of the most successful parks in Europe and uses – just like the 1980 Harbour Island – the narrative potential of surviving industrial relics.

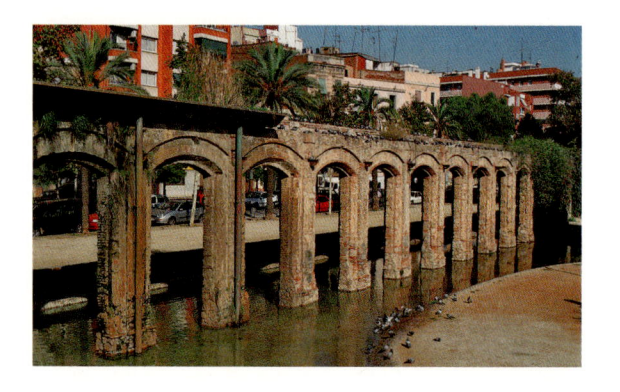

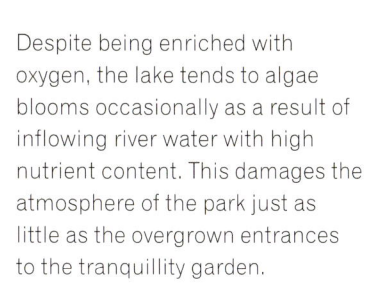

Despite being enriched with oxygen, the lake tends to algae blooms occasionally as a result of inflowing river water with high nutrient content. This damages the atmosphere of the park just as little as the overgrown entrances to the tranquillity garden.

DEALING WITH "BAD PLACES"

a lake that also has ruin-like features scattered about it. This large stretch of water was placed under the bridge to reflect light up into the darkness.

The most important dialogue partners for the new interventions in the eastern half of the park are cleared, formerly buried pavement areas and remains of walls and foundations, but also valuable old groups of trees and luxuriant spontaneous vegetation. In the western section, overgrown mounds of rubble with vegetation growing over them and areas strewn with assorted demolition material define the picture. Essentially the eastern half derives its character from noticeably more intricate, almost garden-like spatial sequences. As well as this, certain quotations relating to the history of the art of gardens were placed among the rubble landscape as new structures, such as the large, red-brick rotunda in the middle of the highest mound of rubble on the site. Peter Latz identifies the circular, 16th century botanical garden in Padua and the Renaissance tomb of Augustus in Rome as models for the sunken circular garden. It was designed with trimmed hedges and individual trees, and visitors are lulled by the soft splashing of the central fountain. Steps that can serve as seats mean that this "hortus conclusus" can also be recognized and used as a theatre garden.

If you leave this tranquillity and theatre garden through one of the exit gates, you find yourself faced with some strangely familiar scenes. Dry, sometimes stony, arid meadows divided into regular squares, oleasters with light foliage, Lombardy poplars and chirping crickets suddenly conjure up Mediterranean images with wild, arid meadows, small cultivated fields, olive trees, cypresses and the song of the cicada:

The architectural and garden design of the sunken tranquillity garden on the Harbour Island borrows unmistakably from historical models, for example the Mausoleum of Augustus in Rome at the time of the Renaissance (Engraving by Scaichi).

Box hedges create a structure and brick walls a clear demarcation line from the surrounding ruderal vegetation. Between them is magnificent, horticulturally cultivated blossom – similar ingredients to Ampertshausen and yet a garden with a different character and its own spatial proportions is created.

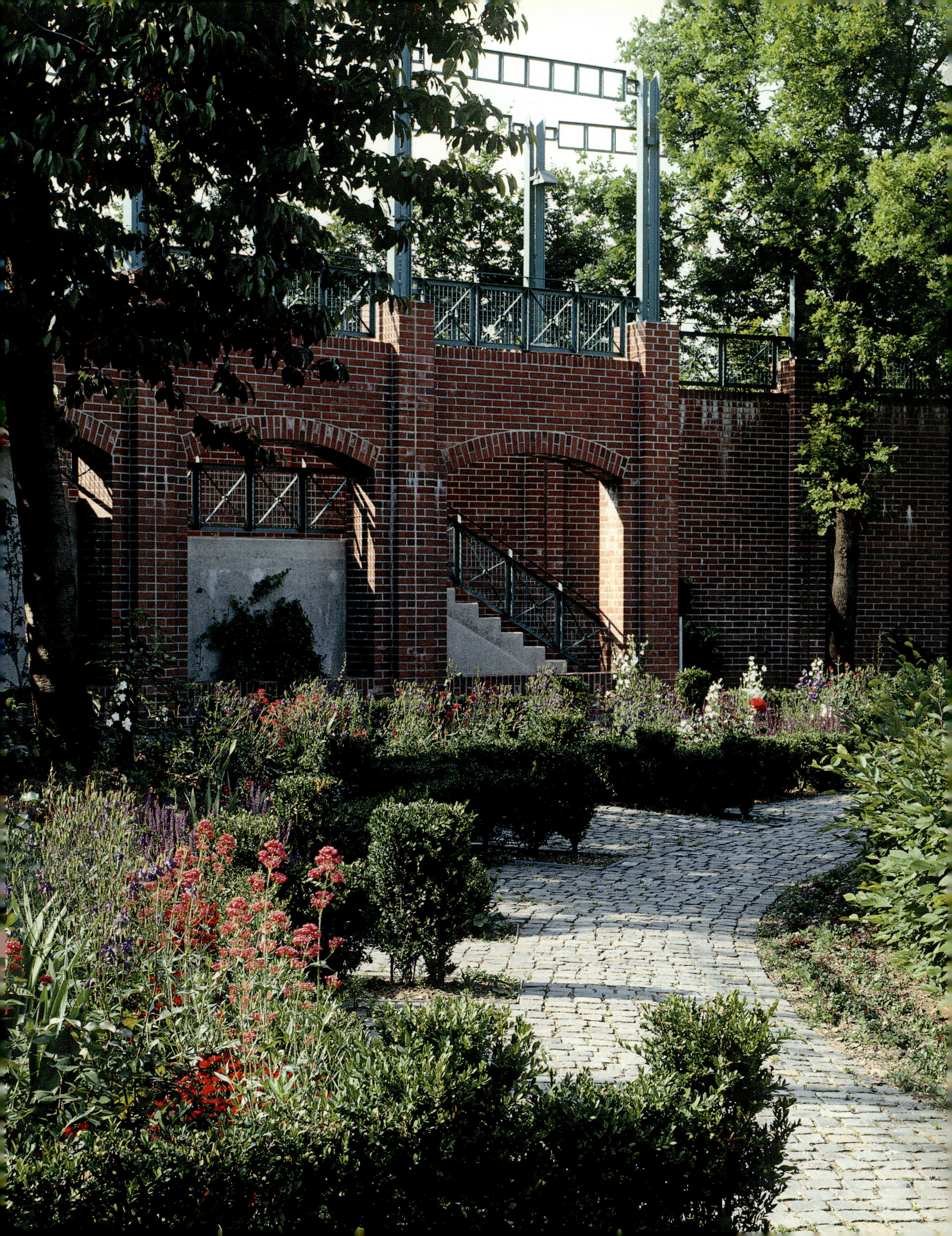

et in Arcadia ego – in the middle of this derelict harbour land! The square fields are bordered by paths, usually lined by broken-brick walls. The aim was to leave the actual final design for these little gardens to people living near the park and to committed campaigners or student groups, in the hope that individuals would take possession of the park and thus bind its users to "their" municipal park more closely. "Widow Weise doesn't go for a walk on the Hafeninsel. She comes into the 'Triangular Field' from her house in Wertweg, waters the plants, hoes the soil and talks to the people watching her. Everyday activities are bound up with the park, and new memories and connections accumulate. Frau Weise's grandsons use the park differently, they gather lilac for Mother's Day or split the carboniferous slate to look for fossils; this attracts amateur photographers, who also take pictures of the beautiful wild flowers in the black substrate of the carboniferous slate. A passer-by tips water into the compacted tailings to rescue the as yet undeveloped tadpoles."[23]

In fact the initial response to the offer that the public should use the experimental fields in the park was eagerly taken up at first, and some people who had known the

Whether it is the meticulously trimmed hedges in the tranquillity garden or the gnarled Russian olives in the Italian valley, there is a Mediterranean atmosphere in the so-called triangle field in the western part of the park, and the rubble walls reinforce this impression.

harbour when it was still intact shared their reminiscences, inspired by the traces of industrial history, which had been commonly accepted as useless and which had been saved during construction. These days people are more likely to meet for a picnic in the "Italian valley", or by the pavilion with a view of the Saar. Groups of students, some with Peter Latz working alongside them, took the opportunity to plant experimental gardens. They invented very simple working rules for sorting out the building rubble or for building "patchwork" walls from all the materials the place had to offer – from sandstone door lintels to old lorry tyres, achieving some aesthetically appealing results whose archetypal forms could remind observers of familiar landscape art projects. *"Essentially it was about accepting the materials found on site, without placing them in traditional categories like beautiful or not beautiful, but just looking at whether they could fit in with the language system or not. A lot of people found that a bit hard to take. Things didn't start to change until the Duisburg-Nord days, but then increasingly did in the course of a long process lasting over 12 years. But after that, people accepted it very quickly."* But at first, the Saarbrücken project was fiercely resisted.

"The profession campaigned actively against the Hafeninsel park, and there was widespread resistance to our project. Incidentally, it was like that in Duisburg as well, the professional organizations published large numbers of letters and newspaper articles, denouncing the project as impossible and professionally damaging in a certain sense. But I saw it quite differently, in fact mainly as a chance to broaden the professional field and the range of jobs for landscape architects." The supporters of the "Kassel School" that had built up around the vegetation expert Karl Heinrich Hülbusch in particular, who

The rubble wall is of local provenance, but the pavilion at the western end of the park is in new brick, thus creating an exciting dialogue between old and new.

DEALING WITH "BAD PLACES"

were hostile to the planning and design[24], and whom Peter Latz had already had to confront as professor of landscape architecture at the Gesamthochschule in Kassel, objected sharply to a so-called rubble aesthetic, the "syntactical design tricks" and an almost indescribable "chaos of materials, forms and figural elements". The Harbour Island won the Federation of German Landscape Architects BDLA award in 1989, but almost simultaneously the aforementioned design critics provocatively prophesied, in their "notes on the anatomy of a piece of bad planning", that the project would fail in *Bauwelt* in 1990: "According to park planner Peter Latz of Weihenstephan, this is the first development phase for the park. Others are supposed to follow. But realistically, it makes more sense to assume that the park will be gradually taken back, in order to deal with the damage that has already resulted from its design."[25]

Peter Latz asserted his qualifications and legitimacy as a landscape architect firmly, and he had dared to take up a clear position running counter to the customary practices of a profession that otherwise tended towards opportunism. So at first he had to come to terms with his position as an outsider. He still refuses to present nature exclusively in terms of long-forgotten Arcadian ideals, instead pointing out the value of the everyday nature that has much more to offer our lives than the cultivated sterility that has to satisfy functional criteria all the time and everywhere. On the Harbour Island, Peter Latz had to accept the risk of open-ended planning, because the collective creative will and the inherent dynamic of urban ruderal vegetation can also work in unexpected ways. Every "open work of art" in Umberto

Many structures of artistic inspiration in the rock gardens, like for example the spiral, now largely overgrown, result from simple, systematic material sorting, carried out on the spot with students in workshops.

Eco's sense[26] lives with this risk of the unforeseeable and is understood as a dynamic structure that does not fit in with any rigid ideals, but always signals freedom and the ability to change. The Harbour Island is an open work of art in this sense, and it was started with the risk of an open outcome. It gave European landscape architecture a substantial boost. But for Peter Latz and his team, the Harbour Island in Saarbrücken was just a preliminary step towards a much more complex and momentous enterprise in the Ruhr district.

"Something incomplete, already like a ruin, is the opposite to the 'neat solutions' that destroy our world, always insisting on being right and always ending in disaster," explained the Swiss sociologist Lucius Burckhardt as early as 1973.

Duisburg-Nord Landscape Park

New York journalist Arthur Lubow called Peter Latz an "Anti-Olmsted" because the landscape architect decided not to stage an Arcadian counter-world to the industrial age in Duisburg-Nord, but to make the industrial landscape speak.

"THERE IS ABSOLUTELY no need for parks anymore because the 19th century problems have been solved and a new type of city has been created. The park and greenery have become worn-out clichés. Our parks will never have the beauty and the power of those in the 19th century. But that is not the only reason. This century created a new type of order. Order can be based on disconnection and superimposing."[27] Adriaan Geuze made this provocative suggestion about the future of parks on the occasion of an international symposium called "The Park" in Rotterdam in 1992. Peter Latz took part, along with many other distinguished European landscape architects, and presented his plans for a new "Park for the 21st century". Geuze said that in the course of the 19th century the city had developed into a kind of monster that was destroying its occupants, and so the invention of municipal parks like the Parc Buttes Chaumont in Paris or Central Park in New York with their exquisite illusion of nature, borrowed from popular 18th century landscape painting, had been absolutely essential for survival, but today?

Since the late 20th century, the radical transition from an industrial to an information society had brought about a radical change in general living conditions. Parks still have a key role to play in urban open space systems, but as Peter Latz had already made clear with his park in Saarbrücken, the stereotypical reproduction of antiquated nature and landscape images was not the way forward. "When Olmsted designed Central Park with Calvert Vaux in the mid 19th century, he intended 'the

Frederick Law Olmsted's Central Park in New York remains a model for urban parks all over the world: its attractive ideal images of nature and landscape offer an alternative world to the city of the industrial age.

DEALING WITH "BAD PLACES"

spaciousness and tranquillity of a charming bit of rural landscape' to afford 'the most agreeable contrast to the confinement, bustle and monotonous street division of the city.' Refreshment is still what a park promises, but the contrast no longer lies between greenery and cement,"[28] wrote the American journalist Arthur Lubow in *The New York Times Magazine*, calling Peter Latz "the anti-Olmsted" because of his rebellion against the antiquated images produced by traditional parks. But what should a 21st century park actually be like in order to illustrate present-day perceptions of nature and landscape appropriately? And yet nevertheless, just like the American icon, to become an integral part of the world we live in now, indeed possibly even to become a type of open space that can point the way forward for the present day?

There are some particularly revealing answers to this question to be found in the Ruhr, as no other German region was affected on such a large scale and so intensively in the past two decades by structural change, or more precisely by deindustrialization, as this densely populated industrial region extending over 800 square kilometres, with its 17 cities on the left and right banks of the Emscher and a total of 2.5 million inhabitants. The aim of the IBA Emscher Park International Building Exhibition was for the first time in the history of building exhibitions not to address architecture, housing reform, urban development and urban renewal exclusively, but to compile a regional policy programme for sustainable ecological, economic and aesthetic renewal for an industrial region that had been exploited to

When August Thyssen founded the steelworks in Meiderich, Duisburg at the peak of industrialization in 1902 he was already one of the most powerful industrial magnates in the Ruhr. For decades the factory – here in the 1950s – was completely inaccessible to outsiders.

the full. Karl Ganser, managing director of the Gesellschaft Internationale Bauausstellung Emscher Park from 1989 to 1999, pointed out the role model character of this ambitious regeneration programme, also with respect to future urban development programmes in other European regions: "Reconstructing landscape is by no means an isolated problem for old industrial areas. All Europe's major conurbations are happily building tomorrow's discussed industrial areas in their extensive suburban zones. For this reason the idea is beginning to dawn of starting to construct landscape in urban space today, not just to protect the remains of what exists now, but to increase and enrich it."[29]

One of the deliberately conceived high points in the Emscher Landschaftspark was the conversion of the disused and completely intact blast furnace plant at Meiderich in Duisburg to create the "Landschaftspark Duisburg-Nord" as a recreation area near the city. The Meiderich plant was closed in 1985, and about 8,000 steelworkers dismissed. This left desperate working families behind, and 230 hectares of post-industrial polluted landscape, punctuated by large service areas, highly complex industrial plants, blast furnaces, turbines, cooling towers, ore bunkers, machine halls, foundries, gas tanks, storage areas, workshops, sewerage facilities, factory railways and roads. In the eyes of most of the people living nearby the former factory site was "terra incognita" and an ecological disaster area which nature was slowing winning back for herself over the years.

The Meiderich plant produced 37 million tons of pig iron, towards the end in five blast furnaces, before it closed in 1985. Its legacy included an enormous industrial ruin and 230 hectares of post-industrial landscape.

DEALING WITH "BAD PLACES"

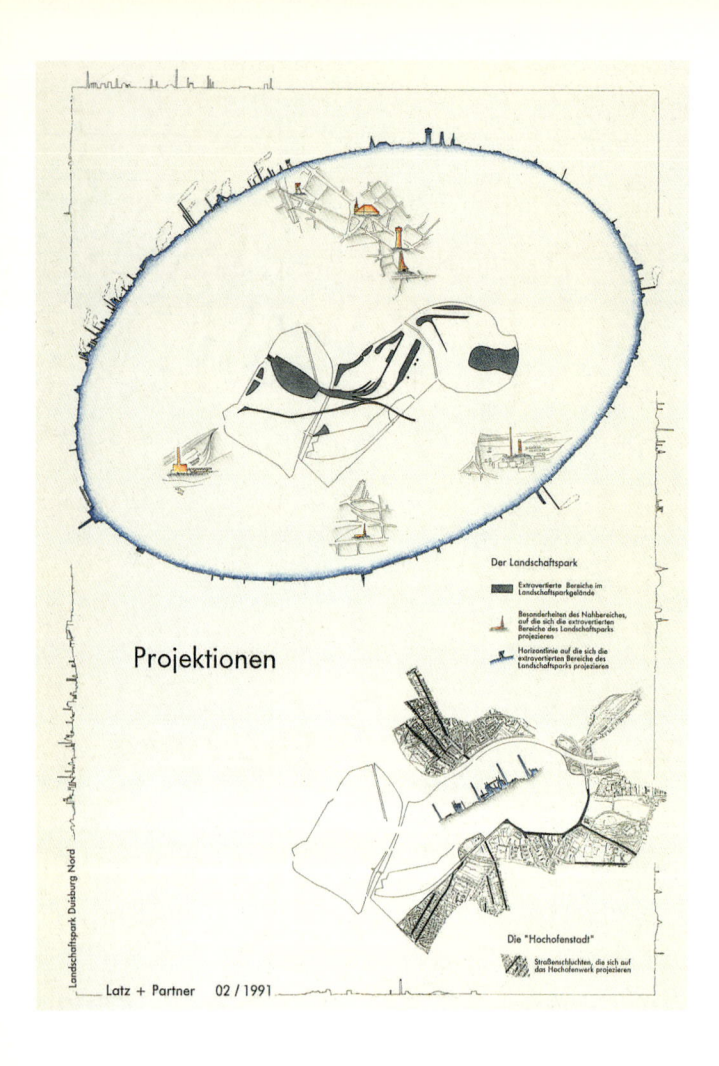

In 1989 this extremely ambitious reclamation idea for the former blast furnace site was added to the IBA Emscher Park project list. Given the complexity of the problems, the competition announced was not a "normal" anonymous one, but a co-operative-concurrent planning procedure involving three German, one English and one French planning team, namely Boyer/Hoff/Reinders from Duisburg, Brandenfels from Münster, Latz + Partner from Freising, Cass Associates from Liverpool and Bernard Lassus et Associés from Paris. All five project groups, who worked on the project in teams including architects, geologists, ecologists, sociologists, energy advisors and engineers "had to commit themselves to work on site during the six month planning phase and to discuss the point their thinking had reached in depth with the client and all those involved, including the active citizens' groups."[30]

Latz + Partner examined the sightlines in various parts of the surrounding area in their analytical drawing called "projections", and also the question of how important the blast furnaces were as a local landmark.

After one year, at the end of the elaborate planning process in which a very wide range of user interests had to be considered, an evaluation commission decided which of the five designs that had been devised was to be used to develop the Duisburg-Nord Landscape Park. The jury was chaired by Donata Valentien, professor of landscape architecture, and she made no bones about how disappointed she was with most of the designs produced. She complained that the special qualities of this extraordinary site had been described and appreciated, but had then simply been forgotten when developing a vision for the future park. "So the ideas remained essentially random, and could just as well have been realized at other, 'normal' locations. [...] The park ideas that were developed were surprisingly conventional in the end, even though they were detached from the real situation and therefore Utopian, derived as they were from classical ideas of the English or French park. They fitted in with the culture of forgetting and suppressing that does have a tradition in the Ruhr – perhaps as a survival strategy. [...] The present situation, which perhaps makes people uneasy because it is so overwhelming, is being confronted with various visions of paradise, though constructing them would mean that the history and nature of the place would have to be more or less completely eradicated. And this cannot be obscured by the fact that the steelworks would survive everywhere inside it, as an alienated, incomprehensible object."[31]

Valentien was thus criticizing the conventional approach of wanting to preserve the industrial relics merely as alienated, incomprehensible monuments, as aesthetically attractive curiosities, without – as Peter Latz proposed in his syntactical planning approach – attempting to tie them into the complex landscape context. Such conventional, essentially one-dimensional approaches had been developed decades before IBA Emscher Park. They usually followed the model of classical landscape parks in which artificial ruins offer reminders of the transience of human works and are intended to support the romantic character of the landscape as a sentimental element. As early as the late sixties the American artist Robert Smithson was photographing pipework, pumping plants and gantries in Passaic, an industrial town in New Jersey, with his instant camera. He called these industrial relics "Monuments of Passaic" and interpreted them – effectively as criticism of the euphoric sixties faith in economic growth – as valuable archaeological evidence of his day, at the same time revealing the transience of man's works in the stranglehold of dynamic natural processes.[32]

A few years later, apparently taking up Robert Smithson's visionary idea of the "Monuments of Passaic", though making a considerably less radical effect, the Gas

The American artist Robert Smithson wrote a visionary article about the town of Passaic in New Jersey as early as 1967, depicting the landmarks in a landscape destroyed by industry, here "The Fountain Monument".

DEALING WITH "BAD PLACES"

Works Park was created in Seattle. It was designed and constructed from 1970 by the American landscape architect Richard Haag. This 9 hectare recreational park is still seen as landscape architecture's first successful attempt to build industrial relics into the design of a modern park deliberately. The landscape architecture world still regularly compares the Gas Works Park with later industrial conversion projects in Europe, and it is frequently identified as the actual precursor of the idea for Duisburg-Nord – but is this correct? Closer comparison with the Duisburg-Nord Landscape Park is instructive for a better understanding of Peter Latz's revolutionary landscape conversion strategy.

The Gas Works Park was created on the site of a former refinery producing gas from coal to supply the city of Seattle from 1906. The highly polluting plant was decommissioned from 1956, when natural gas started to be used as an energy source. The legacy, prominently sited on the north shore of Lake Union with a view of Seattle, consisted of the rusting ruins of the refinery and an ecological disaster area. Richard Haag noticed the area in 1969, and was enthusiastic about the "ghostly spirit" of the place. „I haunted that place and discovered: no sensuous earth forms, but a dead level wasteland; no craggy rock outcroppings, but peaks of rusty roofs; no thickets, but a maze of tubes and pipes; no sacred forests, but towering totems of iron; no seductive pools, but pits of tar; and no plants (not even invasive exotics) had been able to secure a root hold in 15 years. It needed a new vision. Originally I pledged to save the most sacred structure, the largest oxygen generator tower. But why not save its spouse, then the two sets of twins – who would break up a

The illustration on the left shows the former refinery plant in the Seattle Gas Works Park in 1976, 20 years after the plant was closed. The landscape architect Richard Haag made it into a public park from 1970.

family?"[32a] He argued in favour of preserving the industrial ruins, at the time mainly for aesthetic reasons, as he insisted. His ideas were seen as progressive, as monument conservation was still in its infancy and there were no industrial monuments at the time. A public, municipal park following the classical Central Park model was supposed to be created on the site. "We promoted a concept of a new kind of people's park that paid homage to our rich Olmsted legacy, complementing it through contrast. [...] The concept of crafting a park featuring 'forgotten works' greatly appealed to the younger generation while older generations lobbied for the stereotypical image of 'park' such as English pastoralism."[33] Haag did not manage to have all the industrial ruins rescued, and so most of the site was cleared of traces of industrial use, thus rendering the various information strata in the landscape unintelligible. All that remained were the rusting cracking towers as absurd mementos, entirely detached from their historical context.

Today the Gas Works Park looks like a simply designed leisure park, with the industrial monument resplendent at the highest point on the site like one of Jean Tinguely's infernal machines – fascinating in its aesthetic appearance, but puzzling in terms of its significance, and also not accessible to the public, as the industrial ruin was fenced off from the outset for safety reasons: "Keep out". Richard Haag took a first successful step on the path to post-industrial use of industrial sites, though this did not develop further to any notable extent in the USA, not least because there is not the same urgent compulsion for sustainable land conversion in North America as in densely populated Central Europe. The Gas Works Park, with its reduced complexity and low level of processuality, its high degree of predictability and lack of integration into a forward-looking discussion about sustainable urban and landscape conversion is scarcely comparable with later conversion projects in the Ruhr. This region is not just interested in land renewal and preserving monuments, but first and foremost in the process-driven, functional transformation of complex landscape structures with an inevitably high proportion of unpredictability. One crucial difference lies in viewing landscape as a complex structure of meaning and information strata, requiring a complex approach to the design.

In Saarbrücken Latz + Partner themselves took charge of devising clichéd classical park designs which in the course of discussion were proven unviable; the competing planning teams relieved them, so to speak, of this step in Duisburg – with one exception: the French artist and landscape architect Bernard Lassus drew up visionary plans for a radical transformation of the former blast furnace site. His daring design concept was called "The day before yesterday, yesterday, today and

DEALING WITH "BAD PLACES"

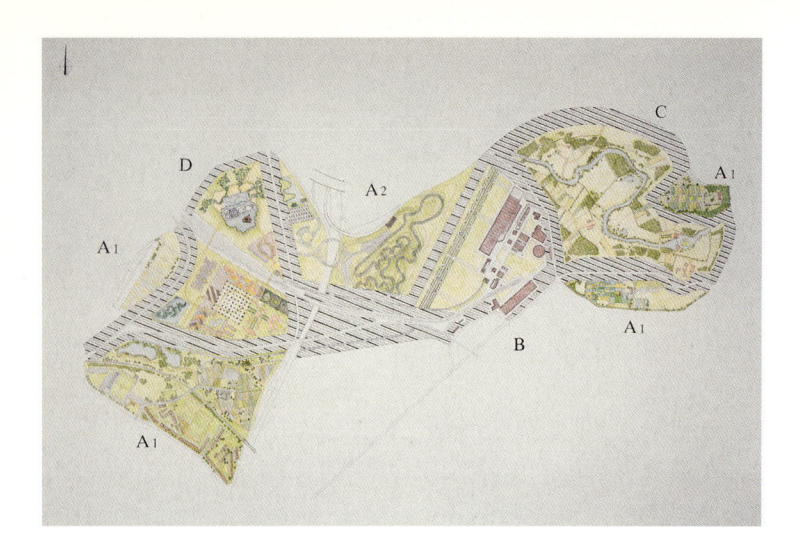

tomorrow". It divided the site into clearly separate sub-areas that he wanted to make more able to meet a very wide variety of demands. Landscape is a world of fragments, and not a world of objects, was his credo. He conceived five peripheral areas for the site under the motto "Everyday leisure extended in the park" as neighbourhood parks intended to cater for the needs of people living nearby, from hobby gardening to motocross adventures. Lassus divided the entire area into four zones in his competition design: Zone A included the neighbourhood parks, and Zone B was set aside for industrial history. The industrial ruins were to be presented on a broad stretch of lawn, as if on a tray. Zone C was intended to reconstruct the Emscher river landscape in pre-industrial times, to give visitors a sense of landscape history. Lassus undertook painstaking research in the Duisburg planning archives to this end, attending to every detail from pasture fencing to windmill. He conceived Zone D as a research zone, with labs and research gardens for conducting forward-

Bernard Lassus called his design concept for Duisburg-Nord "The Day Before Yesterday, Yesterday, Today and Tomorrow". "The Day Before Yesterday" aimed to reconstruct the water meadows, while "Tomorrow" was to be devoted to environmental technology – here with an iceberg and tropical island.

looking science. This zone was called "From ice to steam, experiences for tomorrow's gardeners", and was intended to show how dependent man is on water and what enormous technological power he has at his disposal to influence his environment. The various zones in this journey through time were to have been separated by massive, regular rows of trees, serving as "time locks" or "temporal pens" as he calls them.

Realizing this spectacular vision of a narrative landscape that would have told the story of its own past, present and future in fascinating images, would scarcely have been possible without completely reshaping the existing landscape. As well as this, constructing and maintaining such a park would have been enormously expensive – which would not have fitted in very well with Bernard Lassus's vaunted "minimal intervention" principles. Consequently jury chair Donata Valentien's assessment ran as follows: "But, despite the intellectual temptations, despite the highlights, many of which promised to be powerful magnets for Duisburg: the fascination of the place remained more powerful, every glance past the proposals and out into the future park confirmed that ultimately there was only one solution." And this was proposed by Latz + Partner: "The Latz proposal had been commended from the outset for its solid, sound individual contributions on water, energy, vegetation. It was not possible to enthuse immediately, the penuriousness of the presentation inhibited emotional ardour, and the splintering into a number of strata made for laborious access. Slowly, led carefully forward, mosaic stones, lines and ideas fitting together, we started piecemeal to discover this work's quality. A process that showed surprising analogies with discovering the place."[34]

"Destroying and polluting the environment is certainly still the first thing we associate with the concept of 'heavy industry'", Peter Latz explained. "The general public is more interested in art collections and villas than in industrial buildings from

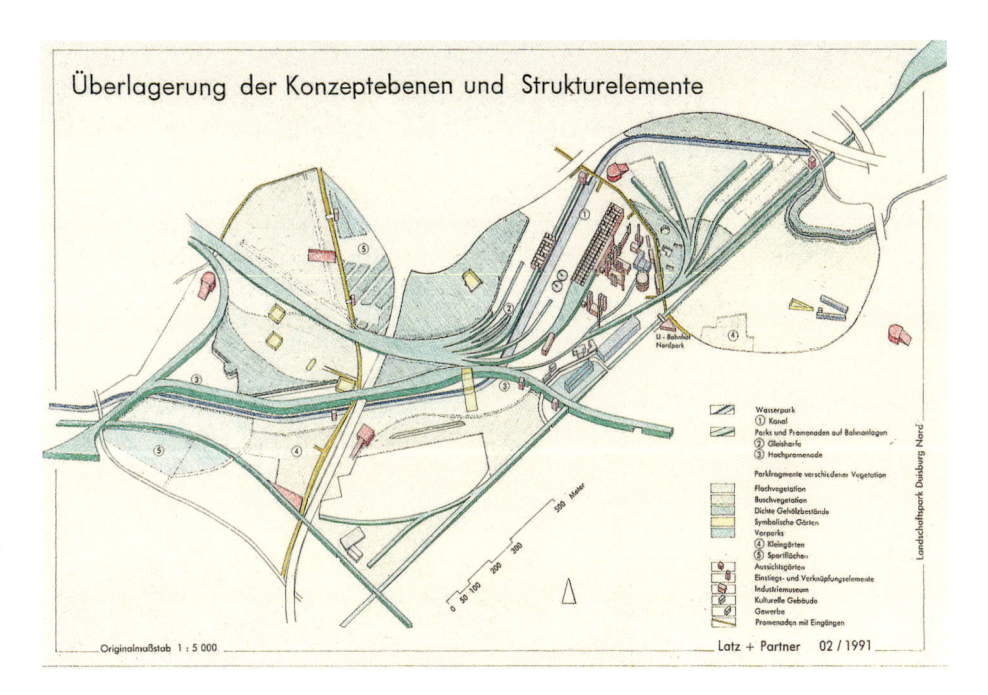

Latz + Partner never wanted to draw an overall plan for Duisburg-Nord, to avoid creating an impression of a complete and objective entity. They were much more concerned about linking independent structural layers in a process-driven approach.

DEALING WITH "BAD PLACES"

industrial dynasties, and our landscape architects tried to combat the pollution with green spaces and strips of green. This natural counter-position, combined with ecological correctness, left as good as no scope for positive associations or even motivation for landscape architects to build up some sort of esteem for these anti-spaces. So that means dismantling, removing the residual pollution and using natural soil to bury all the remains under a stretch of green in the tradition of the English garden – negating the anti-world. But acquiring knowledge about production could be fascinating and it could be possible to discover a new aesthetic perception of gigantic production machines, described as an identification item, 'landmark' or mythological dragon."[35] Duisburg-Nord was different from Saarbrücken: here Peter Latz did not have to peel the traces of history laboriously out of the rubble. He was confronting a largely intact industrial complex that still offered almost all the levels of information needed to fully understand this strange landscape.

Faced with the many, at first mysterious-looking ruins, the landscape architect acknowledged: "As far as I am concerned, the Duisburg-Nord Landscape Park is closely associated with Bomarzo." He discovered a reincarnation of the dragon from ancient mythology that had already been on its threatening rampage in Bomarzo in the monstrous blast furnaces in Meiderich, which once spewed fiery slag and molten iron. His indebtedness to the Renaissance garden's delight in experiment played a central role in Duisburg, as it did for the Saarbrücken Harbour Island project. "In other words, the aestheticization of structure like the sculptures of the Renaissance, simultaneous memory structures, like the waterwheel or the shepherd's bower, an

The ruins of Fountains Abbey in the Studley landscape garden and the dragon in the Sacro Bosco in Bomarzo are reference points and interpretative schemes that also play a key part in Duisburg-Nord.

In Vicino Orsini's Mannerist Garden of Monsters the oriental dragon fights against dogs, but Meiderich's monstrous dragons, which used to breathe fire, have to defend themselves against the tooth of time.

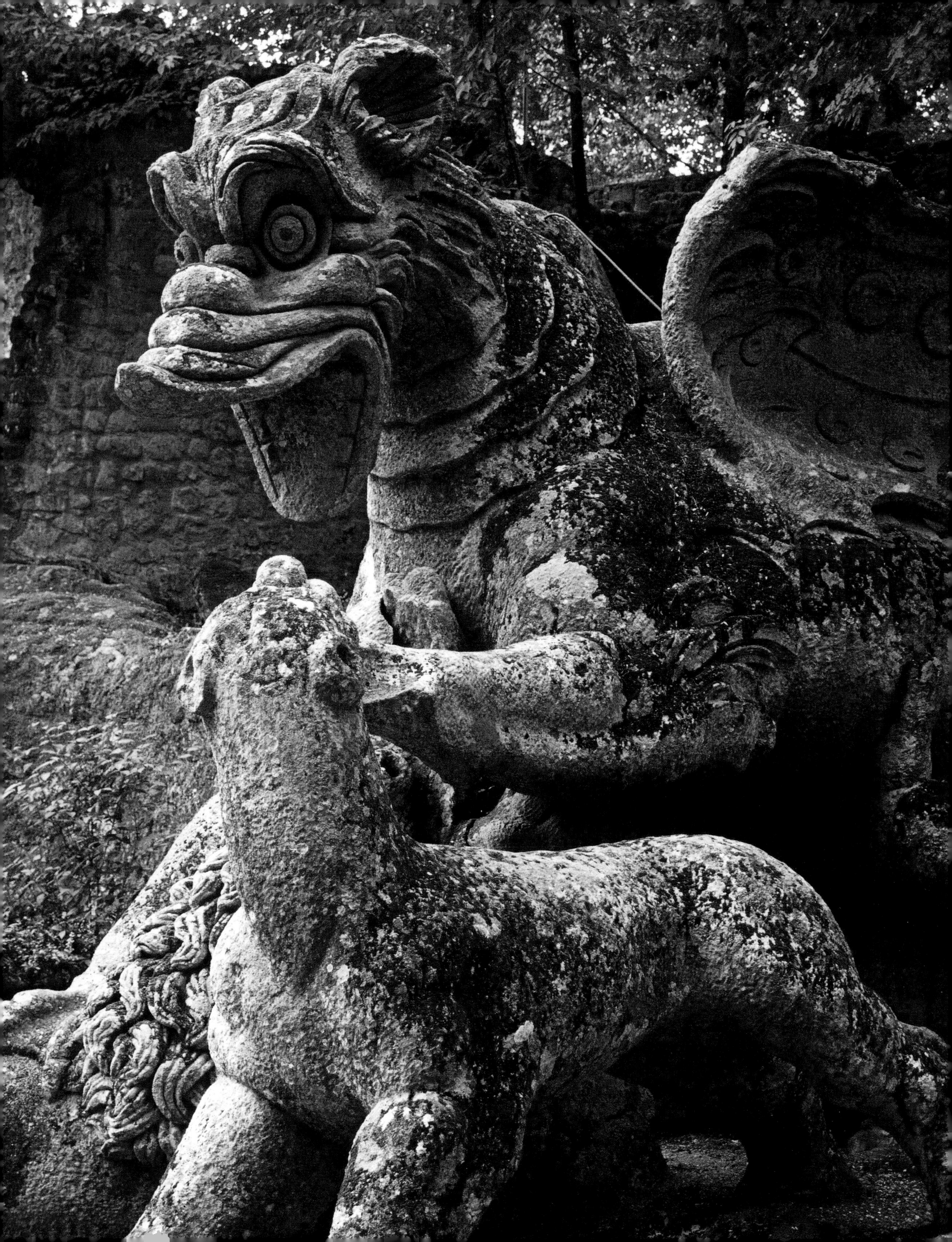

interest in what is past, self experiences, like the journeys of Kent and Fürst Pückler, or historical interpretations conveyed in myth. It is the fantastic landscape that will follow the industrial age that we have to address in a new and careful way"[36], Peter Latz explains. So inventive and experimental design approaches had to be combined with the same horticultural artistry and finesse that Vicino Orsini had brought into play in such a masterly fashion over 400 years earlier in his mysterious Sacro Bosco. "For Duisburg-North Landscape Park I began by writing stories. Stories about a falcon circling a mountain. And it I gradually became clear to me what I would do with the blast furnaces."[37]

Latz urgently defines design as the concrete influencing of the intelligibility of information layers. He mistrusts the credo of spontaneous and intuitive design. For this reason the actual challenge for the landscape architects was firstly to understand the existing entanglement of function and information layers in general, in order to work out how this industrial landscape organism, formerly so alive, used to function. "The contradictory nature of places like this is worrying. The fear of not being able

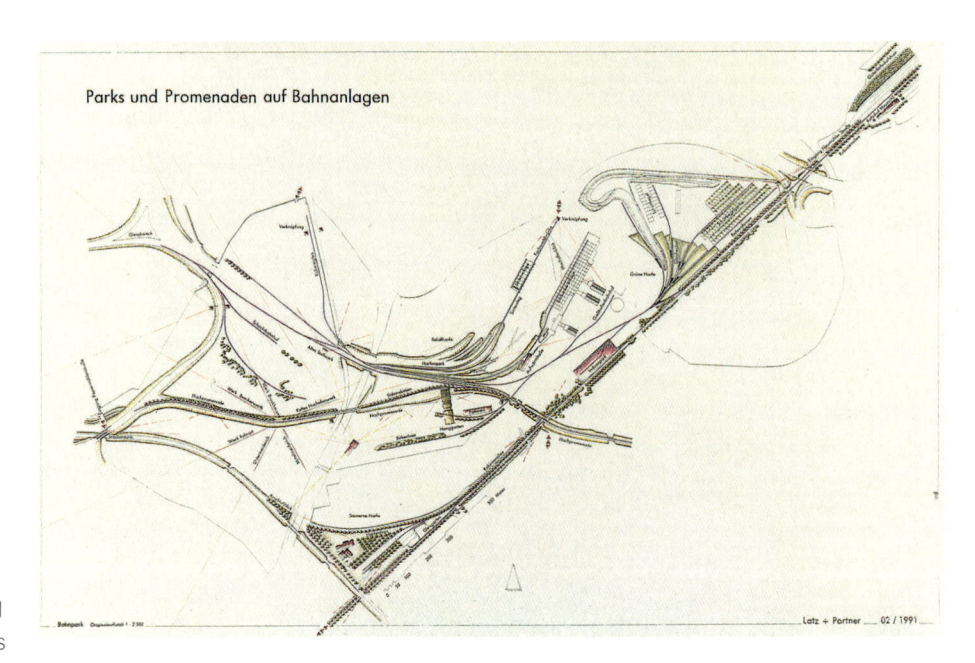

The blast furnaces are obviously very important landmarks, but the value of the extensive rail system on the industrial site as a potential network for parks and promenades was waiting to be discovered.

to see the end, of not knowing the outcome, can be fascinating and at the same time, like the mythical wood, challenge one to get to the spiritual heart of the system. If we assume that the industrial process took a strictly rational approach, that there must have been detailed principles that were clearly comprehensible behind everything incomprehensible, then we are postulating about the existence of rules and systems that make it possible to penetrate the chaos."[38] But this insight did not lead to a complete, overall creative plan, as this would never have been able to reflect the living complexity of the real landscape accurately. Instead the team decided on an abstract portrayal of the most formative basic elements of the landscape and developed four separate, individual park concepts that were subsequently superimposed on each other again. The "water park" consists of the interwoven canals, treatment and settling basins, while the "rail park" uses the old railway facilities. Roads, transport routes and over 20 bridges make up a layer of their own as linking promenades, and so do the many different fields and gardens, some of which were quite deliberately inserted as a contrast to the industrial aesthetic. The four levels of the park are

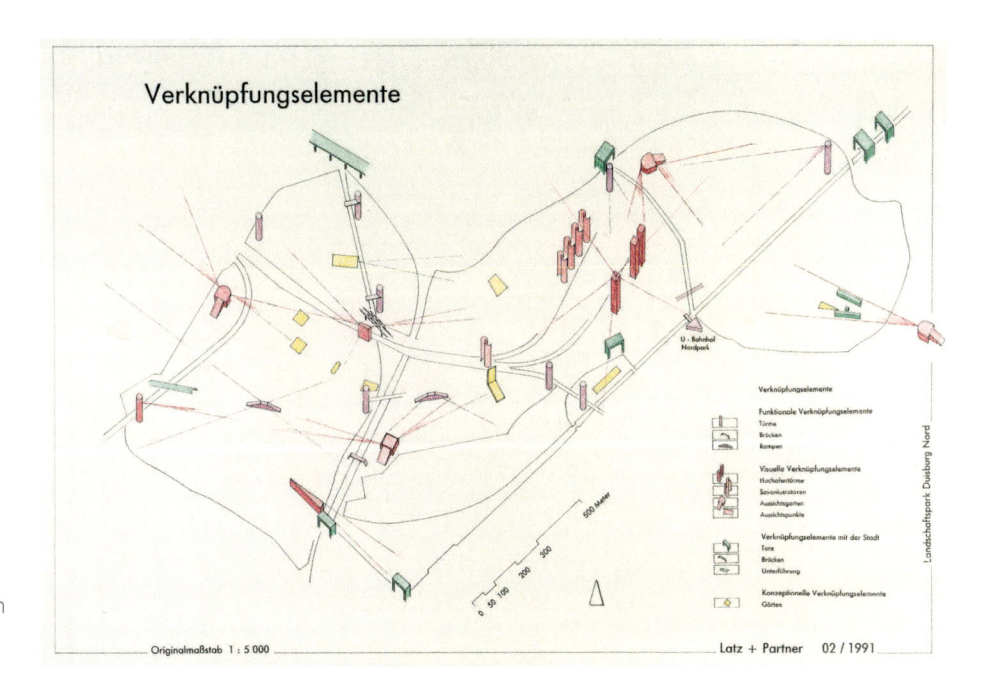

The view from the blast furnace reveals the park's size and complexity. New landmarks like the great wind wheel and a system of linking elements placed at key points tie the landscape sections into a new structure.

DEALING WITH "BAD PLACES"

115

linked together visually, functionally, through ideas or symbolically, using the smallest possible interventions, special connecting elements, ramps, steps, terraces or gardens.

It is particularly remarkable that Latz + Partner were able to hold their own with their strategy of the smallest possible intervention against Bernard Lassus's competition entry: Lassus had in fact already explored this design principle in the sixties in his artistic projects, and he and Lucius Burckhardt made it part of landscape architecture theory.[39] "'Minimal intervention' doesn't mean not wanting to do anything, but using 'espace propre' carefully," Bernard Lassus explained. "When in 1965 I used a red tulip to carry out the important experiment 'Un air rosé', this made clear what minimal intervention is. If you hold a strip of white paper in the goblet formed by the petals of a tulip, you will see that the air colours. This is the principle of minimal intervention: the place is not altered physically in any way and, nevertheless, you change the landscape."[40] But the physical intervention Lassus planned for the Duisburg-Nord industrial landscape was anything but minimal. However, in 1981 Lucius Burckhardt explained another aspect of the this design approach, under the heading "The smallest possible intervention": "The French garden artist Bernard Lassus feels that every intervention in the landscape derives first of all from a misunderstanding of what already exists. Anyone who replaces one landscape view with another one must consider what we are losing and what we are gaining by an intervention of this kind. It is no longer acceptable for the garden architect to say '... but there wasn't anything there before' in astonished self-defence. Anyone designing a landscape must consider whether the meaning he is creating is such that it is comprehensible to other people, and also to people from other cultural backgrounds. In our pluralistic society, a design must be open to multiple interpretations."[41]

Just like Bernard Lassus and Lucius Burckhardt, Peter Latz followed the smallest possible intervention trail, but he had already put this technique into practice for the Harbour Island in Saarbrücken, and even more consistently in his planning for Duisburg-Nord. The intelligibility of the existing information planes in the industrial landscape was preserved almost completely, carefully complemented with new levels of meaning or "culturally recycled" in places. "I never used to call it 'cultural recycling'," explained Latz. *"It is more about taking items over in their totality and understanding their original functions. That is why I find it so important not to put everything into the rubble crusher and use it as road-building material, even though that is often described as perfect recycling. So you could certainly say that our recycling is imperfect, in that on the one hand we do mix certain building or planting substrates from crushed recycling materials.*

The strategy of minimal intervention, vividly demonstrated by Bernard Lassus in his little 'Un air rosé' experiment in 1965, played a not insignificant part in the development of the Duisburg-Nord Landscape Park.

The stump of a former factory chimney sits in the middle of the sage field like an abstract architectural sculpture. The scent of blossom mingles with the scent of coal and rusting iron to create a new aroma.

DEALING WITH "BAD PLACES"

Ein Geflecht industrieller Strukturen wird Landschaft

A second, closer look at the master plan of the Duisburg-Nord Landscape Park reveals how the weaving of industrial structures can form a new kind of landscape without falling prey to traditional bucolic clichés.

Nevertheless we sometimes decide to leave the stump of a factory chimney, say, or whole sections of wall standing, even if they would provide all those many thousand tons of broken concrete for road building. But we want to keep them in their role and in their historical function, and sometimes invest the surviving building components with new meaning that can stimulate new readings of existing material. I think that this is fundamentally different from the traditional recycling approaches. We have sometimes used whole sections of steps and bridges again and then repainted them to show that they can be used and so that they are not confused with the rusty sections with 'keep out' on them."

Blast furnace 5, an 80 metre high steel monster through whose innards you climb, offers a splendid view of the park and the Ruhr. In the shadow of the blast furnace, which Latz sometimes calls the "Matterhorn" of the industrial landscape, is Cowperplatz, named after the mighty blast furnace stoves. The area was planted with a grid of fruit trees, which monument conservationists saw as totally inappropriate at first given the industrial past. But this planting was also deliberately aiming to reinterpret what was here in the spirit of a minimal intervention. There is scarcely any other location in the park where the effectiveness of this principle can be seen more vividly than in the massive, up to 14 metres high, concrete forms of the ore and coke bunkers. Here the park's users have completed the creative reinterpretation themselves by erecting a summit cross on "Monte Thyssino". In this way, a minimal effort permanently changed the way the former industrial landscape is read.

The linear structures of the rail park are another individual park system, another important layer. *"The rail system in Duisburg-Meiderich is available within the gigantic*

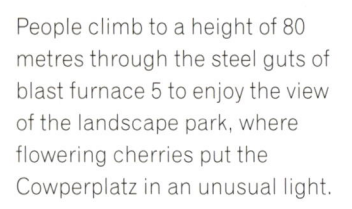

People climb to a height of 80 metres through the steel guts of blast furnace 5 to enjoy the view of the landscape park, where flowering cherries put the Cowperplatz in an unusual light.

park and extends well out beyond the 230 hectares into the adjacent urban spaces as a language system," Latz explains. *"I quickly realized that the team had to learn how the locomotive runs, and thus understand how the rail systems functions, and its movement patterns. This was to produce one of the future language layers, and it was essential to ensure that it was not destroyed at any point."* Straight railway lines and curving loops cover the landscape as an independent, fully functional steel network. It is true that for a long time the railway embankments represented obstacles in the site and sight barriers that were difficult for outsiders to overcome. However, it is now possible to experience the view over the landscape from these earth masses, and is easy to access the adjacent urban districts. At the centre of the site the rail embankments come together to form the so-called "rail harp": "The 'Gleisharfe' ('The Rail Harp') is an intermeshing of railway tracks where every second track leads downwards and the

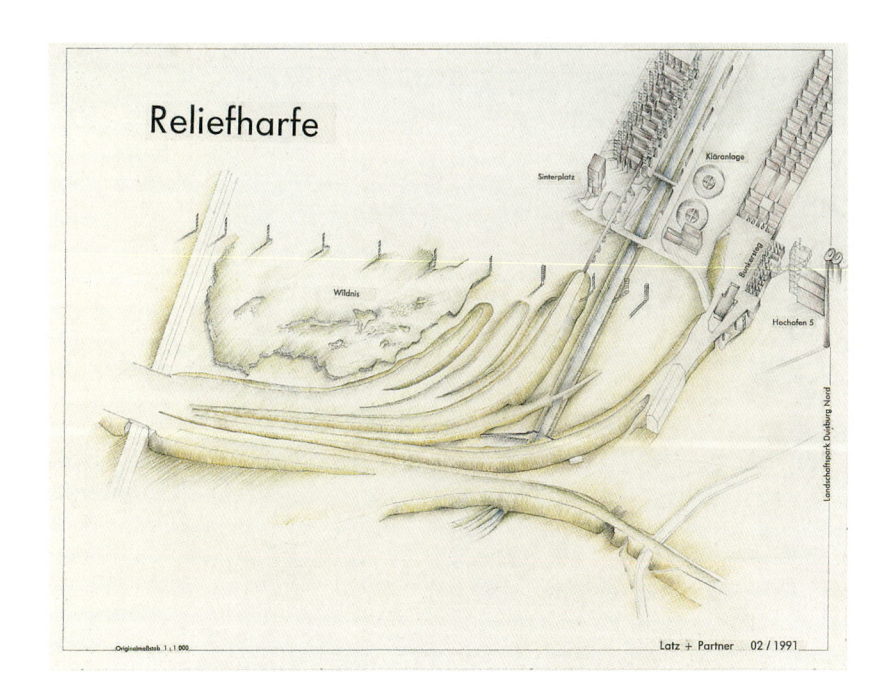

The landscape transformation is most successful where people's activities add the finishing touch, in the climbing garden in the bunker complex, for example. The landscape architects also provided reading aids for new ways of looking at things by using landscape art to interpret existing features.

DEALING WITH "BAD PLACES"

121

ones in between lead upwards – a fantastic, technological object. My affinity for the sensitive railway technology of dividing and recombining strands of tracks led me to discover the rail park in Duisburg very quickly. The movements occasioned by the pattern of the tracks have the complexity of ballet. The engineers who designed this set of tracks over a period of sixty to seventy years certainly had technology in mind and not art. If they had been told at the time that what they were doing was art, they would probably have reacted very negatively and it might even have cost them their job. The history of technology has very often produced fascinating structures. These should be given recognition and supported in their force of expression."[42] To prevent the vegetation from running riot and slowly concealing these earthworks, which reminded him of modern Land Art projects, Latz had the area cleared and then mowed regularly – even this an essentially minor intervention that made a big impact: design through maintenance.

The "bunker gardens" in the large sintering bunkers and the somewhat smaller ore bunkers at the former sintering plant are also experimental and provocative. Special saws were used to cut openings into the massive concrete chambers and then a whole variety of gardens were designed inside them. These flourish exclusively on a substrate of recycled materials from the site, without any added topsoil. It is also possible to look into the gardens in the ore bunkers from above from a long walkway and understand their own charm, somewhere between garden art and industrial nature. Behind this combination of something that is obviously valuable with some-

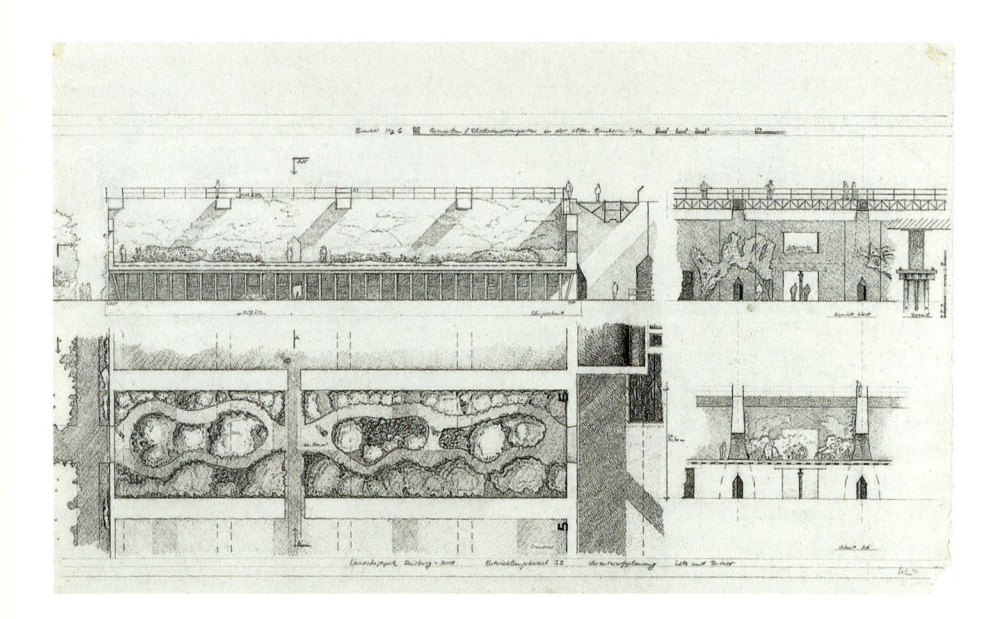

Tilman Latz used drawing to explore the possibilities for transforming some large bunker gardens into unusual small gardens, with raw industrial aesthetics and fine horticulture mingling with each other.

The fern garden in the Duisburg-Nord Landscape Park, embedded in one of the bunker compartments, is again based on the archetypal spiral shape that is also to be seen in the plant microcosm of the hesitantly unfurling fern fronds.

DEALING WITH "BAD PLACES"

thing ostensibly worthless lies the principle of a deliberate aesthetic transformation of perception that had already been used in the design for the Harbour Island and helps to enhance value generally: *"Gardens have high value levels, and certain plants are particularly valuable. For example, if I plant an anthericum in recycling material, then suddenly both the anthericum and the recycling material have the same status. In Duisburg it is the wonderful blue sage, which we could never have introduced without the builders rubble and conversely: the building rubble would have been worthless material without being enhanced by the beautiful blossom, which happens only once a year. So most visitors don't even notice that the flower garden is based on recycled building rubble."*

It is not just carefully tended, domesticated nature comes into its own in the park. Attractive everyday nature has developed all over the site, but there is also a special, sometimes quite rare kind of vegetation that owes its existence to the unusual environmental conditions. Many exotic plant varieties – over 200 non-native species have been recorded – travelled to Duisburg with imported aggregates and found a new home here. Industrial nature took over as the typical design element and demanded a rethink, not just in terms of horticultural management. In the

Dialogues between old and new, wilderness and garden, unfold all over the park, whether it is between the blue railwalk and rusty steel masts or between trimmed hedges and shrubs growing freely.

It looks as though part of the Ampertshausen box garden has been transplanted to Duisburg. It is not just the wine-red of the autumn foliage and the rust-red of the bunker wall that are involving themselves in stimulating conversations.

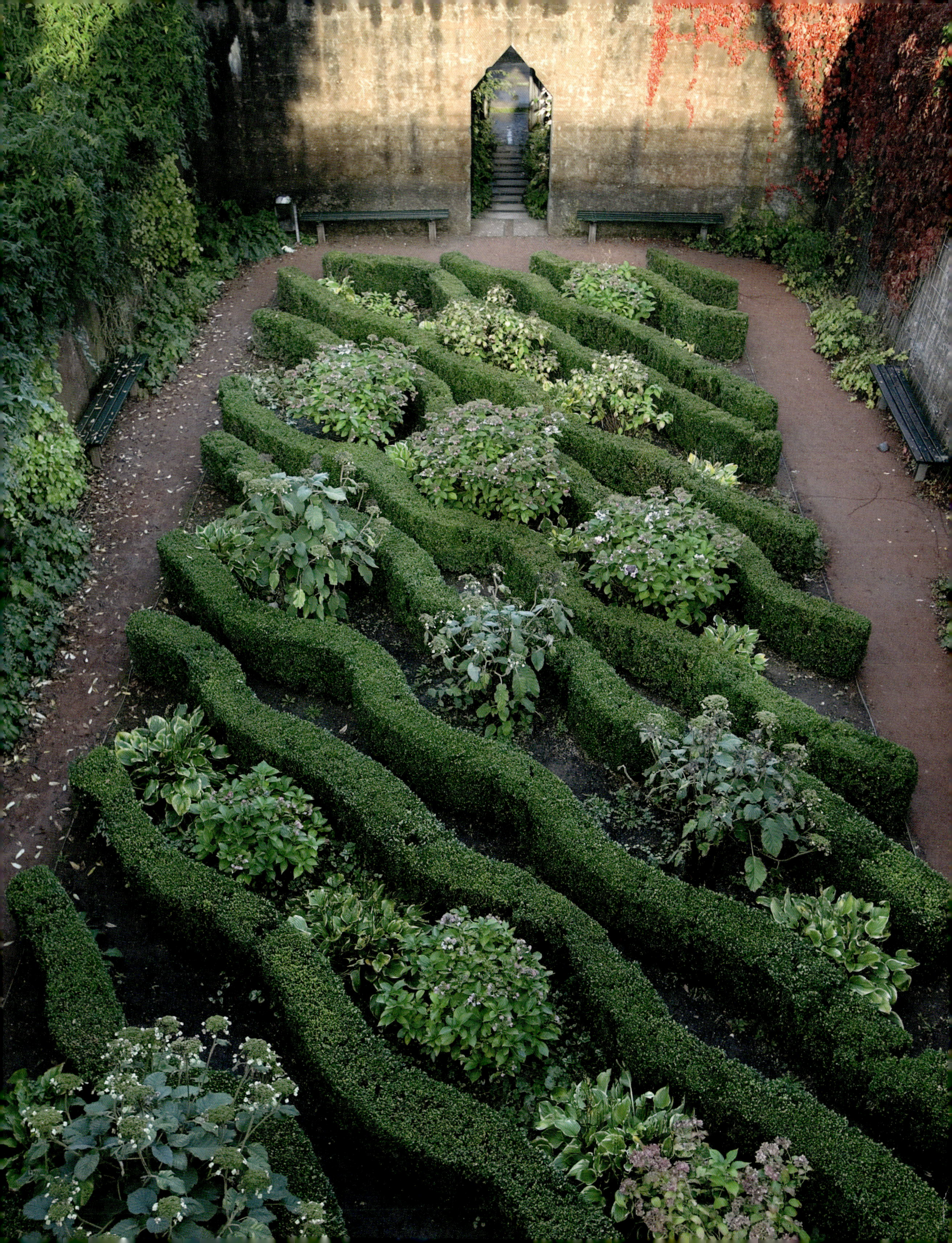

meantime, gardeners have been specifically trained to handle industrial nature in Duisburg-Nord.

Peter Latz also questions traditional views of nature in the "Piazza Metallica", "a plaza that is surrounded by giant industrial structures in the same way that a Renaissance piazza is ringed by palazzos" as Arthur Lubow[43] wrote in the *New York Times Magazine*. The piazza consists of 49 steel slabs, each weighing eight tons. These elements measure 2.2 × 2.2 metres, and were originally used to line pig casting beds. For decades they had to withstand the erosive forces of molten iron at temperatures over 1300 degrees. "This created fluvial systems which are very similar to a glacier's cutting edge, in other words primordial formations which were created by the force of molten elements. As a symbol of nature I find this infinitely

Images of cultivated and spontaneous vegetation impact equally on the park and the provocatively unusual readings of landscape. Extraordinary plant communities with a rich variety of species, some creating their own micro-landscapes, have developed in extreme locations shaped by industry.

The Piazza Metallica with its 2.2 × 2.2 metre steel slabs is an impressive event both of culture and of nature.

126

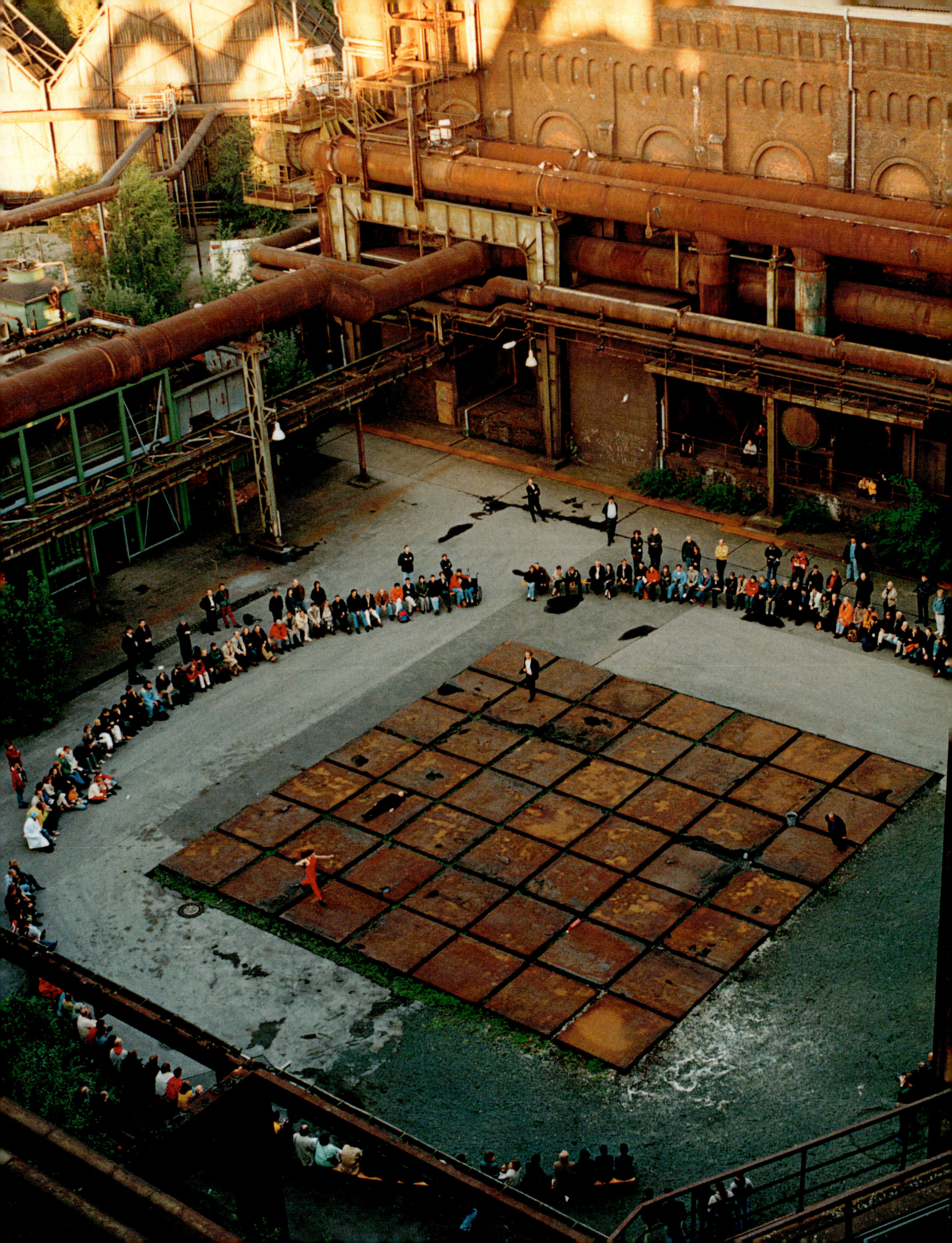

more interesting than a few forlorn birches!"[44] says Peter Latz, and admits: *"But in other Duisburg projects I wanted to develop systems that are both highly artificial and highly ecological."*

There is evidence of this approach in almost every section of the Duisburg-Nord Landscape Park: *"So technology and nature not as a contrasting pair, as in early Modernism, but technology and nature in accord. Here I am interested in a possible congruence within the ecological concept. This is nothing to do with the need for harmony; no, the technical idea is to try to integrate natural sequences as much as possible, and to let nature be nature. On the other hand, nature we create artificially must allow us to find an aesthetic language that is identical with the technical one. For example, if I am working*

The 49 steel slabs in the Piazza Metallica were originally used to line pig beds in the pig casting bay. Peter Latz was particularly fascinated by the traces of enormous erosion forces on the slabs, so he made them visible.

in some technical industrial complex I can't plant clumps of trees in the English style, because that would produce a contrast. But if I plant the trees on a grid or in rows then I am working with the same language as in industrial architecture and the trees will still flourish just as they would in a free, landscape composition. I am absolutely allergic to the idea that nature should reconquer something for itself. That is definitely not what is intended, as it simply means that nature is triumphing over technology. Then we have lost society as a whole. We have to keep a hold on technology, and integrate it into our environment."

This almost educational design approach shows clearly in the example of the restoration of the so-called "alte Emscher", formerly an open sewerage system contained in a dead straight concrete slab channel. This sewerage channel was in urgent need of refurbishment because of serious environmental pollution, and the clear water channel is now part of the water park, which is one of the four key individual park systems. When the restoration of the "alte Emscher" was under discussion, many people anticipated that the canal would be transformed into a meandering river, but the landscape architects refused to create such a pseudo-natural image: *"We had decided against this even in the competition phase because we didn't think it made sense to tackle so much contaminated soil. We wanted to build the phase in which rivers were straightened into the park as a cultural phase and to make sure that we could get hold of clean water, as there is no water to flow or meander, it has to be collected in this channel. This is why we called it the clear water canal. That was quite a struggle, as a lot of people tried to hold us back for years because they had the image of a naturally meandering river in their heads. Later, when the project was completed, people strolled along the left- and right-hand*

Industrial nature took over the ruins, for example the coal bunker, with extraordinary vigour in the past decades. Latz + Partner added cultivated garden and park nature, thus initiating a new reading.

DEALING WITH "BAD PLACES"

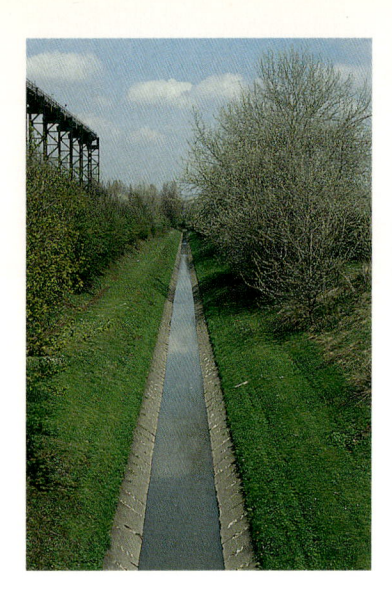

sides of the canal even though it was winter – in other words actually not the season for visiting parks. This element was accepted from the very first day, in fact much more quickly by users than by the appointed authorities in the planning phase."

The Emscher sewerage canal runs under the actual, open clear water canal in which 80 to 100% of the accumulated rainwater from the roads, roofs and squares is collected. Of course, even surface water cannot be introduced into the clear water canal without a certain amount of preliminary purification, so numerous cleaning phases are built into the water system, as a rule using planted settling basins. The existing settling, clarifying and cooling tanks in the disused industrial effluent treatment works were re-used for this purpose after appropriate refurbishment and cleaning. *"The water canal is an artefact aiming to introduce natural processes in a devastated and perverted situation. These processes work according to the rules of ecology, but are initiated and sustained by technological means. Man uses this artefact as a symbol of nature,*

The water system is one of the most important systems in the Duisburg-Nord Landscape Park. The Emscher had previously been hidden away in a culvert but it has now been changed back into a living waterway above the ground, partly using existing sewage treatment facilities in the park.

but is still responsible for the process. It is the most natural and at the same time the most artificial system," Latz explains, pointing out that the depth of the water varies between 10 centimetres and 2.5 metres in the different sections of the canal, thus creating very different habitats for flora and fauna. The water is enriched with oxygen by a wind-driven pump in the nearby crushing tower, from which the water crashes into a gravity-fed tank from a great height.

Something that also fascinates many foreign visitors to Duisburg-Nord is that there is free access over the whole area. Peter Latz is always pleased to repeat that *"This Park is open 365 days per year and 24 hours per day, permanently and even at Christmas,"* particularly to his American colleagues who – just think of the Gas Works Park in Seattle – find this kind of openness inconceivable. Incidentally, it was not easy to ensure this accessibility. *"People kept wanting to charge to come into the park. There were lively arguments about this, and the entire board of directors was in favour of*

The landscape architects call the whole system of waterways the water park, and use existing infrastructure to run this system; it includes a new wind wheel that pumps up water and allows it to trickle down in order to be enriched with oxygen.

DEALING WITH "BAD PLACES"

it. The operating company was supposed to do that. Then partial fencing was suggested, if it proved impossible to fence the whole thing off." But that didn't happen either, because the landscape architects made this part of their creative work as well, rather than leaving the decision to politicians. But fences were designed for particularly dangerous areas, and a number of walls that gave a sense of boundaries were renovated.

The result was a "Volkspark" with predominantly open access. It has developed outstandingly well since it opened, and there is always something going on thanks to outstanding management by Dirk Büsching, director of the "Landschaftspark Duisburg-Nord GmbH" operating company: open-air concerts in the Piazza Metallica or on the open-air stage, theatre performances in the Giesshalle, celebratory banquets and exhibitions in the Kraftzentrale, (a kind of cathedral for work), guided tours on industrial history and industrial nature, photo-excursions by day and night, diving instruction in the gas tank, climbing competitions and a great deal more. After sunset the park, illuminated by the English light artist Jonathan Park in the area near the blast furnaces, invites visitors to undertake nocturnal exploration tours. A new cultural landscape has come into being that intelligently questions the traditional ideal notions of beautiful landscape. Internationally the project had already acquired the first Rosa Barba European Award for Landscape Architecture in Barcelona in

The industrial site is still being opened up in different ways: in the transferred sense by the many cultural events that take place in the park and literally by opening up closed bunker compartments with special saws.

2000, the Grande Médaille d'Urbanisme of the Académie d'Architecture in Paris in 2001, and in 2005 in the USA the Places Award from the Environmental Design Research Association (edra). So it has long been seen as one of the turn of the century's major landscape architecture projects: as the industrial age comes to an end, it is important to manage structural change in terms of environmental design as well, and not to suppress the industrial component of landscape history as "anti-world".

The British light artist Jonathan Park devised a lighting concept based on rich colours specially for the blast furnaces of Duisburg-Nord Landscape Park; it also attracts a lot of interested visitors at night and motivates them to explore the site.

DEALING WITH "BAD PLACES"

Parco Dora, Turin

The tract of derelict industrial land known as Spina 3 covers almost 100 hectares. It is on both sides of the Dora and is the largest subsection of the Spina Centrale, an important main urban development axis running through Turin from north to south.

GIVEN THEIR YEARS of experience with the "anti-world", Latz + Partner threw themselves into a variety of post-industrial use projects world-wide, coming up with a tenacious wealth of invention. *"Each conversion project is different, the preliminary decisions are completely different and the prevailing site conditions are completely different,"* says Peter Latz emphatically with reference to one of the most recent conversions in Italy which he conceptually designed together with Tilman Latz. *"Unlike Duisburg-Nord, the new park in Turin is coming into being in a densely built-up area that will be occupied by the middle class in future. So people will live very close to and with the new park from the outset, and a dense road system will ensure that the park is firmly anchored within the municipal system."* Building the park directly into the urban structure is the first key characteristic of the Turin project.

Turin is Baroque in character but built on the Roman grid system. If one looks at current aerial photographs of the project area on which the Parco Dora, covering about 45 hectares, will come into being not far from the centre of town, it is scarcely possible to explain at first glance how such an extensive, cleared area of land could possibly have emerged on the banks of the Dora. The derelict land north of the city centre covers a total area of about 100 hectares, which will not contain the park alone, but also an environmental technology and research centre, Mario Botta's new Santo Volto church with a converted factory chimney 55 metres high as its steeple, and also large new-build areas with residential high-rise building. These have already been completed, and occupy the most striking edge of the site running down to the river lowlands, where most of the industrial areas used to be.

There are very few industrial relics as reminders of its former use. Almost all Turin's disused industrial areas were cleared as a result of the enormous development thrust fuelled by the preparations for the 2006 Winter Olympics, and used for conversion into building and transport spaces to as large an extent as possible. Peter Latz had critical comments to make about the functionalistic perceptions about landscape that lay behind this: "Industrial archaeology has been in place for a long time, and tries to prevent and compensate for the loss of knowledge that is bound to come about as production ends. On a very different plane, and against a different background, the planning paradigm that form follows a function exclusively is collapsing – in other words leisure architecture for leisure, production architecture for production, a machine means something only in terms of what it has to do, and so should be scrapped as quickly as possible as soon as it is not working to full capacity."[45] The result of this approach identifies the second essential special feature of the initial situation for Latz + Partner when planning the Parco Dora. They were quite definitely too late on the scene here for their insistence on intact information strata.

A far-reaching master plan entitled Programma di Riqualificazione Urbana (PRIU) had been prepared as early as the eighties in the face of profound structural changes in the Italian mechanical engineering and automobile industries. This was definitively finalized in 1998 and aimed to transform extensive areas of Turin's urban structure. Rapid and radical changes were made to areas of the city that used to be industrial in character as part of the preparations for the Winter Olympics. The old north-south railway line that used to divide the city so severely was buried over 12 kilometres so that large areas of it could be built over. The building works,

The revealed concrete foundations of the former Ingest laminating factory look like an archaeological dig. The foundation pit will be restaged as a water garden and surviving hall structures are being transformed into atmospheric garden spaces.

co-ordinated by the French architect Jean-Pierre Buffi, developed over a total area of over 200 hectares along a line running from the northern districts of Turin to the Lingotto in the south. This "Spina Centrale" was divided into four sub-sections, with "Spina 3", which includes the new Parco Dora, as the largest by area of these sectors.

One of the most significant events in the history of how this aristocratically inclined upper Italian provincial capital at the southern periphery of the Alps developed so rapidly into the leading industrial centre was the foundation in 1899 of the Fabbrica Italiana Automobili Torino, FIAT for short, accompanied by the massive expansion of the railway system in the late 19th century. The first Michelin factory outside France was built on the bend in the Dora river in 1908, which even a few decades later covered an area of just under 63,000 square metres of the river flats with its factories. By the twenties, the adjacent areas on the river flats were already accommodating factory sheds for the "Ferriere Piemontesi" Piedmontese

ironworks – from 1917 FIAT ironworks – Vitali, Ingest and Valdocco, producing iron and steel parts for the Italian automobile corporation. The population of Turin, driven by industrial expansion, tripled within a century to over 900,000 – two million in the metropolitan region as a whole. The growth of the city meant that originally peripheral industrial areas had to be integrated into the body of the city. Industrial areas were starting to be abandoned as early as the seventies. Even today about one third of jobs in Turin are tied to industry. But the same structural change in heavy industry that brought the Ruhr to its knees economically in the mid eighties led likewise to large inner-city industrial areas being almost completely abandoned in Turin.

Latz + Partner won the international competition for planning the Parco Dora in 2004, jointly with STS Servizi Tecnologie Sistemi from Bologna, Pfarré Lighting Design, Studio V. Cappato, Studio C. Pession and the artist Ugo Marano. "Coming to terms with the past and the metamorphosis of the place from industrial use to

In the course of Turin developing into Italy's leading industrial centre, the Piedmontese ironworks, Ferriere Piemontesi (FIAT ironworks from 1917), came into being in the early 20th century on the present development site Spina 3.

DEALING WITH "BAD PLACES"

leisure use are fundamental aspects of the planning process. Retaining existing buildings and transforming them is a significant factor," said the explanatory text, but there was a third feature demanding attention apart from tying the park tightly into the urban structure and the industrial architecture, most of which had been demolished: the fact that the structures left behind by the motor car industry were nothing like as aesthetically spectacular as the steelworks in Meiderich, for example.

Once Turin had commissioned them for the project, Peter and Tilman Latz and their team made sure the few industrial relics remaining on the former and centrally located Vitali iron foundry site north of the Dora survived. The neighbouring residential quarter was almost completely built, and a start was being made on clearing up the remaining industrial areas thoroughly. The last large steel-mill factory hall on the Vitali site was due for demolition when Latz + Partner intervened. The hall roof was almost 30 metres high, the Cappannone di Strippaggio building had been 320 metres long and 195 metres wide. Latz asked for it be saved, calling it a "technical canopy", a comparison with a natural tree canopy. Its powerful span affords a large concrete base slab protection from sun and rain, and will in future offer space for a whole range of uses from a market to sporting events.

There is no need for permanent buildings in the park as a lower, former office building survived immediately adjacent to the factory hall, and this can be renovated and converted without difficulty. The surviving hall used to be flanked by an adjacent building of the same kind, but this had already had its roof removed and demolition work had started on the 30 metre tall and three metre wide red-painted steel columns. *"The remains of the hall were actually to have been removed completely, but these*

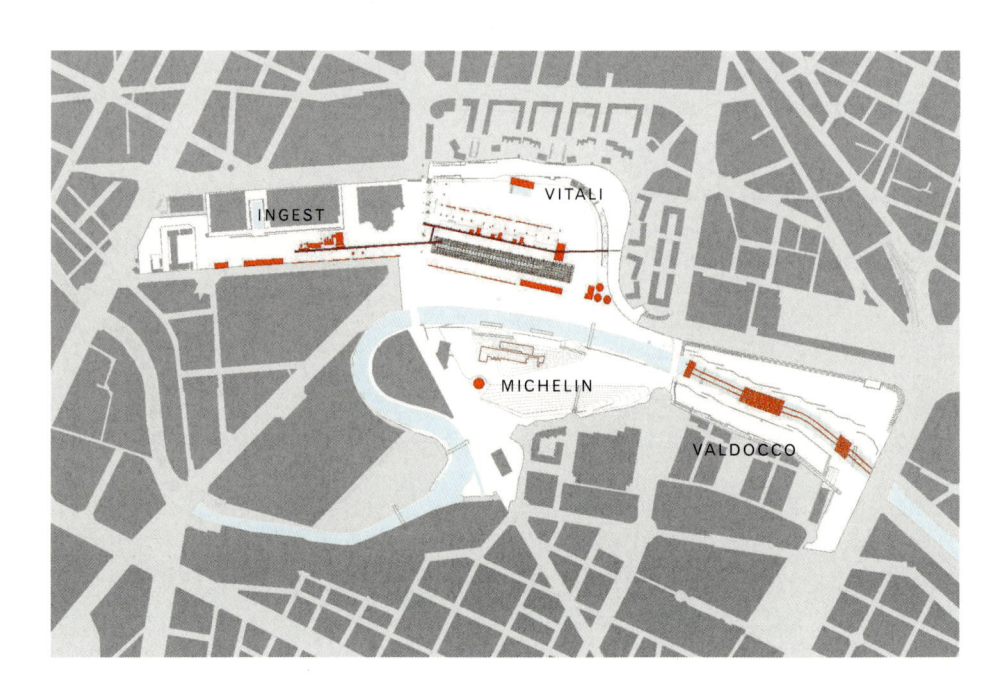

Most of the car industry's derelict industrial plant was removed as part of the preparations for the Winter Olympics. Latz + Partner earmarked the few remaining elements on the four sections for future conversion to other uses.

Peter Latz calls the 30 metre high hall roof of the former Vitali iron factory a "technical canopy" and compares it to a natural canopy of trees, intended to offer a large number of leisure activities in the future.

DEALING WITH "BAD PLACES"

were fixed columns that could be left standing without difficulty," Peter Latz explains. *"The old building plans and the structural engineering were examined, and so we were also able to keep these futuristic-looking elements. Eventually they and the surviving concrete monoliths – covered with climbing plants – will probably establish the character of what may well be the most impressive part of the park. If these structures keep their imposing form and their green cover develops, proliferating all over the monuments, then and only then will we see a new image of technology and nature in harmony."* Some towers will be made accessible to the public, and children's play facilities are to be installed in other concrete structures, similarly to Duisburg-Nord.

Some of the most significant challenges when planning this park came from its relatively low siting in relation to the housing development to the north on the terraced part of the site, as well as the enclosed main road, the new Corso Mortara, which will run through the north of the park site as a busy by-pass, in itself an extensive construction project. Unlike the two German projects described before, there is considerable demand in the Parco Dora for public infrastructure that can be used on a daily basis, and so broad steps and a piazza will accentuate the transition from the higher residential area with its shopping centres. Ramps, promenades, stairs and terraces will in future bridge the striking differences within the site, in

30 tall steel columns were left standing like large sculptures where the hall roof was removed. Latz + Partner are developing a landscape park between them, combining nature and technology in a new way.

order to ensure that the park is linked with the housing development with as few constraints as possible. To serve this purpose, long walkways are to be constructed high above the ground on free-standing steel columns and connecting the different parts of the park, offering a completely different view of the site in the future.

Not much will remain of the abundance of industrial nature that has sprung up spontaneously. The soil is so contaminated that a continuous covering of impermeable clay and unpolluted recycled material up to 60 centimetres thick will be needed, providing a growth medium for the new gardens. But anyway Peter Latz only considers the untouched industrial wilderness on very rare occasions as a planning target: *"The zero variant involving no cultivation and maintenance can only be realized in situations where there are no people living for kilometres around. But at the moment there are people living close by or having their allotments. I have to introduce maintenance to stop the area in question turning into a rubbish dump and running completely wild. And the degree of maintenance increases, up to the areas that are visited daily, or shown off as part of guided tours. These have to be tended meticulously, and where appropriate have rubbish cleared from them daily. Also, a park needs 70 to 80 years of time and care before it can develop its character fully, and all these on-going maintenance interventions, which also have to secure the existence of the historical substance, cost money. Of*

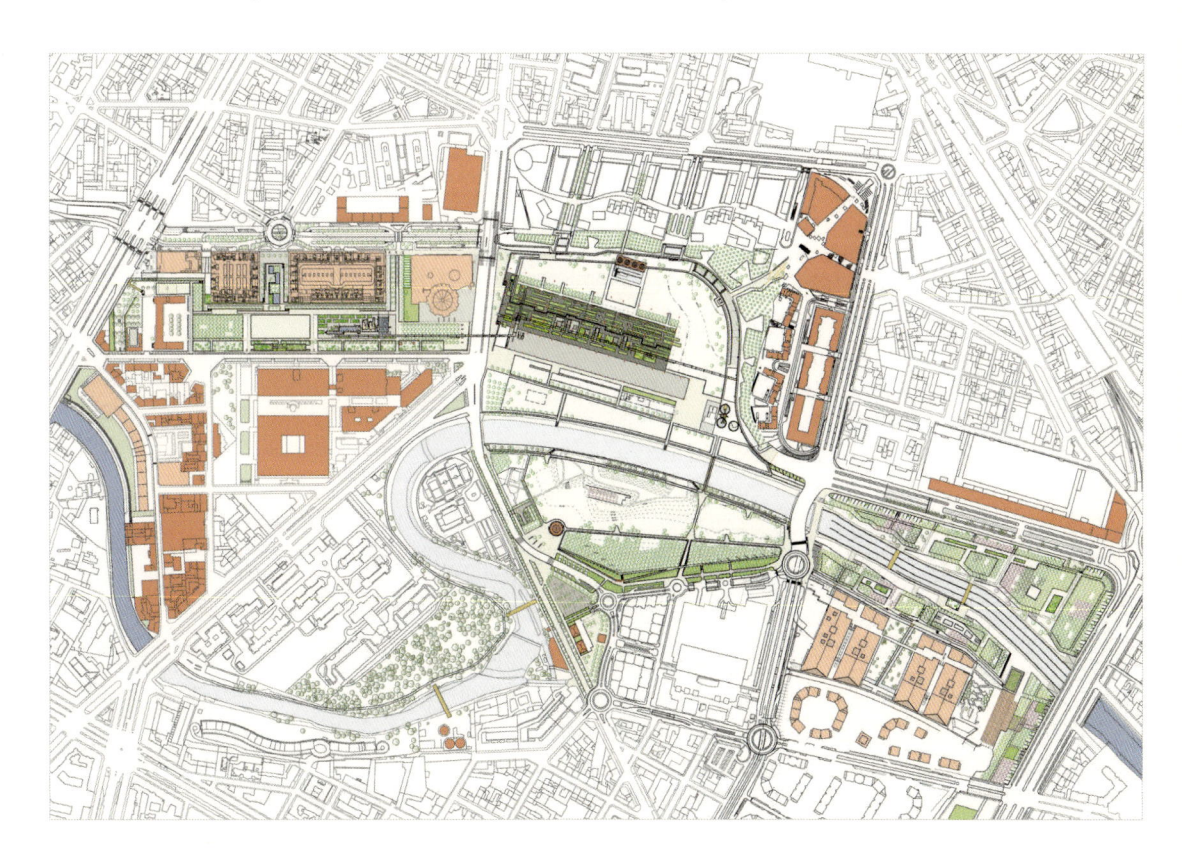

The master plan shows clearly how important the Parco Dora will be as a municipal park for nearby residents in housing originally completed for the Olympic Games.

DEALING WITH "BAD PLACES"

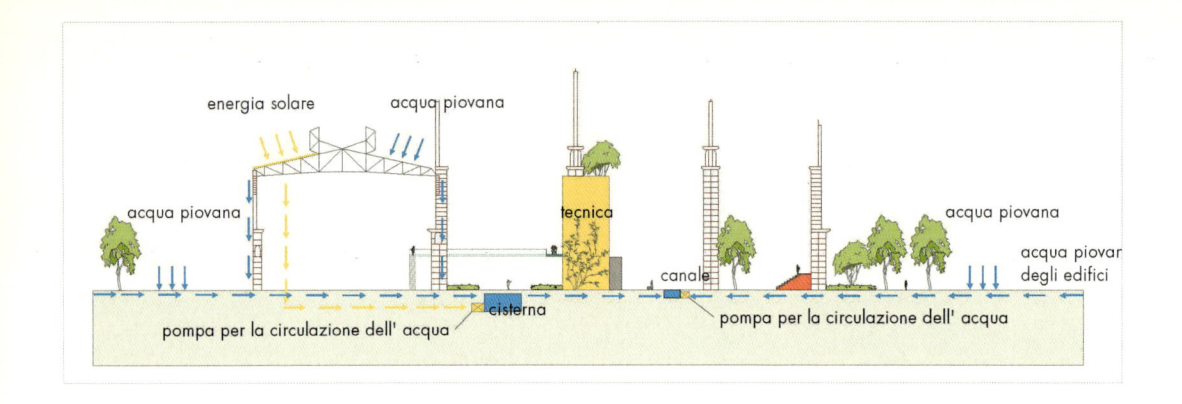

course local authorities don't want to know about that, and of course people often try to pull the wool over their eyes and pretend you can develop parks using the zero maintenance variant. But that doesn't work here in Turin in the city centre."

There is clear evidence of one of the key themes in Peter Latz's work in Turin. "Water systems, the impressive symbol of ecological renewal in open space, also reform modern urban agglomerations. Their rules impose new elements on existing structures: the gutter, brook, and retention pool for rainwater management become an elementary component of the city and its parks. Parks become a component of the infrastructure network and biotope network extending far beyond their limits."[46] An extensive system made up of water channels and former foundation tanks and settling basins is being transformed into luxuriantly planted water gardens, which are intended to ensure that the water system approximates a natural process. But here too Latz + Partner are not trying to harmonize nature and technology.

The course of the Dora river, canalized and regulated for years now, forms the spine of the new park and becomes a central, connecting element defining the various parts

Latz + Partner's planning approach for the Parco Dora is based on the principle that technology and nature are not a contrasting pair but can form a new, complex environment system together.

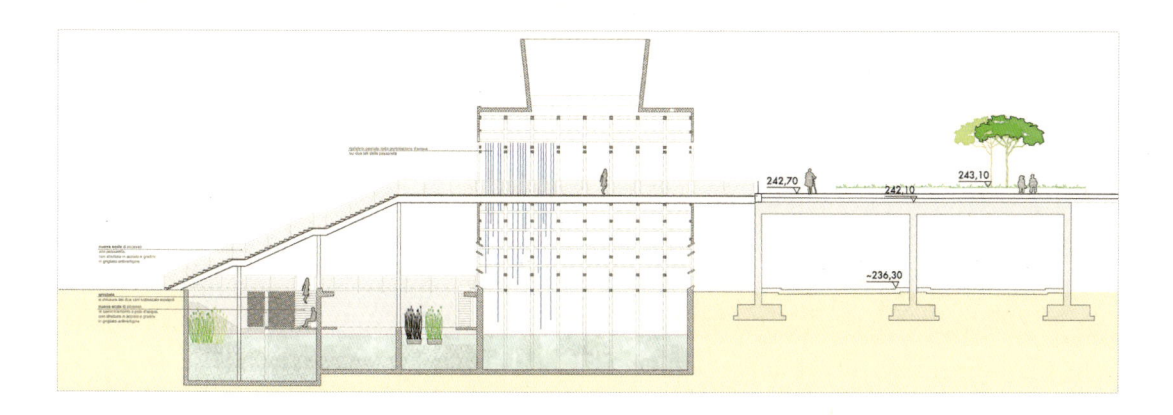

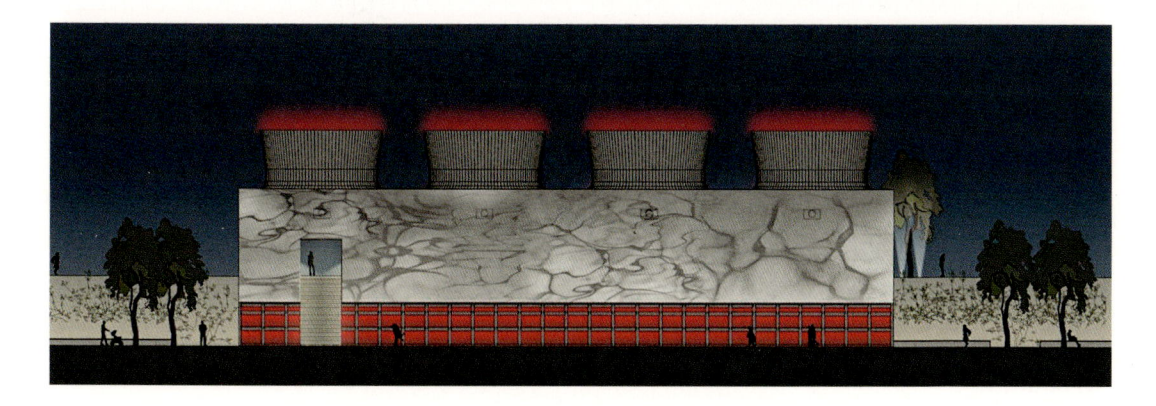

The example of the former power station on the Vitali site shows how the landscape architects intend to use the existing infrastructure to create a working, self-regulating irrigation system for the park.

DEALING WITH "BAD PLACES"

143

of the park on its north and south banks. One crucial feature involves clearing access to the riverside areas, so that visitors can get to the Dora. Pontoons, embankment paths, but also large flood areas of will make it possible to experience the water again in future. Looking at historical photographs of the Valdocco factory site shows how essential such measures are. This used to extend over 237,000 square metres on the eastern periphery of the Spina 3 plot, and pictures show clearly that the river was built over to a massive extent throughout the whole factory area, and disappeared from the landscape completely.

There is scarcely anything left of the old industrial buildings in this section either, which was repeatedly used as an interim topsoil dump. Only a lonely cooling tower

The river in the area of the Valdocco site, previously culverted, is not being restored to its natural condition. Its concrete lid will simply be removed and the fascination of an artificial river gorge will be clearly sensed. Peter Latz is not interested in compulsory harmony.

Landscape architecture's most effective interventions always aim at ideal mental images of nature and landscape as well. Only someone who is aware of this can transform a concrete channel into a gorge.

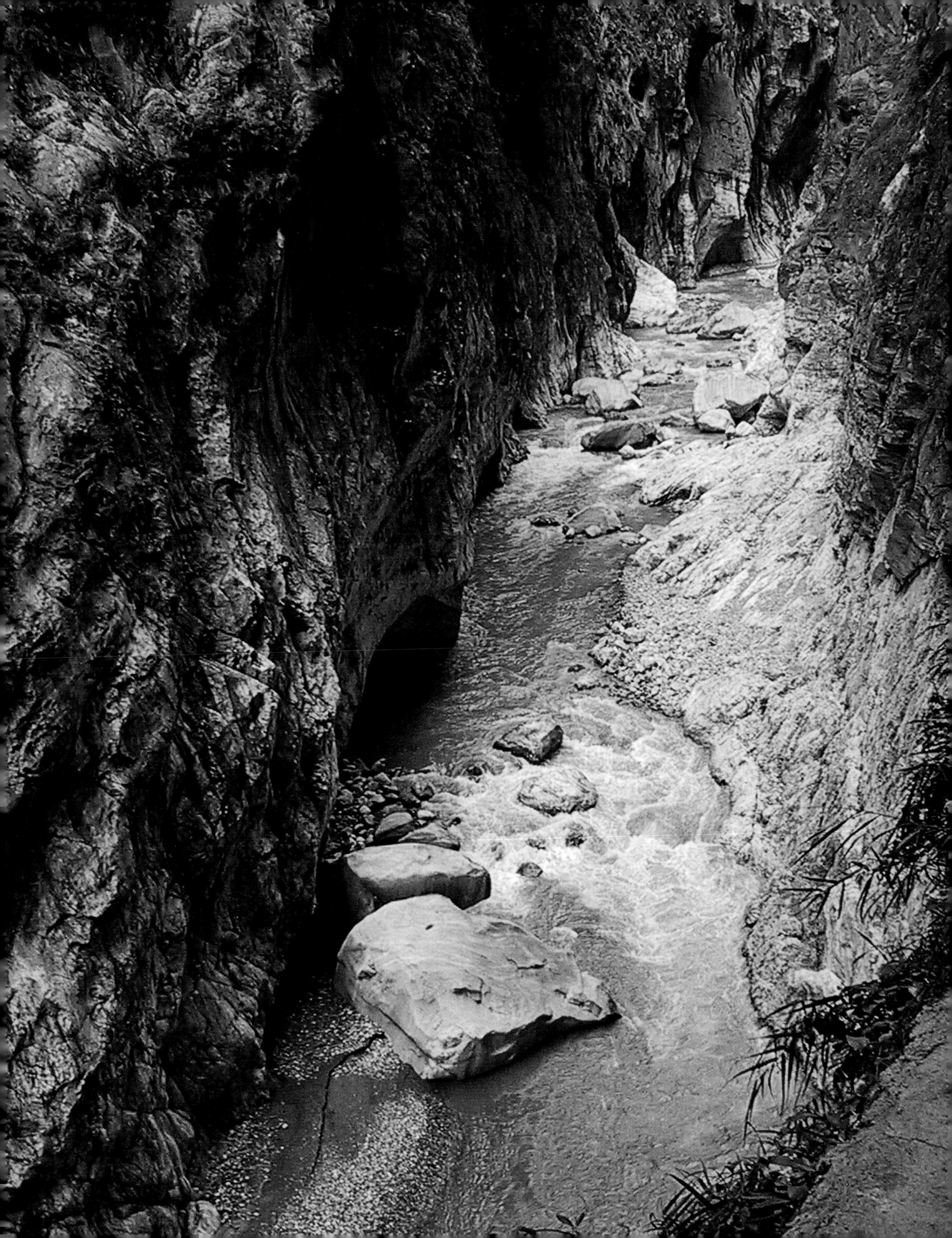

on the site of the former Michelin factory, adjacent to the west, is to be retained as a park landmark. Already today, the tower is a point of orientation visible from afar. In the future it is to be accentuated by special lighting at night as well. The whole southern part of the site, directly adjacent to the urban development, has long since been built over, partly with a very large shopping and office centre and partly with new residential quarters and a so-called "Environment Park". This extensive, 'greened' office building complex, a research and service centre for environmental technology, forms a precise, built boundary to the river flats. All the north-facing office spaces in the centre look out over the emerging park with the Dora flowing through it, though for the time being the river is still invisible.

To explain his concept, Peter Latz takes you very close to one of those mysterious, dangerously deep holes in the overgrown rubble landscape. You can hear the wild gurgles of rushing water coming up out of the depths. If you close your eyes you suddenly imagine yourself in a gorge coursing with white water. These holes in the landscape are nothing other than places where the massive concrete slab, which used to cover the river so that the factories could be built, has collapsed. The water rushes though the solid concrete walls that support the concrete lid, at a depth of several metres. But the design plans do not involve restoring the river, but opening up as much as possible the concrete cap which had been built over the river to enable the siting of the Valdocco factory there, while retaining the concrete walls. The impression of an artificially created river gorge is to be retained, flanked by promenades and avenues of trees. Here too visitors will start to begin to read the industrial

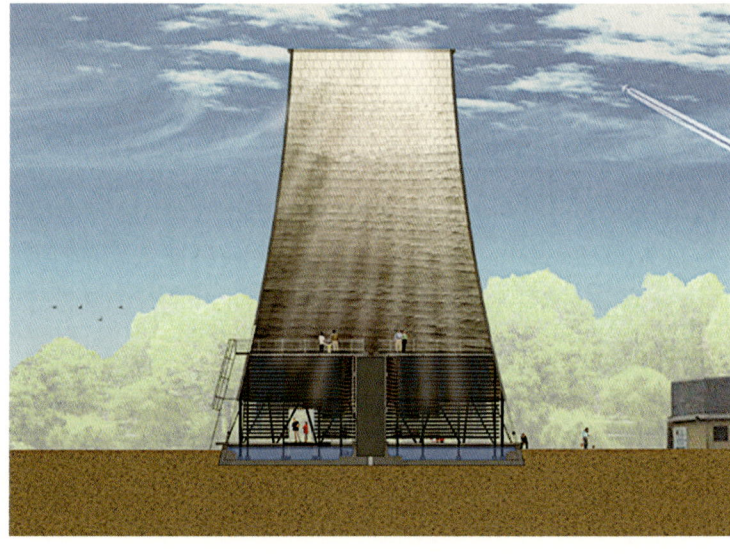

The cooling tower is all that survives on the former Michelin site. It will be presented as a light and sound sculpture that visitors can walk into. The engineering structure is illuminated at night, and stands as a landmark in an open landscape park area.

ruins, just as they look at the remains of Roman aqueducts and ancient building foundations, "eager to find out why what they are seeing looks so strange, to develop recognition patterns, or to learn new ways of dealing with things, relax, and use the objects according to their own imaginations".[47]

The new park in Turin will become an attractive municipal park. It will seem less fragmented and reconstructed than the Hafeninsel in Saarbrücken, as here there is no need to toil over freeing the information strata from the rubble. And the Parco Dora will also be far less complex and authentic in terms of industrial history than the Duisburg-Nord Landscape Park, as in Turin there is very little left of the industrial landscape's original substance, which in any case was nothing like as functionally and spatially complex as the Meiderich blast furnace plant. There is also little scope for a wilderness of post-industrial spontaneous vegetation, as the landscape architects have to bear in mind that this new park will become the most important leisure and recreation area for local housing, and so safety and environmental engineering aspects have a major role to play. These features show clearly how much a particular context is influenced by the development possibilities for derelict industrial land – to say nothing at all about the political background.

The future view from the terrace of higher terrain to the north shows a people's park with clear traces of industrial history. The remains of the Vitali steel-mill factory hall are particularly impressive when seen from here.

DEALING WITH "BAD PLACES"

Hiriya Mountain, Tel Aviv

The 85 metre high table mountain of rubbish – Peter Latz calls it the "mythical mountain" – on the plain outside the gates of the Israeli metropolis Tel Aviv, is a landmark visible for miles around.

ONE OF THE most astonishing mountains in Israel is a lonely, 85 metre high table mountain rising out of the agricultural plain of the small Ayalon and Shapirim rivers with an area of 68 hectares not far from Tel Aviv. This striking earthwork catches your eye as soon as you start the approach to Ben Gurion airport or from the nearby motorway linking Jerusalem with Tel Aviv and Beersheba with Haifa. But this hill with whole flocks of birds, storks, vultures and seagulls circling around it was not created by natural geological forces over millions of years but by half a century's accumulation of a total of 30 million cubic metres of household and commercial waste from Tel Aviv and its metropolitan region. Hiriya is the largest rubbish dump in the country, and at the same time a symbol, "the nation's environmental wart [...] a visual reminder of the consequences of mismanagement and lack of civil responsibility," as Martin Weyl, curator of the momentous "Hiriya in the Museum" exhibition in the Tel Aviv Museum of Art in 1999 puts it.

The rubbish dump was set up without any protective measures in 1952 in a place where the little Arab town of Hiriya had stood until 1948, when its inhabitants abandoned the site after the war of independence. The more successfully the Jewish pioneers managed the settlement and the agricultural reclamation of Israel and the more rapidly the population grew, from fewer than a million in 1948 to over 6.3 million today, the faster the mountain of rubbish outside the city grew. Today almost 2.9 million people live in the Tel Aviv metropolitan region and over 95 per cent of Israel's waste is disposed of on dumps and not recycled. "Hiriya's 'Mount Trashmore' soon became a symbol for a national 'throw-away' mentality and environmental

The rubbish mountain became a serious safety problem for Ben Gurion international airport, visible in the background, as large flocks of birds regularly swooped on the 30 million cubic metres of household and industrial rubbish.

DEALING WITH "BAD PLACES"

neglect," said Alon Tal of Tel Aviv University appositely, describing in an article entitled "A Brief Environmental History of Israel" how environmental requirements were almost completely ignored in the Zionists' ambitious development plans.

Even in the early seventies, the mountain was drawing attention to its rotting internal life, emitting not only evil smells and liquids but also the greenhouse gas methane, which often combusted spontaneously in the summer months and caused stinking, smouldering rubbish fires. In the eighties the mountain was already being fed 2500 tons of rubbish per day. Polluted water seeped into the nearby rivers and flocks of birds gathered around the rubbish mountain; until by the early nineties they represented a serious threat to air traffic at Ben Gurion airport, 3.5 kilometres away. It kept being necessary to suspend air traffic from one to three o'clock in the afternoon, the time when most of the flocks of birds arrived, because of the threat of collisions. By winter 1997, 3200 tons of unsorted rubbish were being dumped per day at Hiriya. The north flank of the mountain started to slip after a heavy thunderstorm, blocking the Ayalon river, an important watercourse for Tel Aviv, for days until a new river bed could be dug for it. One year later the Ministry of the Environment, created in 1988, decided to stop using the mountain as a dump. Instead, it would be used as an enormous holding ground for sorting about 3000 tons of rubbish per day and then transporting it to other dumps in the south of the country. So the mountain of rubbish continued to grow, if no longer in Hiriya, where

Hiriya's "Mount Trashmore" also made a disastrous impact on air quality and the water quality of the rivers Ayalon and Shapirim. Poisonous seepage polluted the water, which was already in short supply in the metropolitan region.

fortunately foundations and museums turned their attention to the environmental problems.

Just one year after Hiriya stopped being used in 1999, Martin Weyl, director of the influential environment and culture trust, the Jerusalem Beracha Foundation took the problem on board and organized the pioneering "Hiriya in the Museum. Artists' and Architects' Proposals for Rehabilitation of the Site" exhibition in the Tel Aviv Museum of Art. Weyl wanted to raise public awareness about the enormous environmental problem outside the gates of Tel Aviv, but he had realized that Hiriya is more than just an evil blot on the landscape: "For years the ugly, threatening monster, Hiriya, has attracted a great number of curious visitors. Some came in order to observe the unlikely phenomenon for themselves: scholars and engineers came to study, bird watchers came to witness one of the largest concentrations and varieties of bird migration, tourists took in the extraordinary vistas, collectors searched for rare specimens to enrich their collections, and young couples simply came to look for discarded furniture or appliances that could still be fixed. [...] Hiriya also had a romantic lure. For many it reflected the quintessential 20th century fascination with the ugly, the decomposing, the rejected, the unexpected, the threatening. Photographers, filmmakers, poets, storywriters and artists frequented the site that contained modern-day Israel's largest concentration of 'objets trouvés' ever. [...] It was to this group, the artists, that we turned, inviting them to elaborate on their observations and their fascination with Hiriya, with the environment, and with ecological concerns, to see whether they could propose a new content and form for the mountain – in the hope that they could turn it into a richer and more meaningful symbol of a different kind."[50]

28 distinguished artists from all over the world sought inspiration from the place and came up with 19 suggestions for transforming the "navel of the country", as Hiriya has come to be known ironically. Designs by artists including Vito Acconci, Shlomo Aronson, Ludger Gerdes, Mierle Laderman Ukeles, Mark Dion, Lois Weinberger and Meg Webster all aimed at retaining the landmark.[51] Many of them took a romantically tinged view of the mountain and proposed that it should be transformed into Land Art, museum complexes, parks and gardens, energy, research and environment parks, indeed even Utopian urban landscapes. A great deal of creative fuel had been created, along with a well-nigh inexhaustible fund of ideas, a real treasure trove for any further planning, but despite the extensive background work, some of it scientifically sound, that many of the artists had put in, none of the projects were built. However, after the exhibition engineers and architects did come

up with the first strategic plans for redeveloping the rubbish mountain, and in 2001 a team of international experts was summoned to define the specific conditions and aims of the redevelopment project. Representatives of the ministries and regional planning authorities examined and approved the plans, while the Beracha Foundation secured the enormous financial resources the project would require.

The aim was by 2020 to create the so-called Ayalon Park. The park was to occupy a total area of more than 300 hectares around the rubbish dump, providing public nature and open space for the 3.3 million inhabitants prognosticated at the time for the densely populated metropolitan region of Tel Aviv, a city in itself not rich in parks and green spaces. The Beracha Foundation announced an international competition for converting the mountain of rubbish that would in future represent the largest part of the Ayalon Park. Eight teams from Holland, the USA, Spain, Israel and Germany were invited to take part in the competition. Latz + Partner won the competition and started to take the first project steps, working with SCS engineers from the USA. One of the most fortunate aspects of the project was that the Beracha Foundation under the direction of Martin Weyl was the project client: his sensitivity, openness to new ideas and delight in experiment meant that Hiriya would not just become a pragmatically revegetated rubbish dump with clichéd landscaping.

"This rubbish tip is the other side of progress," says Peter Latz, refusing to deny the place an identity. Nevertheless, it has to become a place that it is good to live in.

As early as 1999, 28 international artists, such as the group Albatross with its collage, came up with visions for Hiriya. Many thought of reshaping the mountain completely as Land Art.

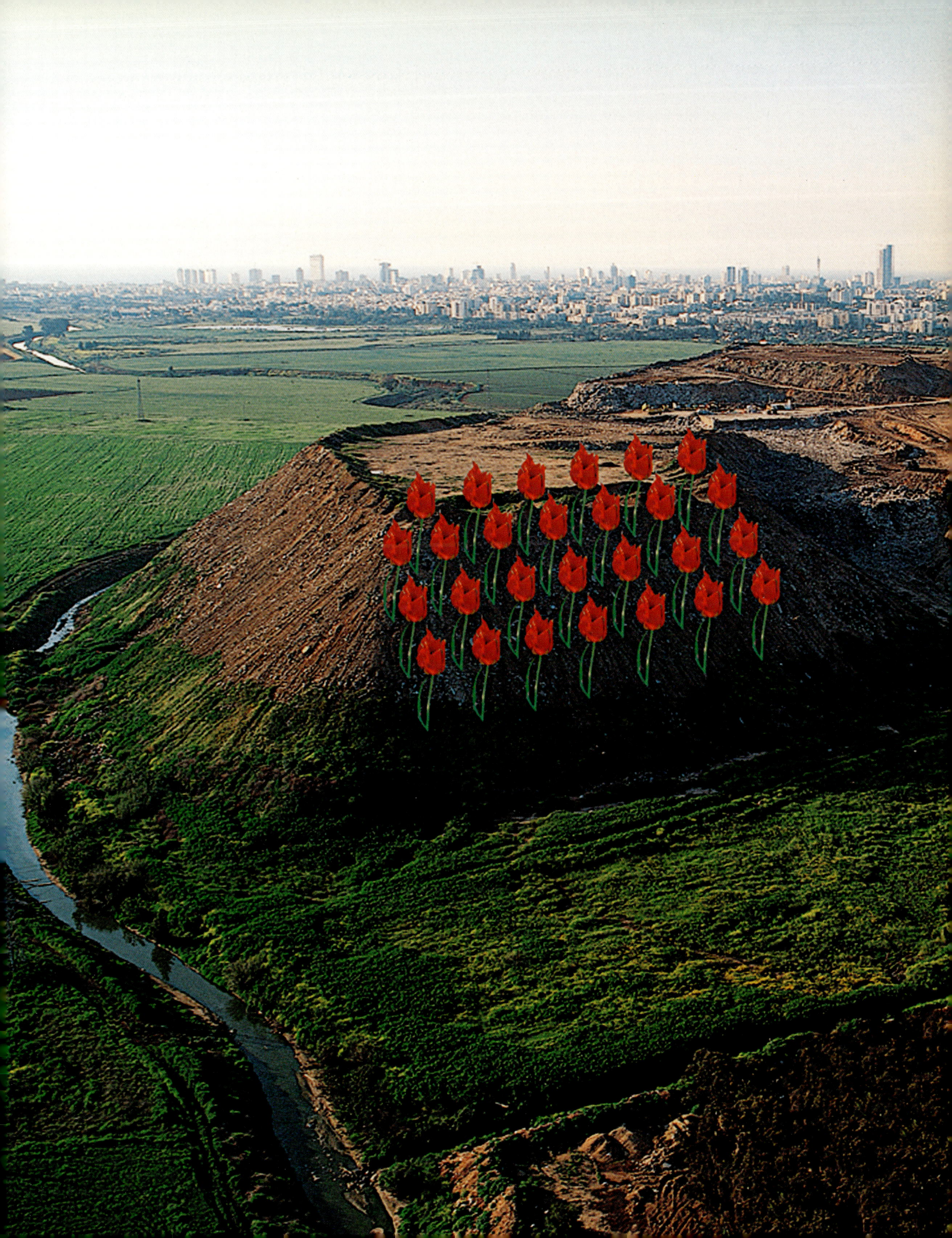

How does one tackle a bad place on this scale? *"First of all, you try to understand the 'production process' for the dump,"* Peter Latz explains. *"The second question is: what happens there of its own accord, and what processes are going on inside the rubbish mountain? This requires a certain knowledge of chemistry. Other questions are: what is the best available technology for dealing with structures like this? What sort of scale am I working on? We realized immediately that the dump would have to be sealed, so that no rainwater could get in and cause poisonous seepage. Then comes the resource analysis: how can I get hold of natural or artificial materials that will guarantee sufficient stability and safety for the mountain over the next 100 years? What conditions do I need for applying sealing substrates, and so on. So I have to put a very different building team together from the one I would recruit for constructing a school yard, for example. This all means that you have to work with a lot of information layers at the same time, and develop a scientifically sound basic concept first of all, based on engineering principles. But then you suddenly throw everything in the wastepaper basket and have to think what other cultural elements you have at your disposal for coping with a structure like this, one apparently without any cultural background."*

Central to all the landscape architects' recultivation and design measures is commitment to the identity of the place. Many of the landscape art projects that had addressed Hiriya in the past took up ideas from "Earthworks: Land Reclamation as Sculpture" dating from the late seventies in the USA[52], and recommended changing the mountain into a gigantic Land Art object. But the artist Lois Weinberger, whose work happened to be following the same theoretical trail as the landscape architects,

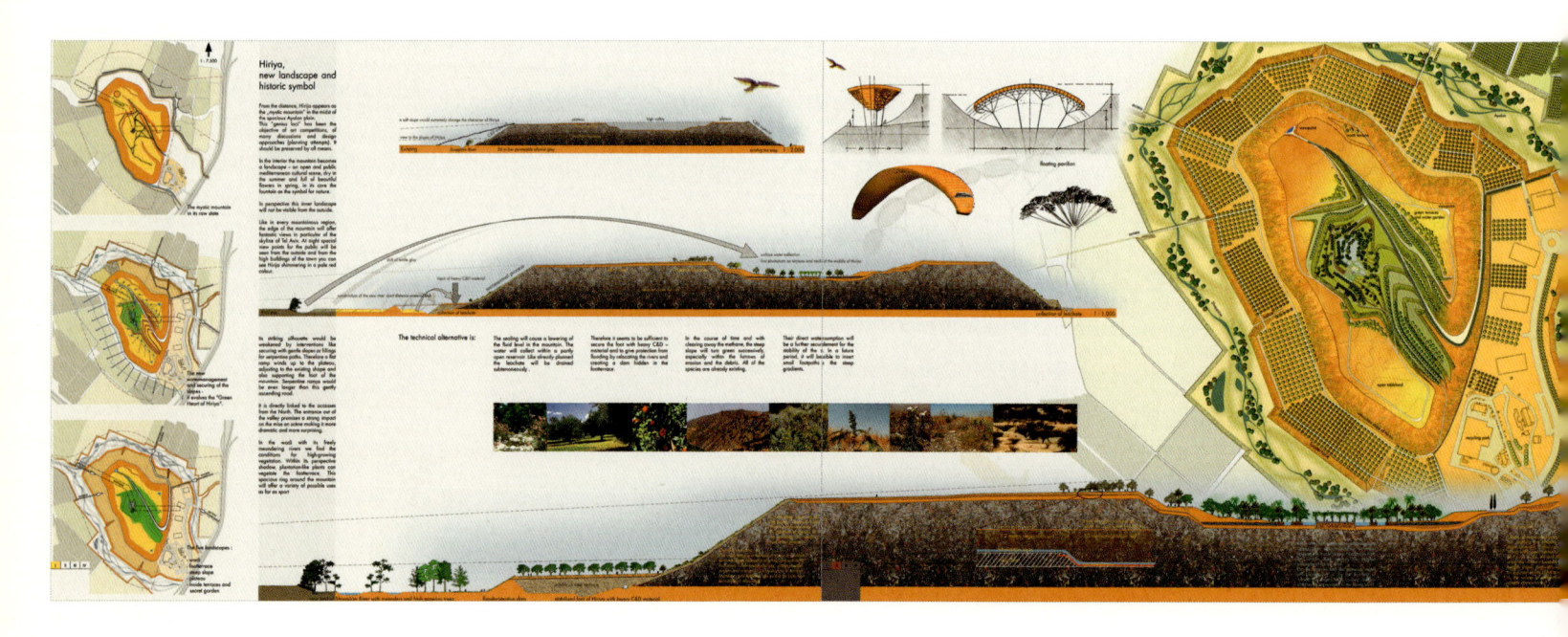

Latz + Partner won the 2004 international competition for transforming Hiriya with a concept intending to retain the characteristic mountain silhouette and to reinterpret the place with acupuncture-like interventions.

spoke out unambiguously against this one-sidedly aesthetic approach: "Examining the materials / the content of the rubbish tip / unmistakeably indicates / that it is not possible / to get rid of something / to conceal the disagreeable / extinguish it / to make behaviour not have happened / a condition / that shows itself to be as depressing as it is relieving. There can be no silent burning and burying / without reading what is burned in advance / without registering what is buried and reconstructing it afterwards by cross connections. [...] I have decided for myself / to like the rubbish sites / at least not to suppress them / nor subject them to faith in boundless feasibility / for me there are links with the stork / with the seagull and the raven at the Hiriya dump / they use the rubbish / possibly / they see it as a gigantic garden / but they do not dispose of the mountain. I cannot spare myself from that."[53]

Peter Latz's approach largely fits in with this theoretical stand, even though he never worked with Lois Weinberger and, as he stresses, was never influenced by his ideas. But as far as strictly rejected suppression strategies and exaggerated manipulation in the spirit of Land Art are concerned, the positions taken up by the artist and the landscape architects are interestingly similar. The landscape architect is particularly certain that the rubbish mountain is part of a complex dynamic structure of spaces created by man that become a landscape, a living culture landscape, that is closely linked with the way our society lives today. *"Hiriya is not an object for us, but a landscape. It must be possible to be able to understand this formation as a mountain of rubbish for as long as possible. Society cannot simply say that it no longer exists, because this*

DEALING WITH "BAD PLACES"

rubbish tip is the other side of the progress coin. The key to developing this place lies in creating spaces that make a cultural identity possible, and this is probably most likely to be of a literary nature, because it is not to be found on the rubbish mountain itself."

"The work on the rubbish mountain could be called poetical fieldwork / if poetry is seen as the most precise means for admitting reality," explains Lois Weinberger germanely in this context. He had planned to build a fragile "museum from the rubbish" as a "perfect temporary measure" called "Present Time Space" on the Hiriya plateau, which would be left completely raw, in the middle of second-hand nature. This museum, conceived as an endless glazed covered walk without a beginning or an end, was intended to bring out the variety of associations and cultural links between rubbish and society, the complexity of what has been used, oscillation between ideal nature and real nature as an actual exhibit. Peter Latz also refers to the contrast between ideal nature and real nature for his cultural recycling of the rubbish mountain, but carefully implants archetypal symbols of positive landscape and of the garden at various points on the mountain in order to change the way the place is read. A special part here is played by the fascinating visual link

The central motif for the planned Hiriya project is a green oasis on the dry plateau of the table mountain with its sparse vegetation. The oasis among the spontaneous vegetation in its original conditions is fed by an ingenious stormwater system.

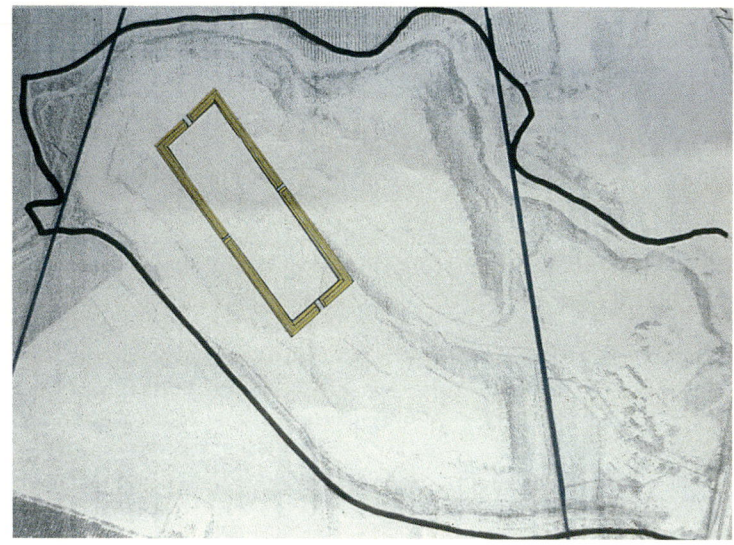

between "Mount Trashmore" and the "Hill of Spring", as the Hebrew name "Tel Aviv" translates. *"From this mountain I see the silhouette of the city of Tel Aviv, which is the epitome of Modernism from its very foundations. This silhouette is quite fantastic, particularly at night. So this means that the place will be developed as a belvedere. That too is a cultural archetype."* The plateau of the rubbish mountain is one of a total of five archetypal landscape sections following each other in sequence that Latz + Partner distinguish for their planning: the wadi, the terrace at the foot of the mountain, the cliff and the inner oasis with its terrace and secret gardens complete the sequence.

The beds of the Ayalon and the Shapirim will be deepened in the future to form the arteries for two wadis. These and the river flats around them will serve as efficient water retention systems in the case of heavy winter rainfall, and are intended to protect southern Tel Aviv from flooding. Here the landscape architects will have to take care that the river beds are sufficiently far away from the foot of the mountain to avoid the influx of polluted seepage water and the accumulation of mud. The wadis will have typical vegetation and freely grouped trees, thus offering a special landscape experience in future, both for walkers in the shade of the trees and also for visitors to Ayalon Park, who will cross the dry valleys on raised pedestrian bridges in order to reach the terraces at the foot of the mountain.

These terraces are there for a number of purposes. They have a significant role as massive volumes of earth for stabilizing the steep mountain slopes. The engineers originally planned to flatten the sides of the mountain, which sometimes slope by up to 45°, to remove the risk of slippage. But Peter Latz saw these steep slopes, which

The artist Lois Weinberger planned a "museum out of rubbish" for Hiriya called *Present Time Space*, intended to address the cultural links between rubbish and society. His photographic works from 1998 depict multi-coloured hens on a rubbish dump, coloured by broken colour containers.

DEALING WITH "BAD PLACES"

already have vegetation on them despite constant methane pollution, as an essential, indeed almost symbolic characteristic of the rubbish dump, and developed an alternative strategy for securing them. Six million cubic metres of demolition material and rubble, covered with the excavated material from the wadis, can be deposited permanently in the terraces. The terraces also include special devices for retaining the poisonous water seeping from the dump. Large areas of these earthworks will be planted with fruit trees, offering an image of cultivated landscape, interspersed with shady picnic gardens, sports facilities, playgrounds and other park features. In contrast, the steep slopes will retain their raw character and wide-ranging varieties of spontaneous Mediterranean vegetation.

In just the same way as the steep slopes, the characteristic artificiality and rawness of the rubbish mountain will be noticeably present on the plateau as well. Only in the centre of the high area, where the driving up of the dustbin lorries and tipping

View from north-west towards the wadi **Perspective**

In future the wadis, a typical landscape element in the region, will offer a special landscape experience, especially for visitors to the Ayalon Park, who cross the dry valleys on raised pedestrian bridges at treetop height.

158

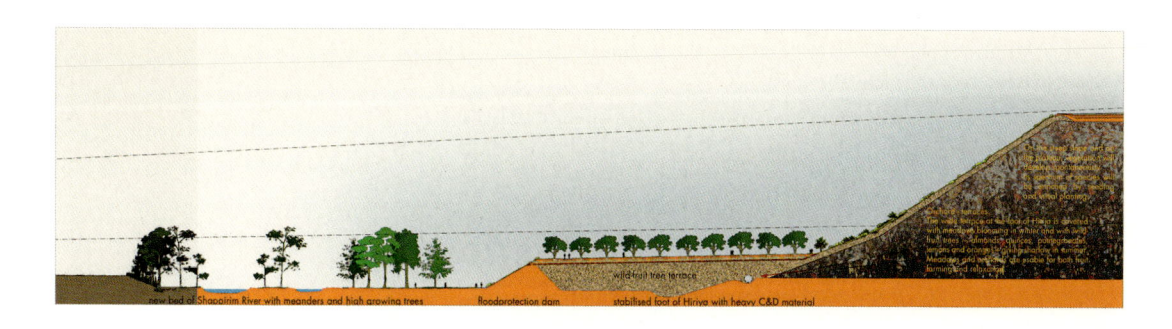

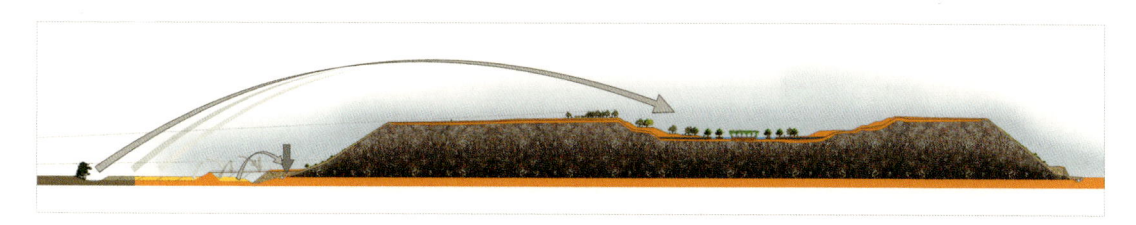

Latz + Partner wanted to retain the characteristic steepness of the rubbish mountainsides, so they developed the strategy of securing the foot of the mountain slope with high-volume terraces that can be used for agricultural purposes.

DEALING WITH "BAD PLACES"

View from the south over the upper plateau **Perspective**

of the rubbish has created a dip from the edges to the middle, a deliberately artificial piece of landscape is to be staged. This will remain almost invisible from the outside and will not change the silhouette of the mountain. *"Here I am referring specifically to the image of the oasis. In the middle of the mountain there is a trough that is ideally suited to creating the cultural archetype of an oasis in modern form."* The laborious climb up the mountain in the heat of the Mediterranean climate is to be rewarded by a lush green oasis – a response to the inhospitality of the place that may seem cliché at a first glance. It gives the impression that the landscape architect wants to implant a pulsating green heart in the seemingly dead rubbish mountain, and that this should stimulate the revival of the whole landscape organism from the inside out.

Creating the oasis with its planted terraces and secret gardens serves the purpose of initiating an emergence of meaning that will affect the surrounding area, but the acupuncture-like placing of this impulse is not an easy undertaking in construction terms. The artist Lois Weinberger criticizes "faith in boundless feasibility", and it is precisely this that is particularly helpful to landscape architect Latz. But the goal cannot be reached without sound specialist knowledge. The hollow has first of all to be provided with a protective layer to stop methane from being emitted. This will at

The high mountain plateau is still furrowed by access routes for the refuse lorries, but spontaneous vegetation has already established its habitats. It is to be retained, enriched by images of cultivated nature.

the same time provide a reservoir for rainwater, which will be kept in a porous drainage layer. Then the layer of vegetation is finally placed on top of this, which will prevent the water from evaporating too rapidly and give the oasis the nutrients it needs. Only a few areas, about 25 per cent of the entire water surface, will be designed as open water. The oasis will be watered with accumulated rainwater and cleaned water from the neighbouring recycling plant, so that the green heart – even with tropical vegetation at its innermost point – can flourish all the year round.

Anyone leaving the oasis on the north side and wandering along the edge of the mountain plateau will arrive at a little hollow that suddenly opens up to reveal the

In future Hiriya will be the core and landmark of the Ayalon Park, an extensive recreational area intended to offer people in the Tel Aviv metropolitan region a new nature and leisure experience.

DEALING WITH "BAD PLACES"

The oasis will be one of the highlights of the new landscape experience. Its heart bursting with tropical lusciousness owes its existence to a technically sound stormwater management concept.

breathtaking view over the Ayalon plain to the skyline of Tel Aviv – fascinating by day and night. Observing the hawks that use the updraughts from the steep slopes of the rubbish mountain to glide suggested the idea of shading the viewing point with a canopy shaped like a paraglider. This original intention was then developed further into an artificial tree canopy. It will have a very shallow span and look almost temporary, and it is intended to crouch down into the landscape to avoid compromising the silhouette of the mountain. In future, this is to continue to act as an orientation point in the Tel Aviv metropolitan area, rather than a "natural" mountaintop, and make it possible to control the space aesthetically and visually, something that had never seemed possible in this area before.

The route from the viewing point back to the foot of the mountain leads – lit at night – past the oasis via a wide, gently sloping path to the south. At the point where the path has to take a sharp bend into order to lead down to the terraces almost par-

Visitors find a pleasant place with a fascinating view of Tel Aviv under tensioned shade canopies spreading out like treetops, erected in a dip to keep the mountain's silhouette unchanged.

DEALING WITH "BAD PLACES"

allel with the edge of the slope, the landscape architects are deliberately directing visitors' eyes to the huge modern recycling plant set up at the foot of the mountain in 2003 to hydro-mechanically and biotechnically sort, clean and separate about 200 tons of rubbish per day. Those interested will be informed in the recycling park's visitors' centre about how fertilizer, water and biogas can be extracted from the rubbish, and how the methane gas can be used more efficiently than burning it off in two special burners at the top of the mountain as has hitherto been the practice. The original intention was to hide the recycling park behind trees and shrubs, but Latz + Partner want to lay this part of the mountain open to experience as well, to a certain extent as part of the process by which it came into being, and are planning a special viewing walkway on the edge of the rubbish processing plant.

The design walks the fine line between admiration for what is here and worth retaining, and the urge to reshape particular key areas horticulturally and in terms of landscape architecture. Nevertheless, Peter Latz still regards rubbish dumps as *"the worst thing [...] we can inflict on our landscape"*. Tolerating such "bad places", which threaten man's existence, is fundamentally out of the question for the landscape architects, however great may be the aesthetic fascination that such places may exude. So Hiriya will become a landscape puzzle picture that is developing dynamically in the Ayalon Park. It will still be ambiguous when read in the future, but will ask important basic questions, especially with respect to socially acceptable ideal notions of landscape.

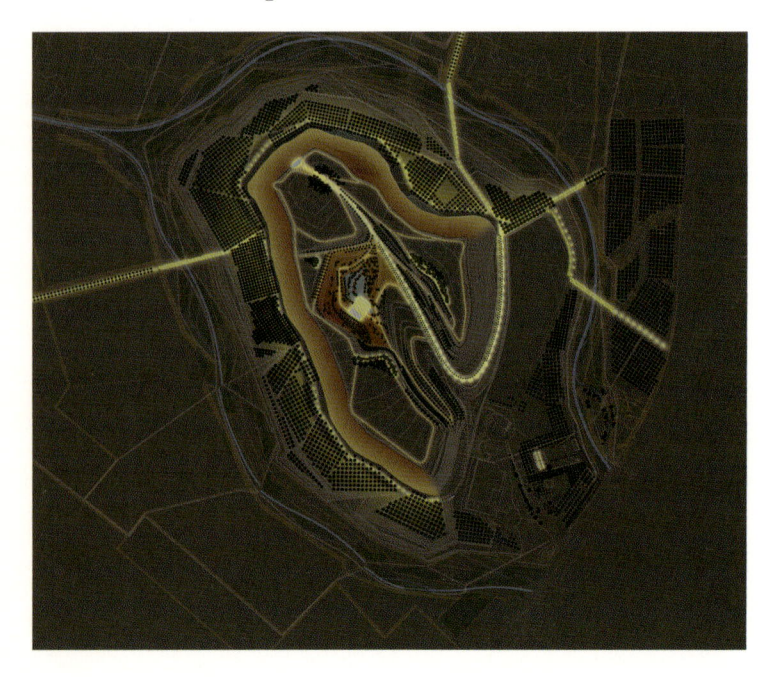

The light concept for Hiriya does not simply provide the necessary illumination for the major access routes, but is also intended to identify the landscape discreetly at night, as a landmark and reference point visible over a great distance.

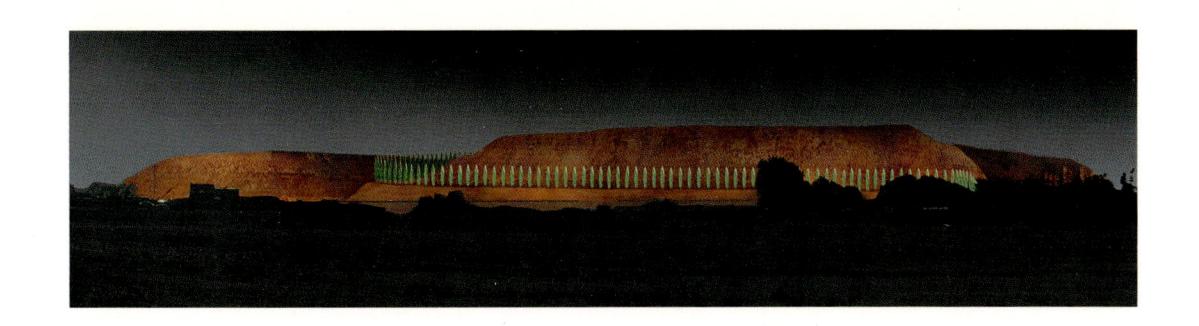

The rubbish processing plant at the foot of the mountain is already working, and is one of the most up-to-date in Israel. Latz + Partner do not want to hide this complex away behind greenery, but devised a viewing platform instead.

DEALING WITH "BAD PLACES"

165

Design as experimental invention

FRANKFURT AM MAIN 1:30000

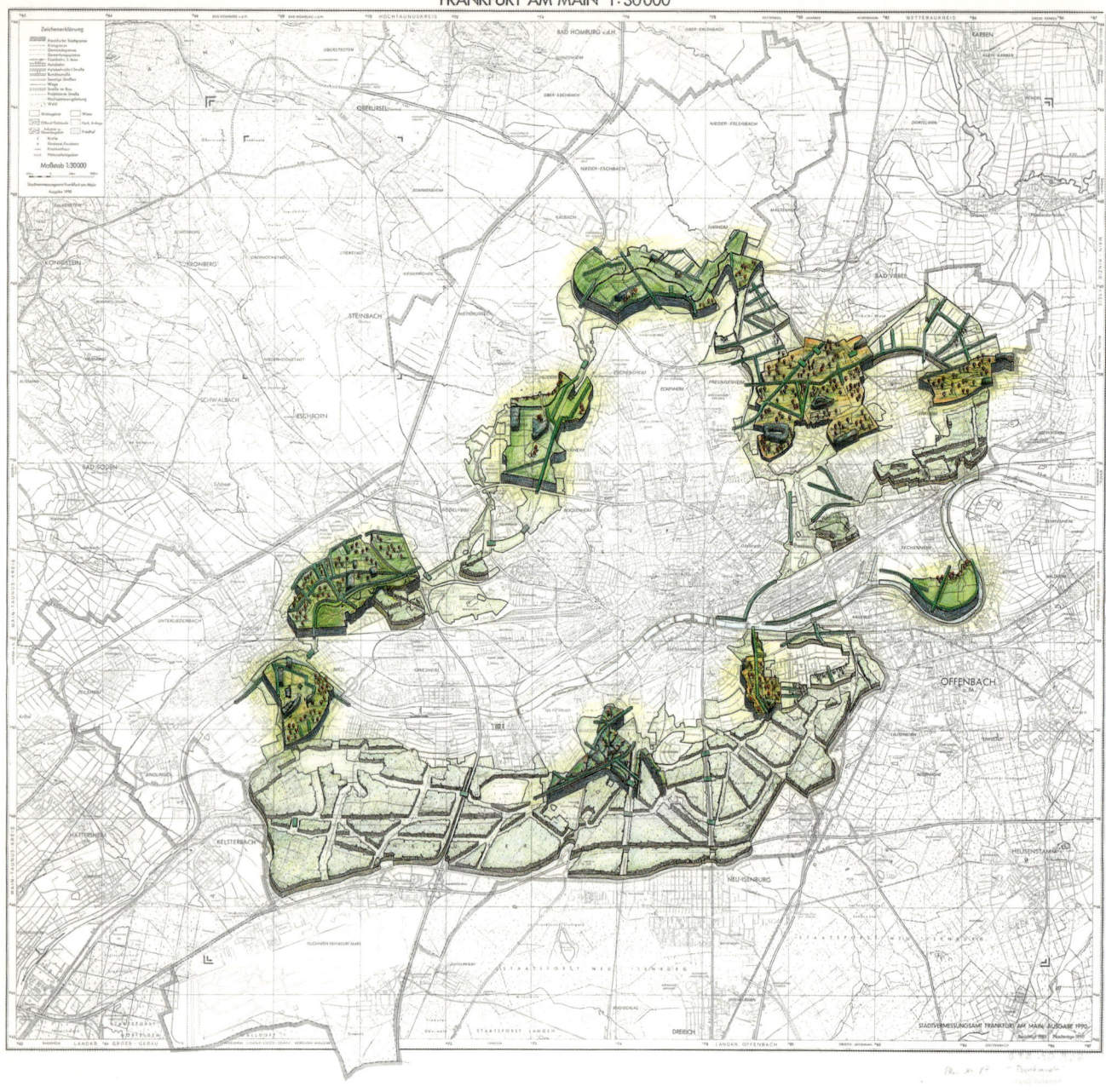

In 1989 the city of Frankfurt am Main decided to conduct a project year developing a viable concept for a Frankfurt GrünGürtel (green belt) covering about 80 square kilometres. Concepts were developed in the following year at summer academies and in competitions involving politicians, administrators, citizens and national and international planners. In 1990/91 Peter Latz, Peter Lieser, Walter Prigge and Manfred Hegger in the GrünGürtel office developed the planning and the Green Belt Charter questioning traditional landscape images. The city of Frankfurt passed a GrünGürtel act in the same year, securing existing green belt land and the further development of this area. Today the GrünGürtel, covering 80 square kilometres, is a landscape conservation area and Frankfurt's most important recreation area close to the centre.

PETER LATZ INSISTS that his students at the Technische Universität München-Weihenstephan, where he is professor of landscape architecture and planning, should also explore theoretical notions about landscape, and do so from the very beginning of their course. For Latz, design is a reflective process, aiming to affect planes of information and the elements directly embedded in them. Put in another way: design means "inventing" information systems or layers. Here he finds it better to design strategies for achieving his aims rather than hunting down good form, and he thinks it is more important to establish viable structures than to create beautiful individual objects. Deciding which of the numerous planes of information could be the crucial ones for a particular design which elements are the key to the overall structure is a central challenge in the design process. It is only after these decisions have been taken that it is possible to use the syntactical approach to bring together the finely woven networks and scattered components of a landscape and, following a particular set of grammatical rules, to create a new structure. Critical awareness of imaginary images of nature and landscape is essential if the enormous variety of visible and invisible information levels is to be handled skilfully in terms of planning and design. "Landscape only exists in our minds, and we all compose it differently in our own minds, so it is an intellectual construct and thus different for each individual"[55], Peter Latz points out, by analogy with Lucius Burckhardt's early eighties thesis about nature being invisible as such.[56]

One of the fundamental difficulties in our highly visual age – and incidentally not just for new students of landscape architecture – is being aware that landscape by no means exists on a pictorial level only. It is never mere scenery, but there could well be an infinite number of invisible, inextricably linked components that shape the essence, the meaning and ultimately the way that landscape is perceived overall. "Not least it is the variety of association patterns that are invoked at the same time as the actual perception process, and can thus influence our insights into space and how we interpret it," Latz suggests. "Could it not be that we mean our memories of the fresh fragrance of a flower meadow, the twittering of the birds and the mild air when we find an open space, a landscape, beautiful? Could it not be that the bitter cold that burns our faces, the fresh wind tousling our hair and the powdery snow our feet are crunching through make us find a landscape beautiful – the space is also only or above all a possible source of experiences?"[57]

A second fundamental source of problems applies to the general understanding of landscape that has essentially been rooted in certain ideal notions for over two centuries. These make it more difficult to generate the necessary new design and development approaches to dealing with today's landscape phenomena, with "bad places" like the Hiriya rubbish mountain. The geographer Gerhard Hard once stated appositely in the context of "Landscape as a professional idol": "If one explores the potential for stimulation and seduction – or put more neutrally, the semantic space – of the linguistic concept of landscape directly (using psycholinguistic and linguistic resources), then one finds an intellectual item something like this: any landscape worthy of the name. I.e. the true, whole and man-made landscape, is quiet, beautiful, rural, green, healthy and healing, harmonious, varied and aesthetic. It is also surrounded by a mass of Arcadian associations: happiness, leisure, love, peace, freedom, seclusion, home ... it symbolizes mature and rooted culture as opposed to false progress and empty civilization, and it is at the same time *the* object, *the* ideal counterpart for (naturally) experiencing a spirited and soulful modern subject."[58] This ideal Arcadian image of pre-industrial landscape is still an influential moral authority within the discussion about landscape and nature conservation. It is driven by the idea that here we are dealing with a statically ordered totality that has to be protected, or at least developed as a target notion. Ideologically it insists on the allegedly insuperable conflict between nature and technology.

In Peter Latz's view, ideas of this kind do not admit understanding technical and natural structures as a complex whole. He sees landscape much more as a spatial structure shaped by people that develops permanently and dynamically, which is often influenced by unforeseeable interactions and never reaches a final state of static climax. "Technical structures or elements of landscape architecture are artefacts aiming to create natural processes. These processes function according to ecological rules, and are initiated and sustained by technological means. People can use these artefacts as a symbol of nature, and see them as life with nature, but they remain responsible for the process. These are natural systems, yet at the same time they are highly artificial."[59] There are certain traditional components of the landscape concept that Latz by no means rejects in principle, but includes them as a matter of course as archetypes in his structuralistic idea of landscape. Despite the danger of being dubbed Postmodern, he often uses quotations from garden history or ideal landscape images to trigger the conversion process, like for example the image of the oasis on the rubbish tip or the garden rotunda on the mound of rubble. "Our new conceptions must design landscape with both accepted and disturbing elements, both harmonious and interrupting ones. The result is a metamorphosis of landscape without destroying existing features, an archetypal dialogue between the tame and the wild. The image of nature can be made of the 'untouched' and the 'built'. Accepting a fragmented world means doing without the complete overall picture and leaving room for the coincidence of nature in the web of the layout. Almost programmed, the 'unreal landscapes that follow industry' are turning up at the moment."[60]

How does one convey such an unconventional view of landscape to students, and distance them critically from traditional ideal notions? It is obviously essential to teach the basic tenets of landscape theory in lectures and seminars, but is it possible to move beyond this and sensitize the students to the invisible information planes and structure-forming elements of a landscape? *"Detailed analyses are made and stock taken – sometimes in a way that new students find meticulous to the point of torment. These are linked with clear questions about the existence, the actual nature and the invisible information contained in the planes or layers of meaning. The object that is being studied has to be explored in great depth. This was a completely new experience for my American students in Harvard and Pennsylvania particularly. They thought at first I was trying to force them to do something that they did not need at all. They thought that all you needed to prepare a design was to study the basic plan and look at a few photographs of the location. I see this completely differently, and so I – even though I have never suggested this quite so specifically – resist so-called spontaneous and brief designs, started at eight in the morning and having to be handed in at three in the afternoon."* Peter Latz is definitely determined that clichés should be removed consistently: "Design languages can emerge spontaneously in fringe situations, but this has to be viewed with considerable caution. Usually they are design languages that have been in place for a long time that come into mind at

Meticulous surveys of buildings and site, here in the Saarland industrial region, are intended to open up information levels well beyond what can be seen in the landscape.

DESIGN AS EXPERIMENTAL INVENTION

moments like these. They turn out to be repetitions, as self-quotations or even as quotations of existing designs, frequently also called models. One strategy would be to eliminate clichés people inevitably have in their heads systematically, so that you can then thrust forward to the actual experiment of a new structural edifice."[61]

Design as experimental invention is a complex process, and the analytical phase is never complete in a reflective creative process of this kind. Intermediate design products must continue to be assessed, especially in terms of the future development perspectives they create. And just as difficult as it is crucial is the constant assessment of which parameters could actually be changed within the tighter framework of the design task, and which pieces of information are in fact essential and important for the project – also called the "object" in design theory – but yet are part of the context peripheral conditions and thus can neither be changed not designed in the context of the design process. The aim is to remain able to act and make decisions in the design process. This is why Latz requires "radical concentration on the object, the actual item that is being considered: in other words, developing the space in all its facets and values and raising the quality of its elements, but not aspirations to improving social conditions, hygiene, politics or even human beings. These aspira-

Peter Latz requires his students, seen here taking part in a building survey in the Saarland in the eighties, to conduct intense on-site surveys – seemingly anachronistic at first, in an age of rapid digital data collection.

tions are context, and important as such, responsible for decisions, responsible for the peripheral conditions under which change can take place."[62]

Working with his colleagues in the department of landscape architecture and planning at Munich's Technical University, Peter Latz conveys a selection of alternative views of design and planning strategies to his students, pointing out, *"that there have to be more out there"*. In this way he puts them in a position to use various design instruments to devise different approaches to solutions. This theoretical knowledge is not dealt with only in lectures, planning surveys, design projects and excursions, but also explored in greater depth in concrete project and studio work that the department has been realizing jointly with the students for decades. Here an important part is played by interdisciplinary co-operation, especially with architects, town planners and landscape ecologists: the "building team" is always appropriately composed. Students have realized building and garden projects on a scale of 1:1 in numerous workshops, including the Hafeninsel in Saarbrücken, the 1985 National Garden Show in Berlin, the 1998 Garden Festival in Chaumont-sur-Loire or in small garden projects in Regensburg, gaining experience in handling different materials, building and design processes, and, much more importantly, of interdisciplinary teamwork.

Students of the Munich Technical University were also actively involved in constructing the spiral mist garden for the Festival des Jardins de Chaumont-sur-Loire in 1998. Standing limestone slabs, spray mist and planted ferns created mysterious nature impressions.

DESIGN AS EXPERIMENTAL INVENTION

This teaching method has left particularly striking traces around the faculty's building in Weihenstephan, in the Munich district of Freising. The four chairs and 340 students took possession of the new site in 1988, after a construction phase of three years. As the professor appointed to succeed Günther Grzimek in 1983, Peter Latz made a substantial contribution even at the planning stage in ensuring that the building would satisfy not only the functional requirements for the teaching and research work, but ecological principles as well. He paid particular attention in Weihenstephan to the climate and energy-related aspects that he had been working on intensively for decades. As in his first house in Kassel in the early eighties and his home and office building in Ampertshausen in the nineties, he made sure that the university building in Weihenstephan had a large conservatory facing south and a central, glazed atrium for the passive use of solar energy. Accumulated rainwater is stored in an ingenious collection system with a large pool in front of the conservatory. All the roofs that sensibly can be are planted, and some of them used for research and experiments. But really experimental are the two hectares around the university building. Even while it was still under construction the students created

Five architecture practices, including Thomas Herzog and Otto Steidle, working with Peter Latz, designed and built innovative "Green Houses" for the 1985 National Garden Show in Berlin. Some of the gardens were laid out in student workshops.

gardens here, planted hedges and trees, built fountains, watercourses and pergolas in workshops, or constructed rubble walls and paths from demolition material and rubble which were available free of charge. The pleasure the students took in creating things made an impact on the whole site in the form of experimental art installations as well over the years.

Work in a real location on a scale of 1:1 reveals that the analysis and design processes are never really over, even when the plans are completed. And basic problems relating to changes of scale and media, along with special design communication requirements, also crop up. These are often underestimated in landscape architecture. "Our specialist languages and presentations are codings that relate to reality only indirectly in terms of both analysis and design. [...] Many changes of media occur in landscape architecture, and the greater the scale, the more frequent they are. These media changes represent a problem in terms of training, learning and teaching, as well as a problem within the profession's everyday work. They change the reality on paper, in sketches, in analytical drawings. [...] Medium and scale can even lead to changes of meaning that distract from the actual

The landscape architect Gunter Bartholmai, Peter Latz's academic assistant, directed the 1988 student workshop called "Regensburg Small Natural Garden Plots". Students created one of three sample gardens in a model small garden complex that opened in 1989.

DESIGN AS EXPERIMENTAL INVENTION

space or object. Paper is available as a mass-produced product, and since the twenties landscape architects like architects are required to make themselves understood by drawing sketches. [...] The ideas that an author has about something are put on paper using a drawing system, and assessed by this means. The idea becomes clearer and clearer via alternative or improved sketches, and comes ever closer to the intended result. This runs the risk of looking for quality in the medium itself, and losing sight of the quality of a real result. And this is a dangerous deficit in precisely those places where the medium is taught and also used almost exclusively as a basis for judgements."[63] André Corboz once wrote with striking relevance about this dangerous deficit in his ground-breaking essay "Das Territorium als Palimpsest": "Every map is a filter. [...] It is a model, and carries all the fascination of a microcosm, it is a simplification that is easy to manage to an extent that can be taken to extremes, and is inclined to replace reality."[64]

The principles of complex design, supported by theories relating to town planning and architecture, were developed in part in the late sixties. Peter Latz was finishing his post-graduate studies in urban development at the Rheinisch-Westfälische Technische Hochschule RWTH in Aachen at the time, and shortly afterwards worked hard at coming to terms with criticism of modern functionalistic urban development at the time, and also with major urban development projects. And so he did not only get to know the implications of the close links between landscape architecture, architecture and urban development emphasized in his training, but had direct experience of it in his early working years. And this is not the least of reasons why

After the new Institute for Landscape Management and Botany building in Freising-Weihenstephan, Munich, was completed in 1986, students had the chance to gather practical experience over the years in workshops for designing the outdoor areas.

Students can only experience the key problems of changes in scale and medium by working on a scale on a real site, here constructing a large retaining wall in 1986.

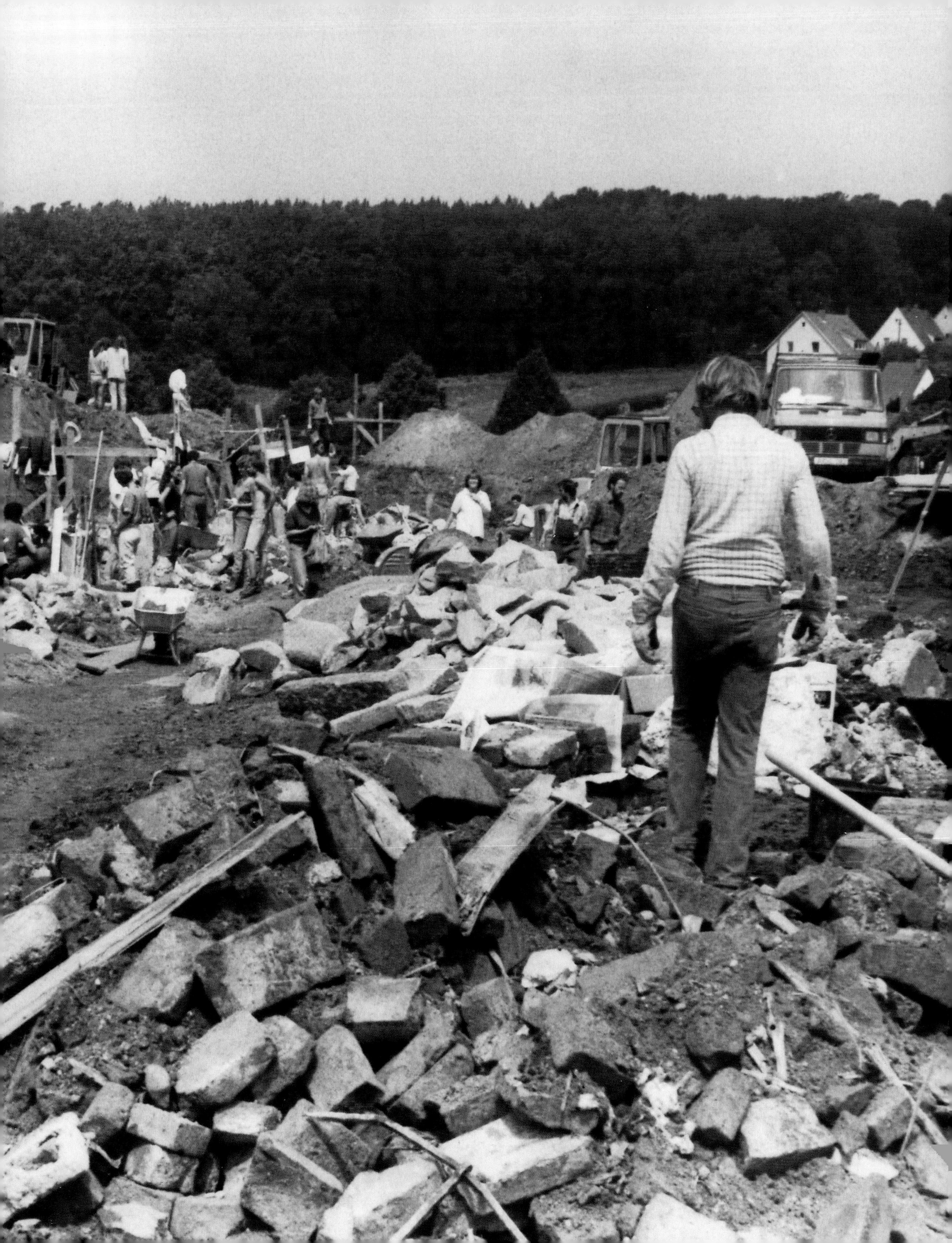

In Weihenstephan, the southerly orientation of the Institute's conservatory with the rainwater pond in front became the building's trademark, as it had in Peter Latz's private residences in Kassel and Ampertshausen.

Students were given a sense from the outset of how closely design methods and construction techniques are linked by being involved in building brick and rubble walls and creating areas with plants and pathways.

DESIGN AS EXPERIMENTAL INVENTION

179

Latz takes it for granted that landscape architecture is part of building culture, and his students benefit from this broad horizon. Because his own profession is not large enough to encompass all the fields of knowledge relevant to landscape architecture with sufficient sophistication there is lively interdisciplinary work in the university teaching, involving related disciplines like forestry, dendrology, tree and shrub horticulture, geobotany, ecology, the engineering sciences, architecture, urban development and many others.

Peter Latz found his way to structuralism via the writings of architects like Aldo van Eyck and Herman Hertzberger, the philosopher Claude Lévi-Strauss, the astrophysicist Fritz Zwicky and the designer Horst Rittel. Here he came across helpful design methods that he started to adapted to certain aspects of landscape architecture. These include for example methodological approaches like the morphology developed to a considerable extent by Fritz Zwicky, though Peter Latz has now come to feel that it is of limited significance. The so-called performance model still plays a considerably more important part in the landscape architect's university design theory. Horst Rittel used it in an attempt to render the complex, usually iterative process of planning and designing large buildings abstract to the extent that a set of systems that could apply elsewhere are revealed. He made a clear distinction between issues applying exclusively to one's own design project or object and those that should be seen as part of the context. The performance model relates two subsystems, the object model and the context model, to each other. The aim of this control model was to find the best possible configuration of values for assessing different

Students can find out on the two hectare institute site that the design process does not end on paper, but rather in constructing and later tending the results of their work.

design variants under given circumstances and particular judgement standards. This was intended to launch a learning process by continually changing variables; the way the problem was understood was changed permanently and systematically intensified.

Rittel's method came into being at a time when architects and industrial designers were tying to make design more scientific with the aid of formulae that are as objective as possible and can be applied operationally. Many of these attempts were pronounced failures by their own "inventors" such as Christopher Alexander and others, even in the seventies, and people returned to seeing design as a mainly intuitive and creative activity. Peter Latz was aware of this, but adapted the performance model, combining it with mainly intuitive design components and developing it further as a meta-theory of design and applying it beneficially to landscape architecture. "The exciting thing about this method is that the analysis becomes an integral part of the model and is not separated from the design process, as tends to be the case in landscape planning, for example," explains Peter Latz. "The analysis is not limited in our case. The particular advantage of the method is that the design process can be embarked upon in a controlled way practically as soon as the first pieces of information have arrived, and then made more precise by multiple repetition of the process."[65]

"This method imposes organization. This is not innovative in itself, but it does ensure innovative approaches, because these are not immediately swept under the table in the discussion, instead certain ideas can be assessed at the same time for their potential value and

Climate and energy considerations where taken into account when conceiving the faculty building, such as that the large areas of grass should face south. Peter Latz influenced the building design considerably.

DESIGN AS EXPERIMENTAL INVENTION

relevance. [...] There are many people who poke fun at this model because they have been socialized into expecting great artistic genius. But if you ask these critics if they have never worked in a team, the criticism usually collapses upon itself. In fact the performance model is a very important method to use in teamwork, where everyone knows his or her place, and when it is his or her turn." It is about systematizing complex tasks and planning requirements to a greater extent and to make them operable and organized within a team, in the interests of greater manageability. This method particularly proves its worth as part of a project-based course as at the Technical University in Munich, where the preferred approach is to work in small student project groups on solving a whole variety of design problems.

Exponents of "free creative design" often see design methods like the performance model as obsessive attempts to make the design process more scientific that would ultimately lead to the "death of imagination". Peter Latz takes up a clear position on this: *"Almost all our most successful projects would not have been possible without making the approach more scientific to a certain extent. So it is about making decision processes soundly comprehensible. It is complete nonsense and usually mere camouflage tactics to keep asserting that designing is a process in which comprehensibility has no part to play. You can only make associations if you can put your hand into a very big box full of things you are familiar with and have studied. How else is it possible to test the viability of spontaneous ideas that are far away from being plans at this stage? It can only be done with criteria that have been cleanly developed in the context. If for example you have a project where you cannot establish any historical planes of meaning or corresponding elements in the context,*

After about two decades the wisteria has taken over the glazed entrance hall of the Weihenstephan faculty building. It displays the splendour of its blossom to the outside and bathes the inside in shadily muted light.

then all historical reminiscences are simply left out of the planning – this also means omitting the chapter on the identity of the location in the project report, the one that says that the history of the location has to be studied. Unless the context is clarified you can't give comprehensible reasons for insisting that very particular remains of former uses and designs should be retained in the project. It is only knowledge about the history of garden culture in particular that puts you in a position to develop sensible approaches in this direction."

Peter Latz demands nothing less of landscape architecture graduates than that they should have all the knowledge at their fingertips that has enriched the profession in the last 500 years, complemented by knowledge of engineering techniques. This has always made it particularly difficult for students with artistic ambition striving exclusively for creative freedom to find their way through the course easily. Peter Latz feels that even with the best working and design methods it is not possible to cover up a lack of background, of repertoires, and you have to expect that sooner or later inspiration through "gut feelings" will hit a barrier or run out. *"Fundamentally designing is about acquiring a depth and breadth of content that can also stand up to cultural examination. So it is not about creating something pleasant at first sight, you need timeless qualities, particularly in open spaces. We want our projects to be complete at some point, and that means they have to last at least 60 to 70 years old. When they have got that far, you think: they can easily get to 100 years or more. But that means that their information levels and languages must contain an appropriate number of timeless aspects if they are to keep communication over a long period. They must also always have some information levels in reserve in case some are destroyed, and they need to be the kind that it is not so easy to*

Trellises were attached also to the south-facing façades of the university building so that plants can climb up. Here students experience the lively interplay of nature and architecture in their immediate vicinity.

DESIGN AS EXPERIMENTAL INVENTION

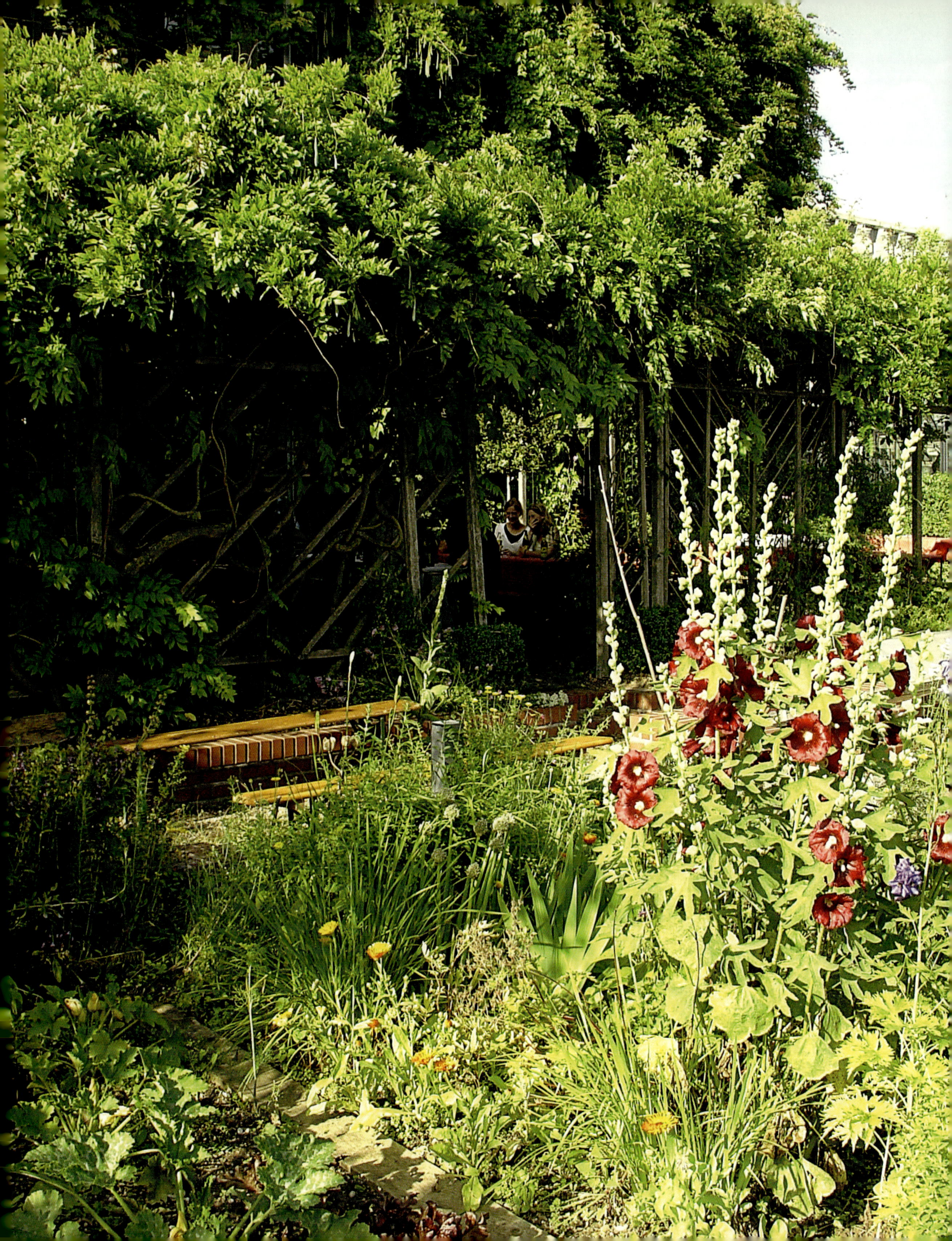

destroy. So it is extraordinarily dangerous to link information to the shortest-lived elements that could well be temporary, as sometimes happens at garden shows. The aesthetic language and the elements that belong to it thus need a good deal of information that can survive for long periods."

Because Latz always builds detailed knowledge of the art of garden design into his own projects and is not afraid to implant historical set-pieces or quotations – as in the Hafeninsel Saarbrücken, for example – his design approach is sometimes called Postmodern. In its rejection of historical connections, classical Modernism preferred landscape that was designed close to nature, as a background with a great deal of contrast, as a partner in dialogue with architecture and technology. From the point of view of complex design, the end of the Modernist paradigm does indeed seem like liberation: "This opened up a great deal and allowed landscape architecture to detach itself for the first time from the paradigm of presenting wild nature, and to use a variety of elements more freely. This certainly did not always lead to positive results, but opened up major new possibilities."[66] Design as experimental invention has become richer and more varied as a result. But this also brings increased responsibility for a profession intended to create lastingly viable living environments. Unduly free experimentation intended to release creative associations is not the aim of Peter Latz's design approach, which is aimed at precision. He is much more committed to the responsibility landscape architecture has for the long-term development of settled areas and landscape. Garden and landscape images that are effective with the public, easier to market and consume may be formally elegant, but they can scarcely show the degree of saturated depth and timeless quality that seem essential to ensuring long life for "good places", whatever their provenance.

"We do not create picturesque gardens, but they take on picturesque forms from time to time," insists Peter Latz with reference to his own garden. This applies equally convincingly to his students' university gardens.

DESIGN AS EXPERIMENTAL INVENTION

Notes

1 Latz, Peter quoted from: Weilacher, Udo: Between Landscape Architecture and Land Art, Basel Berlin Boston 1996; p. 125

2 Alberti, Leon Battista. On the Art of Building in Ten Books. Transl. Joseph Rykwert, Neil Leach, and Robert Tavernor. Cambridge, MA: The MIT Press, 1988. Book 9, II, 159v–160v, p. 255. Darmstadt 1989; p. 32

3 for this cf. Lévi-Strauss, Claude: The Raw and the Cooked. New York 1970

4 Pehnt, Wolfgang: Deutsche Architektur seit 1900. Munich 2005; p. 511

5 cf. Lévi-Strauss, Claude: The Raw and the Cooked. New York 1970

6 Luxembourg City Tourist Office (ed.): Architektur und Kunst im öffentlichen Raum – Kirchberg. Luxembourg die Stadt. Luxembourg 2006; no page

7 Latz, Peter: "Umweltspezifische Fachperspektiven. Die Sicht der Grüngestaltung" in: Kossak, Andreas (ed.): Visionen für eine umweltgerechte Gestaltung des Verkehrs in der Metropole Berlin/Brandenburg. Berlin 1994; p. 70

8 ibid.; p. 68

9 Latz, Peter quoted from: Weilacher, Udo: Between Landscape Architecture and Land Art. Basel Berlin Boston 1996; p. 132

10 Luxembourg City Tourist Office (ed.): Architektur und Kunst im öffentlichen Raum – Kirchberg. Luxembourg die Stadt. Luxembourg 2006; no page

11 cf. Burckhardt, Lucius: "Vom Entwurfsakademismus zur Behandlung bösartiger Probleme" (1973) in: Burckhardt, Lucius: Die Kinder fressen ihre Revolution. Wohnen – Planen – Bauen – Grünen. Cologne 1985; p. 226 ff.

12 Rittel, Horst/Webber, Melvin M.: "Planning Problems are Wicked Problems" (1973) in: Cross, N. (ed.): Developments in Design Methodology. Chichester 1984; pp. 134 – 144

13 Rittel, Horst/Webber, Melvin M.: "Dilemmas in der allgemeinen Theorie der Planung" in: Rittel, Horst: Planen, Entwerfen, Design. Stuttgart 1992; p. 21

14 Latz, Peter/Bartholmai, Gunter: "Die Hafeninsel – Visionen vom Wandel" in: Arcus 1984; p. 211

15 ibid.; p. 213

16 ibid.; p. 214

17 Latz, Peter quoted from: Weilacher, Udo: Between Landscape Architecture and Land Art. Basel Berlin Boston 1996; p. 128

18 ibid.; p. 130

19 Latz, Peter in: Garten und Landschaft 11/1987; p. 42

20 Reisinger, Claus: "Die Hafeninsel in Saarbrücken" in: Die Gartenkunst 1/1991; p. 99

21 cf. Weilacher, Udo: In Gardens. Profiles of Contemporary European Landscape Architecture. Basel Berlin Boston 2005; p. 164 ff.

22 Cf. Burckhardt, Lucius: "Der kleinstmögliche Eingriff" (1981) in: Burckhardt, Lucius: Die Kinder fressen ihre Revolution. Wohnen – Planen – Bauen – Grünen. Cologne 1985; p. 247

23 Latz, Peter in: Garten und Landschaft 11/1987; p. 48

24 cf. Hülbusch, Karl Heinrich: "Zur Ideologie der öffentlichen Grünplanung" in: Andritzky, Michael/Spitzer, Klaus (eds.): Grün in der Stadt – von oben, von selbst, für alle, von allen. Reinbek bei Hamburg 1981; pp. 320–330

25 Lührs, Helmut: "Der Bürger(meister)park Hafeninsel Saarbrücken" in: Bauwelt issue 39, 1990; p. 1973

26 cf. Eco, Umberto: Das offene Kunstwerk. Frankfurt 1990

27 Geuze, Adriaan: "Moving beyond Darwin" in: Knuijt, Martin/Ophuis, Hans/van Saane, Peter (eds.): Modern Park Design. Recent Trends. Amsterdam 1993; p. 38

28 Lubow, Arthur: "The Anti-Olmsted" in: The New York Times Magazine. May 16, 2004/section 6; pp. 47–53

29 Ganser, Karl: "Die Strategie der IBA Emscher Park" in: Garten + Landschaft 10/1991; p. 15

30 Forssmann, Jörg: "Landschaftspark Duisburg-Nord" in: Garten + Landschaft 10/1991; p. 21

31 Valentien, Donata: "Ein Park des 21. Jahrhunderts?" in: Garten + Landschaft, issue 10/1991; p.25

32 cf. Smithson, Robert: "The Monuments of Passaic" in: Artforum, December 1967

32a, 33 Haag, Richard quoted from: Pirzio-Biroli: "Adaptive re-use, layering of meaning on sites of industrial ruin" in: Arcade journal 23/2004

34 Valentien, Donata: "Ein Park des 21. Jahrhunderts?" in: Garten + Landschaft 10/1991; p. 30

35 Latz, Peter: "Industriefolgelandschaft als Aufgabe der Gartenkultur – Drei Annäherungen" in: Rohde, Michael/Schomann, Rainer (eds.): Historische Gärten Heute. Leipzig 2003; pp. 61/62; unpublished manuscript

36 Latz, Peter: "Drei Annäherungen", original manuscript dated 13.11.2002 on "Industriefolgelandschaft als Aufgabe der Gartenkultur – Drei Annäherungen" in: Rohde, Michael/Schomann, Rainer (eds.): Historische Gärten Heute. Leipzig 2003; p. 63; unpublished manuscript

37 Latz, Peter quoted from: Weilacher, Udo: Between Landscape Architecture and Land Art. Basel Berlin Boston 1996; p. 126

38 Latz, Peter: "Industriefolgelandschaft als Aufgabe der Gartenkultur – Drei Annäherungen" in: Rohde, Michael/Schomann, Rainer (eds.): Historische Gärten Heute. Leipzig 2003; p.64; unpublished manuscript

39 The symposium "l'intervento minimo" was held by Bernard Lassus together with Lucius Burckhardt in Gibellina-Nuova on Sicily in 1981. Among the participants were the art historian Stephen Bann, the vegetation expert Karl Heinrich Hülbusch and the artist Bazon Brock. Bernard Lassus was visiting professor at the Gesamthochschule in Kassel in 1985.

40 Lassus, Bernard quoted from: Weilacher, Udo: Between Landscape Architecture and Land Art. Basel Berlin Boston 1996; p. 117

41 Burckhardt, Lucius: "Der kleinstmögliche Eingriff" (1981) in: Burckhardt, Lucius: Die Kinder fressen ihre Revolution. Wohnen – Planen – Bauen – Grünen. Cologne 1985; p. 241

42 Latz, Peter quoted from: Weilacher, Udo: Between Landscape Architecture and Land Art. Basel Berlin Boston 1996; p. 132

43 Lubow, Arthur: "The Anti-Olmsted" in The New York Times Magazine. May 16, 2004/ section 6; p.52

44 Latz, Peter quoted from: Weilacher, Udo: Between Landscape Architecture and Land Art. Basel Berlin Boston 1996; p. 131

45 Latz, Peter: "Drei Annäherungen", original manuscript dated

13.11.2002 on Industriefolgelandschaft als Aufgabe der Gartenkultur – Drei Annäherungen" in: Rohde, Michael/Schomann, Rainer (eds.): Historische Gärten Heute. Leipzig 2003; p.62; unpublished manuscript

46 Latz, Peter: Über die Idee, Zeit sichtbar zu machen. The idea of making time visible" in: Topos. European Landscape Magazine. Issue 33, December 2000; p. 98

47 Latz, Peter: "Drei Annäherungen", original manuscript dated 13.11.2002 on – Industriefolgelandschaft als Aufgabe der Gartenkultur – Drei Annäherungen" in: Rohde, Michael/Schomann, Rainer (eds.): Historische Gärten Heute. Leipzig 2003; p. 62; unpublished manuscript

48 Weyl, Martin: "Hiriya as a Symbol" in: Tel Aviv Museum of Art (ed.): Hiriya in the Museum. Artists' and Architects' Proposals for Rehabilitation of the Site. Tel Aviv 1999; p. 155

49 Tal, Alon: "A Brief Environmental History of Israel" in: Tel Aviv Museum of Art (ed.): Hiriya in the Museum. Artists' and Architects' Proposals for Rehabilitation of the Site. Tel Aviv 1999; pp. 133 – 140 cf. also: Zitterbart, Eva: "Herzls Traum hat seinen Preis. Israels Umwelt ist in keinem guten Zustand" in: Wiener Zeitung, 1 Mai 1998

50 Weyl, Martin: "Hiriya as a Symbol" in: Tel Aviv Museum of Art (ed.): Hiriya in the Museum. Artists' and Architects' Proposals for Rehabilitation of the Site. Tel Aviv 1999; p. 153

51 cf. also: Weinberger, Lois: "Das Verlassen der Gärten. Die Müllhalde als Garten oder erster Entwurf 'Hiriya Dump'" in: Kunstforum International, vol. 145, May – June 1999; p. 224–232

52 cf. Seattle Art Museum (ed.): Earthworks: Land Reclamation as Sculpture. Seattle 1979

53 Weinberger, Lois: "Das Verlassen der Gärten. Die Müllhalde als Garten oder erster Entwurf 'Hiriya Dump'" in: Kunstforum International, vol. 145, May – June 1999; p. 230

54 ibid.; pp. 226/232

55 Latz, Peter: "Experimentelles Entwerfen", unpublished manuscript for a lecture on 21.2.2006 at the Leibniz Universität in Hanover

56 cf. Burckhardt, Lucius in: Ästhetik und Ökologie. Reprint Nr. 20. Gesamthochschule Kassel 1990; p. 7

57 Latz, Peter: "Experimentelles Entwerfen", unpublished manuscript for a lecture on 21.2.2006 at the Leibniz Universität in Hanover

58 Hard, Gerhard: "Landschaft als professionelles Idol" in: Garten + Landschaft 3/1991; p. 14

59 Latz, Peter: "Experimentelles Entwerfen", unpublished manuscript for a lecture on 21.2.2006 at the Leibniz Universität in Hanover

60 Latz, Peter: "Über die Idee, Zeit sichtbar zu machen. The idea of making time visible" in: Topos European Landscape Magazine, issue 33, December 2000; p. 96

61 Latz, Peter: "Experimentelles Entwerfen", unpublished manuscript for a lecture on 21.2.2006 at the Leibniz Universität in Hanover

62 ibid.

63 ibid.

64 Corboz, André: "Le territoire comme palimpseste", in: Diogeste, Diogène, no. 121, January – March 1983

65 Latz, Peter: "Experimentelles Entwerfen", unpublished manuscript for a lecture on 21.2.2006 at the Leibniz Universität in Hanover

66 ibid.

Project data for the projects shown in this book

P.13 ff.
Studio, house and garden in Ampertshausen, Kranzberg
Planning and construction: 1991 to today
Architect: Peter Latz, Landscape architect:
Anneliese + Peter Latz

P.15
House in Christbuchenstrasse, Kassel
Converting an old building: result of the "Pullover" research project by Prof. Peter Latz, Prof. Thomas Herzog, Dr. Rudi Baumann at the GH Kassel
Planning and construction: 1979 – 1983
Self-supply unit on 800 sq m of garden, built and run by Anneliese, Peter, Tilman and Jan Latz 1979 – 1988

P.34 ff.
University of Marburg on Lahnberge
General development plan for open spaces and infrastructure as a set of instruments for developing the general building programme
Planning: 1976 – 1980
Landscape architect: Dipl.Hort. Anneliese Latz ? Prof.Dipl.Ing. Peter Latz
Client: Land Hessen
Total area: 170 hectares

P.37 ff.
Hospital of University of Marburg on Lahnberge
Outdoor spaces, roofs, courtyards and terraces
Planning and construction 1st building phase: 1976 – 1985, gardens on buildings based on the "Green Roofs" research project with Dr. Fritz Duhme, TU Munich,
2nd building phase: 2000 – 2004
Client: Land Hessen
Architect 1st building phase: Staatl. Hochschulbauamt
Landscape architect 1st building phase: Dipl.Hort. Anneliese Latz – Prof.Dipl.Ing. Peter Latz
Architect 2nd building phase: AEP Stuttgart
Landscape architect 2nd building phase: Latz + Partner
Project director 2nd building phase: Burkhard Krüpe
Site management 2nd building phase:
Latz – Riehl – Schulz, Kassel
Overall area open spaces: 15 hectares

P.46 ff.
Ulm Science City on Eselsberg, University Section West
Planning and construction after competition (1st prize): 1988 – 1995 and 1997 – 2001
Client: Land Baden–Württemberg
Architect: Steidle + Partner, Munich
Landscape architect: Latz + Partner
Project director: Christine Rupp–Stoppel
Site management: Berthold Stückle, Ulm
Total area outdoor spaces incl. ecological compensation areas: 13 hectares

P.56 ff.
Plateau de Kirchberg, Luxembourg

P.56 – 58
Master plan for urban, landscape and artistic renovation
Planning: 1990 – 1993
Client: Fonds d'Urbanisation et d'Aménagement de Plateau de Kirchberg
Project team: Prof. Peter Latz – Prof. Jochem Jourdan, Prof. Kasper König (Frankfurt) – Christian Bauer (Luxembourg)
Total area: 220 hectares
Sub-projects commissioned by the Fonds d'Urbanisation et d'Aménagement de Plateau de Kirchberg and by the Ministère des Travaux Publics:

P.59 – 63
Boulevard John F. Kennedy
Conversion of the urban motorway into a boulevard
Planning and construction: 1993 – 2008
Project team: Latz + Partner – Lux Consult, TR Engineering, ARCOOP (Luxembourg)
Overall length: 3 km

p.64 – 66
Klosegroendchen, dune and water park with arboretum
Planning and construction: 1994 – 1996
Landscape architect: Latz + Partner
Total area: 30 hectares

p.68 – 78
Parc Central, Ecole Européenne et Centre National Sportif et Culturel
Planning and construction: 1995 – 2006
Architect Ecole Européenne: Christian Bauer, Luxembourg
Architect CNSC: Roger Taillibert, Paris
Landscape architect: Latz + Partner
Project directors: Aléth de Crécy, Stefanie Hackl, Christine Rupp-Stoppel
Site management CNSC: Latz – Riehl, Kassel
Total area: 20 hectares

p.70
Parc de la voie romaine and European arboretum
developed from existing reafforestation
Planning and construction: 1993 – 1999
Landscape architect: Latz + Partner
Total area: 10 hectares

p.66 – 68
Hôpital Kirchberg, Luxembourg
Planning and construction: 1998 – 2003
Client: Fondation François Elisabeth
Architect: INCOPA Saarbrücken
Landscape architect: Latz + Partner
Project director: Christine Rupp–Stoppel
Site management: Dutt – Hegelmann, Saarbrücken
Total area outdoor spaces: 2.5 hectares

P.73
Pedestrian precinct, Melsungen
Planning and construction after competition (1st prize): 1996
Client: Stadt Melsungen

Project team: Latz + Partner, HHS Planer und Architekten (Kassel)
Landscape architect: Latz + Partner
Site management: Latz – Riehl – Schulz, Kassel
Total area: 4500 sq m

p.82 ff.
Bürgerpark Hafeninsel, Saarbrücken
on the site of the old coal harbour
Planning and construction after specialist reports (1980 / 81) and political decision-making process (1981 – 1985): 1985 – 1989
Client and site management: Stadt Saarbrücken
Landscape architect: Dipl.Hort. Anneliese Latz – Prof.Dipl.Ing. Peter Latz
Project director: Gunter Bartholmai
Total area: 9 hectares
Award of the German Federation of Landscape Architects BDLA 1989

p.102 ff.
Landschaftspark Duisburg-Nord
Metamorphosis for the Duisburg-Meiderich steelworks
Planning and construction after international competition (1st prize): 1990 – 2002
Initiator and mentor: Internationale Bauausstellung Emscher Park, Prof. Dr. Karl Ganser
Client: LEG NRW, Emschergenossenschaft, KVR Essen
Project team: Latz + Partner (planning and general direction), Latz – Riehl (site management), G. Lipkowsky (architectural sub-projects)
Lead Design: Prof. Peter Latz
Project directors: Christine Rupp-Stoppel, Karlheinz Danielzik
Overall area (9 sub-projects): 230 hectares
EDRA Places Award, Edmond, OK 2005
Play & Leisure Award, Friedrichshafen 2004
Grande Medaille d'Urbanisme of the Académie d'Architecture, Paris 2001
First Rosa Barba European Award for Landscape Architecture, Barcelona 2000

P.134 ff.
Parco Dora, Turin
on former industrial sites
Planning after international competition (1st place):
from 2004
Client: Stadt Turin
Project team: Latz + Partner – STS Servizi Tecnologie Sistemi (Bologna) – Ing. Vittorio Cappato, Arch. Carlo Pession (Turin), Ugo Marano, Art (Cetara) – Gerd Pfarré Lighting Design (Munich)
Lead Design: Prof. Peter Latz, Tilman Latz
Project directors: Dörte Dannemann, Daniela Strasinsky
Total area: 37 hectares

P.148 ff.
Hiriya Landfill Restoration, Ayalon Park, Tel Aviv
Planning after international competition (1st prize):
from 2004
Client, initiator and mentor: Beracha Foundation Jerusalem, Dr. Martin Weyl
Landscape architect: Latz + Partner, after approval phase with Moria & Sekely, Tel Aviv
Project directors: Ulf Glänzer, Tobias Kramer
Total area: 118 hectares

P.168
Green Belt, Frankfurt am Main
Development planning 1990 - 1992
Client, initiator and mentor: Stadt Frankfurt, Tom Koenigs
Project team: Manfred Hegger – Prof. Peter Latz – Peter Lieser
Total area: 8000 hectares

P.173 ff.
Jardin de brume, Festival International des Jardins, Chaumont-sur-Loire 1998
Planning and construction: 1997/98
Client: Conservatoire International des Parcs et des Jardins et du Paysage, M. Jean Pigeat
Landscape architect: Latz + Partner
Construction: student workshop, directors Prof. Peter Latz, Albert Gründel, Stefanie Hackl

P.174
5 gardens for the 1985 Berlin International Garden Show, "Green Houses", Berlin – Britz
Planning: 1981 – 1985
Client: DEGEWO Berlin
Landscape architect: Dipl.Hort. Anneliese Latz ? Prof.Dipl.Ing. Peter Latz
Project director: Gunter Bartholmai
Gardens made and run for BUGA 1985 Berlin GMbH with student groups from TU Munich, directed by Prof. Peter Latz, Daniel Sprenger, Gerhild Lögler

P.175
Small natural gardens
Planning as part of the "Small natural gardens – model designs in Regensburg und Schweinfurt" research project by the landscape architecture and planning department 1985 – 1989
Client: Bayerisches Staatsministerium für Landesentwicklung und Umweltfragen
Model small gardens realized in student workshop, direction Prof. Peter Latz, Dr. Gunter Bartholmai

P.176 ff.
Technische Universität München, Institute for Landscape Management and Botany
Main structure open space, roofs, green façades
Planning: 1986 – 1988
Client: Land Bayern
Landscape architect: Dipl.Hort. Anneliese Latz – Prof. Dipl.Ing.Peter Latz
Total area: 1 hectare
Individual items designed and realized via student workshops and in the Institute for Landscape Architecture and Landscape Planning from 1986 to today

Illustration credits

"Albatross": Duby Tal, Moni Haramati 152, 153
Administration des Bâtiments Publics Luxembourg 62
ALIFOTO s.r.l. Torino 134
Gunter Bartholmai 20 r., 171, 172, 175 t.l., b.l., b.r., 176, 177, 178, 179, 180, 183, 184
Beracha Foundation 149, 150
Chair for Landscape Architecture and Landscape Planning, TU München 103
Città di Torino 137
Fonds d'Urbanisation et d'Amenagement du Plateau de Kirchberg 76 r.
from: Marieluise Gothein: Geschichte der Gartenkunst. Leipzig 1926 96 b.
GrünGürtel-Projektbüro, Frankfurt am Main 168
from: Robert Hobbs: Robert Smithson: a retrospective view. New York, no year 107
Kommunalverband Ruhrgebiet; image no. 1082/85 105
Landeshauptstadt Saarbrücken 82
Bernard Lassus 110, 116
Anneliese Latz 21, 145
Michael Latz 47 r., 50 t.l., t.r., 54, 58, 65 t.m., t.r., 67 l., 72, 73 b.l., b.r., 74, 75 t., b.l., b.r., 78, 102, 114 t., 115 t.l., t.r., 117, 125, 129, 131 b.
Peter Latz 20 l.
Latz + Partner 13 t.r., 15, 22 r., 24 b.r., 28 l., 34, 37, 38, 40 l., 41 t.l., 42, 46, 48, 51 l., 56/57, 64, 65 t.l., 68 l., 69, 71, 85, 88/89, 100, 106, 111, 112 b., 114 b., 115 b., 118/119, 121, 122, 128 b., 132 r., 136, 138, 139 t.r., b., 140 b.l., t.l., t.m., b.r., 141, 142 t., b.r., 143, 144, 146, 147, 148, 154/155, 156, 158, 159, 160, 161, 162, 163, 164, 165, 173, 181, 182
Peter Liedtke 126 t.r., b., 127
from: Sutherland Lyall: Designing the new landscape. New York 1991 84
Sara Cedar Miller, Central Park Conservancy 10
Monika Nikolic 12, 13 t.l., 14, 16, 17, 18, 19, 22 l., 23, 24 t., m., b.l., 27, 28 r., 30, 31, 32, 86, 87, 90, 92 t., 93, 94 t., 96 t.l., 97, 99
outdoor.webshots.com 65 b.

Christa Panick 39, 40 r., 41 t.r., t.m., 43, 44, 45, 98 b., 101, 121 t.l., 123
Brigitte Schmelzer 47 l.
Jane Sebire 126 t.l., 128 t., 130 b.
Mary Randlett 108
Stein + Design 67 r.
Berthold Stückle 53 t.l.
ThyssenKrupp AG Corporate Archives 104
Susanne Wamsler 174
Udo Weilacher Cover, 20 l., 29, 41 b.l., 49, 50 b., 51 r., 52, 53 t.r., b.l., b.r., 55, 59, 61 l., 66, 68 r., 73 t., 76 l., 91, 92 b., 95, 96 t.r., 98 t.l., t.r., 112 t.l., t.r., 113, 120 l., 121 t.r., 124, 130 t.l., t.r., 131 t.l., t.r., 132 l., 133, 139 t.l., 140 t.r., b.m., 142 b.l., 175 t.r.
Lois & Franziska Weinberger 157
André Weisgerber 60, 61 r., 63, 77
Harf Zimmermann 120 r., 121 t.m.

Further selected projects and competitions

Crystal Palace Park, London
Master plan with Meadowcroft Griffin Architects and specialist planners, from 2006, comm.* LDA London

Kaohsiung Waterfront Renovation at Wharfs 1 – 22
2nd prize 2006 with LEF Cons.Env.- YCFA Arch.- EDA Int. Landsc. Arch. (Taiwan), Arch. M. Atzinger, G. Pfarré Lighting Design, WTM Ing.

Port Rambaud, Lyon
New design with Seralp, Solpaysage, G. Pfarré Lighting Design, from 2005, comm. SEM Lyon Confluence

Place Flagey, Brüssel
1st prize with D+A International, G. Pfarré Lighting Design, from 2005, comm. Ministère de la Region du Bruxelles-Cap.

Tangshan – Nanhu South Lake District, China
1st prize, development planning 2005/06, 2nd phase with Prof. Liu Xiaoming, comm. Stadt Tangshan

Orange County Great Park, USA
2nd place, 2005 with Royston Hanamoto Alley & Abey

Göttelborn Brownfield
1st prize, revitalization, from 2005, comm. IKS

Heidelberg Rail City
Open spaces with Iris Dupper, Belzer-Holmes Lighting Design, B. Stückle, from 2004, comm. Stadt Heidelberg

St. Chamond
Conversion and development planning with Seralp, Beterem, G. Pfarré Lighting Design, 2004–06, comm. EPORA

Urban squares, Esch-sur-Alzette
1st prize with Arch. Ch. Bauer Assoc., G. Pfarré Lighting Design, from 2004

Rainham Conservation Park, Rainham Marshes
Study with Arch. Peter Beard, 2003, comm. LDA London

Main station, Munich
1st prize 2003, Arch. Auer + Weber

Fazenda Paz, Maxaranguape/Natal, Brasil
Infrastructure consultancy 2003 – 06, comm. Peter Wiese

‚Wetterwechsel'
National Garden Show exhibition garden, 2005 Munich

Technical secondary school, Friedberg
1st prize, Arch. Auer + Weber, open spaces 2002–05, comm. Landratsamt Aichach-Friedberg

Stadt-Umland-Bahn Munich
Development study 2002–03, comm. Stadtwerke München

Primary and secondary school, Holzkirchen
1st prize, Rheinpark – Architekten, open spaces 2002–05, comm. BG Markt Holzkirchen – Landkreis Miesbach

Central bus station, Munich
1st prize, Arch. Auer + Weber, 2002–03 comm. LH München, from 2005 comm. Hochtief Projektentw.

Dachau Memorial
Main entrance and visitor centre (Arch. F. Nagler), from 2002, comm. Staatsbauamt

Main street and spa park, Bad Ems
Development planning 2002–03, comm. Stadt Bad Ems

Old/new port, Bremerhaven
New design with Latz – Riehl Partner, from 2001, comm. BEAN.
International Illumination Design Award of Merit, IESNA, New York 2006

Völklinger Hütte World Heritage Site
General plan, open spaces 2001–03

Jardin Public Aval, Lyon
1st prize with Kazuo Katase, 2001–04, comm. SEM de la Cité Internationale Lyon

Euregio Park Terres Rouges, Esch-sur-Alzette
1995–2002, comm. Stadt Esch

Deutsche Bundesstiftung Umwelt, Osnabrück
Arch. Herzog + Partner, open spaces 2000–02, comm. DBU

Solar-City Linz – Pichling
Masterplan with architects N. Foster – Th. Herzog – R. Rogers 1995–96, comm. Stadt Linz
Open spaces residential quarters (Arch. Herzog + Partner) 2000–04, comm. GWG, WAG
1st prize Central Square, Arch. Auer + Weber, 2000–06, comm. Stadt Linz

Konversion Base de Sous-Marins de Keroman, Lorient
1st prize 1999, with Arch. Paczowski/Fritsch

Döppersberg, Wuppertal
District development, work in interdisciplinary workshop 1999, comm. Stadt Wuppertal

Finsbury Square, London
New design 1998, comm. Jones Lang LaSalle

Strada Interquarters North, Milan
Development planning 1998/99, with Hanno Dutt, comm. City of Milan

Terminal II, Munich Airport
1st prize 1998, Arch. Herbert Kochta, open space concept

Tunnel under Mittlerer Ring, Munich South
Town planning report with Stracke und Zurmöhle 1997/98, open air spaces and roads from 1997

Shell Research Centre, Thornton
Open spaces with Ian Hamilton Finlay 1997–99

Potsdam Volkspark and National Garden Show, 2001
1st prize with F. Jourda Arch., HHS Planer + Arch., general plan 1996–97, construction of south park in 2001, comm. ETBF

Fröttmaning model building project
Arch. Herzog, Steidle, Hilmer + Sattler, from 1998, comm. BLS

Solar – City, Regensburg
Masterplan with Herzog + Partner, Foster + Partners, 1995–99

Mondorf-les-Bains
Urban development study with Arch. Ch. Bauer, F. Thyes 1997, homes and urban square with Schröder Ass. from 2001

Granta Park, Abington
Master plan with E. Parry Architects 1996–97, open spaces 1997–99, comm. TWI

SOKA – Bau, Wiesbaden
Arch. Herzog + Partner, open spaces 1995–2003, comm. SOKA – Bau.
Architectur + Technology Award Frankfurt 2006

Revitalization Böhlen – Lippendorf industrial landscape
1st prize 1996

Urban square at Kirschallee Barracks, Potsdam
1st prize 1996

Continuing education academy, Trier
Arch./comm. Bischöfl. Generalvikariat, open spaces 1995–98

Housing complex, Dortmund – Immermannstraße
1st prize, Arch. Steidle – Schmitz, open spaces 1995–98, comm. Stadtwerke Dortmund

Streets and squares, central Saarlouis
2. Preis 1995 with Arch. Ch. Bauer Assoc.

DeTeMobil headquarters, Bonn
Arch. Steidle – Schmitz, courtyards, roofs, energy concept 1993–96, comm. C+G Montag Verm. Verw.

Lechwiesen motorway service station
Arch. Herzog + Partner, open spaces 1993–96, comm. Autobahndirektion

Wacker office and housing complex, Munich
1st prize, Arch. Steidle + Partner, open spaces on roofs 1991–97, comm. Wacker Pensionskasse

Revitalization of coal and salvaged material works for Völklinger Hütte World Heritage Site
1st prize 1995, with Arch. Ch. Bauer Assoc.

Heiligenstock play park
Structural park concept 1992–93, comm. Stadt Frankfurt

Conversion of Mont – Cenis colliery, Herne – Sodingen
1st prize 1992

Windberg Abbey
Arch. Th. Herzog, open spaces for youth education centre, courtyard of cloister 1990–96

Wilkhahn, Bad Münder
Arch. Th. Herzog, open space development 1989, sub-sections built 1989–94

Landeszentralbank, Kassel
Arch. PAS, municipal gardens 1985–89

Landeszentralbank, Bad Hersfeld
Arch. and comm. LZB Frankfurt, 1984–88

"Grüne Häuser", Berlin
Arch. Steidle, Herzog, Schneider-Wessling, Faskel, Stürzebecher, open spaces 1982–85, comm. Degewo

Nicolaizentrum housing complex, Osnabrück
Arch. Schneider-Wessling, 1982–84

IBZ International Meeting Centre, Berlin
Arch. Steidle + Partner, 1980–83

Courtyards and streets in Nauwieser district, Saarbrücken
Analysis and general planning with Sabine Schmelzer-Biegler, 1979–80

Technische Hochschule Darmstadt, Campus Lichtwiese
1st prize und master plan with Haus-Rucker-Co 1977, sub-sections built 1977–83, comm. Staatsbauamt

Museum, Mönchengladbach
Arch. H. Hollein, open spaces 1976–82

Ecological and solar construction
Small projects planned and built from 1976

Saar – Hunsrück nature park
Research programme and general landscape planning with G. Kaule, P. v. Pattay, E. Schneider, M. Sittard, 1973–76, comm. Ministerium für Umwelt, Saarland
Landscape plans for sub-sections

Wattenscheid – Höntrop
General direction of town planning, open spaces and circulation, 1970–85, comm. DSK

Urban renewal, Dillingen / Saar
Refurbishment and land use planning with Arch. C. Schmitz und Prof. O. Neuloh, 1969–70

D S D headquarters, Saarlouis
Open spaces and development, 1969–71

Development of construction system for schools
SLS research project with Arch. C. Schmitz, Höhler/Weiß Ing., comm. Homburger Stahlbau

*comm. = commissioned by, given only if not clear from project title

Selected publications

Latz, Peter in *TOPOS: Grow! Current Tendencies in Architecture and Landscape*, Callwey, Munich 2006: "Metamorphosis". 60–65

in *TOPOS 50: Reflections*, Callwey, Munich 2005: "Landscape Architecture as an Intercultural Principle". 6–12

in *Historic Gardens Today*, ed. M. Rohde, R. Schomann, Seemann Henschel, Leipzig 2003: "Post-Industrial Landscape as a Task for Garden Culture". 60–65

in *TOPOS: About Landscape*, Callwey, Munich 2003: "The idea of making time visible". 77–82

in *Penser la ville par le paysage*, dir. A. Masboungi, ed. F. de Gravelaine, Projet Urbain, Éditions de la Villette et DGUHC, Paris 2002: "L'eau et la vegetation, strate écologique essentielle au projet". 44–52

in *TOPOS 41*, Callwey, Munich 2002: "Reclaiming public open space". 85–89

in *Manufactured Sites,* ed. Niall Kirkwood, Spon Press, London/New York 2001: "The metamorphosis of an industrial site". 150–161

in *do.co.mo.mo Ibérico – Arquitectura e Industria Modernas 1900 – 1965*, dir. p. Landrove, 2nd seminar report 2000: "Los extraordinarios jardines posteriores a la era industrial". 199–209.

in *IndustrieKultur – Mythos und Moderne im Ruhrgebiet*, Klartext Verlag, Essen 1999: "Spurensuche und Landschaftsarchitektur". 29–31

in *IndustrieNatur – Ökologie und Gartenkunst im Emscher Park*, Eugen Ulmer, Stuttgart 1999: "Der Blick hinaus...". 168–173

in *TN Probe 6/1998*, Tokyo: "Re-Discovering the Landscape". 113–097

in *Die Gartenkunst 1/1996*, Wernersche Verlagsgesellschaft, Worms: "Die Grünflächen auf dem Plateau de Kirchberg in Luxembourg". 153–160

in *Landscape Transformed*, Academy Editions, London 1996: "Emscher Park Duisburg". 54–61

in *Stadtparks Frankfurt*, ed. Tom Koenigs, Campus, Frankfurt/New York 1993: "Paradigma Park". 22–27. "Spielpark Heiligenstock". 28–33

in *Vision offener Grünräume*, ed. Tom Koenigs, Campus, Frankfurt/New York 1991: "Zwischen Bebautem und Belassenem". 39–61

in *Garten und Landschaft 11/1987*, Callwey, Munich: "Die Hafeninsel in Saarbrücken". 42–48

in *anthos 4/1984*, Hrsg. BSG/FSAP, Graf + Neuhaus, Zurich: "Visions of Change". 18–23

in *Werk, Bauen und Wohnen 9/1982*, Zurich: "Idyll or reality?". 28–31

Latz, Peter; Bartholmai, Gunter in *Gemeinsames Wohnen am Rüdesheimer Platz*, "Reihe Werkstadt" 12, Archibook, Berlin 1983:"Zur Grünplanung". 72–77

Latz, Peter; Herzog, Thomas in *Werk, Bauen und Wohnen 9/1982*, Zurich: "House and garden – an eco-system". 23–27

Latz, Anneliese in *Die Gartenkunst 2/2000*, Wernersche Verlagsgesellschaft, Worms: "Die Pflanze als Hauptdarsteller". 203–216

Latz, Anneliese und Peter in *Cities for The New Millennium*, ed. M. Echenique/A. Saint, Spon Press, London 2001: "Imaginative Landscapes out of Industrial Dereliction". 73–78

in *UIA Work Programme: Architecture of the Future*, ed. JIA, Tokyo 1999: "Water – a Symbol for the Ecological Rehabilitation". 113–097

Weyl, Martin in *TOPOS 51: Prospective Landscapes*, Callwey, Munich 2005: "Hiriya Dump Conversion". 76–80

von Behr, Karin; Nickig, Marion in *Künstlergärten in Deutschland*, Ellert & Richter 2005: "Duisburg-Nord: Auf der Suche nach neuen Naturbildern". 198–207

Lubow, Arthur in *The New York Times Magazine*, New York 2004: "The Anti-Olmsted". 46–53

Xiangrong, W; Qing, L. in *The new landscape in Europe*, Southeast University Press 2003: "Landschaftspark Duisburg Nord". 65–75. "Bürgerpark Hafeninsel Saarbrücken". 87–97

Jones, Louisa in *Reinventing the Garden*, Thames and Hudson, London 2003: "Mist Garden". 110–111

Diedrich, Lisa in *TOPOS: Parks – Green urban spaces in European Cities*, Callwey, Munich 2002: "No politics, no park: the Duisburg-Nord Model". 29–38

Tate, Alan in *Great City Parks*, Spon Press, London 2001: "Landschaftspark Duisburg-Nord". 114–122

Schröder, Thies in *Changes in Scenery*, Birkhäuser, Basel Berlin Boston 2000/2002: "Constructing physical nature". 64–77

Holden, Robert in *International Landscape Design*, Calmann + King, London 1996: "Landschaftspark Duisburg Nord". 12–17. "Hafeninsel, Saarbrücken". 22–27.

Herzog, Thomas in *Solar Energy in Architecture and Urban Planning*, Prestel, Munich/New York 1996: "Solar City Linz Pichling".

Weilacher, Udo in *Between Landscape Architecture and Land Art*, Birkhäuser, Basel Berlin Boston 1996/1999: "The Syntax of Landscape – Peter Latz". 121–136

Burckhardt, Lucius in *Eden – Rivista dell'Architettura nel Paesaggio 2/1993*, Berenice, Milan: "La memoria, come renderla visibile?". 46–51

Reisinger, Claus in *Die Gartenkunst 1/1991*, Wernersche Verlagesgesellschaft, Worms: "Die Hafeninsel in Saarbrücken". 73–101

Schille, P. in *Geo 2/1985*, Gruner & Jahr, Hamburg: "Grüner Wohnen". 10–32

Selected exhibitions and exhibition catalogues featuring work by Latz + Partner

"Groundswell – Constructing the Contemporary Landscape" Museum of Modern Art, New York, 25 February – 16 May 2005

Reed, Peter in *Groundswell – Constructing the Contemporary Landscape*, Museum of Modern Art, New York 2005: "Duisburg-Nord Landscape Park". 124–133

"graublaugrün" Museum für Europäische Gartenkunst, Düsseldorf, 28 March – 9 May 2004, from 2005 a travelling exhibition in German cities

Nathalie Collinet in *graublaugrün – Das Revier atmet auf: Der Emscher Landschaftspark*, Benrath Palace and Park Foundation 2004: "Landschaftspark Duisburg-Nord"

"Infrastrutture e Paesaggi Contemporanei" Istituto Universitario di Architettura di Venezia, September 2002

Maffioletti, S.; Rocchetto S. in *infrastrutture e paesaggi contemporanei*, Il Poligrafo, Padova 2002: "plateau de kirchberg luxembourg 1990–1999". 88–91

"Territories: Contemporary European Landscape Design" Harvard University, Graduate School of Design, 19 April to 24 May 2001: Duisburg-Nord Landscape Park; Kirchberg, Luxembourg

"100 Years of Landscape Architecture" Harvard University, Graduate School of Design, April/May 2000: Duisburg-Nord Landscape Park

"Rehacer paisajes – Remaking landscapes", 1a Bienal de Paisaje de Barcelona – The 1st Barcelona Landscape Biennial, March 1999

Fundación Caja de Arquitectos in *Rehacer Paisajes/Remaking Landscapes*, Font i Prat Ass. S.L., Barcelona 2000: "Klosegroendchen, parquet dunar y estanques de reteción / Klosegroendchen, dune park and retention ponds". 79

"Parque Duisburg Nord / Duisburg Nord landscape park". 138 "Revitalización de planta industrial en Völklingen / Steelworks in Völklingen". 237 "1er Premio Europeo de Paisaje Rosa Barba / 1st Rosa Barba European Landscape Prize". 256–267

"La Reconquista de Europa. Espacio público europeo, 1980–99", CCC – Centre de Cultura Contemporània de Barcelona 1999

Linne, Martin in *La reconquista de Europa, espacio público urbano 1980–1999*, CCC, Barcelona 1999: "El parque paisajista Duisburgo-Norte". 164–169

"Vertigo: The strange new world of the contemporary city", Glasgow 1999 Festival Company, 26 February – 16 May 1999

Leppert, Stefan in *Vertigo*, Ed. Rowan Moore, Laurence King, London 1999: "Landschaftspark Duisburg Nord – The rust belt blooms". 178–191

"VI Venice Biennale of Architecture", 15 September – 17 November 1999

Wachten, Kunibert in *Change without growth?* Ed. K. Wachten, Fr. Vieweg & Sohn, Braunschweig/Wiesbaden 1996: "The Ruin in the Park". 34–35

Prigge, Walter ibid.: "Superpositions". 99–107

"Par Exemple", Interréseaux with Patrice Goulet and Karl Ganser, April 1995 Paris, May 1995 Karlsruhe

Goulet, P.; Wustlich, R. in *Par exemple – Abbilder zeitgenössischer Architektur in Deutschland und Frankreich – Images d'architecture contemporaine en France et en Allemagne*, H. Schmidt, Mainz 1995: "Hafeninsel in Saarbrücken / Ile portuaire de Sarrebruck". 106–110

On Peter Latz and Partners

Peter Latz

Peter Latz was born in Darmstadt in 1939 and grew up in the Saarland as the eldest of eight siblings. At the age of 15, he helped his father, Heinrich Latz, to build a house. Then he left school to try working on landscape gardening in Hans Lang's firm in Bous, and to plant an orchard on his grandmother's plot of land. After graduating from high-school he studied landscape architecture at the Technische Hochschule in Munich, and after taking his diploma from 1964 followed the four year post-graduate education in town planning led by Prof. Kühn at the Institute of Urban Development and Regional Planning at the RWTH university in Aachen. This was linked with intensive practical involvement in urban renewal projects – mainly in the Ruhr district.

Peter Latz and his wife Anneliese founded their landscape architecture practice in Aachen and in partnership with Herbert Kuske in Saarbrücken in 1968. In 1970, he set up the SLS practice for interdisciplinary urban planning, system planning and landscape planning with the architect Conny Schmitz, and directed it until 1976.

Peter Latz was appointed as a university teacher at the Gesamthochschule in Kassel in 1973, and his family and practice followed one year later. He built his first home for his own family in Kassel; it tied him, his wife and their two sons Tilman and Jan into a long-term research project on passive solar energy and self-sufficiency. He was offered a professorship at the Technische Universität München-Weihenstephan in 1983, and the main practice was moved to this new workplace in 1988.

Kranzberg-Ampertshausen has housed the practice and the family home since 1991. Peter Latz built his second house there, turning a 100-year-old agricultural estate into an experimental field for horticulture and an ecological demonstration object.

Peter Latz won the First Rosa Barba European Landscape Prize, awarded in Barcelona, in the year 2000 for his pioneering planning for the Duisburg-Nord Landscape Park, and the Place Planning Award from the Environmental Design Research Association (EDRA) in Edmond, USA in 2005.

The Académie d'Architecture in Paris awarded Peter Latz the Grande Médaille d'Urbanisme in 2001.

University career

Peter Latz started teaching in 1968 as a lecturer at the Limburgse Akademie voor Bouwkunst in Maastricht, running architecture training projects that were closely linked with practice. He became full professor of landscape architecture at the Gesamthochschule in Kassel in 1973, advocating project-oriented studies from the outset, and running applied research for alternative construction technologies in open spaces and architecture with his colleagues. In 1983 came the call to the Landscape Architecture and Landscape Planning department at the Technische Universität München-Weihenstephan, from which he will retire in spring 2008 after 25 years of increasingly international teaching activity.

Peter Latz has been active in higher education seminars, workshops and symposia all over the world since the nineties. He has been visiting professor at the Harvard University Graduate School of Design and is Adjunct Professor at the University of Pennsylvania School of Design.

Anneliese Latz

Anneliese Latz, née Riedl, was born in 1940 in Linz an der Donau. She grew up in the Tyrol as the eldest of four siblings. After graduating from high-school and practical work in horticulture she studied landscape architecture at the Technische Universität München-Weihenstephan, graduating with a diploma in 1963. After working in local and regional planning in Munich and Saarbrücken and on a free-lance basis in the Prof. Kühn – Dipl.Ing. Meurer town planning office in Aachen she founded her own landscape architecture practice with her husband Peter Latz in 1968, in which she still works as partner and managing director.

Tilman Latz
Tilman Latz, the elder of two sons, was born in 1966 in Aachen. After graduating from high-school in Kassel and practical work in horticulture he studied landscape architecture at the Hochschule für Bodenkultur in Vienna and then at Kassel University. He graduated in 1993 with a Diploma II, worked in his parents' practice for a year and then started post-graduate studies in architecture at the Architectural Association in London. After graduating at RIBA I level he completed his Diploma II in architecture at Kassel University.

Then came four years as project leader with Françoise Jourda Architectes in Paris. In 2001 Tilman Latz came back to Germany with his wife, the landscape architect Iris Dupper, to join the Latz + Partner practice as third partner.

Tilman Latz teaches and lectures in many countries, including as part-time lecturer during the winter terms 2001/02 and 2003/04 at the University of Pennsylvania School of Design.

The practice
The practice was launched in 1968 as "Dipl. Hort. Anneliese Latz · Dipl. Hort. Peter Latz · Landschaftsarchitekten", planning private gardens and outdoor public spaces. The most important project in the early years was access and open spaces for the Dillinger Stahlbau headquarters building, which demonstrated early entrepreneurial understanding of sustainable ecological design for the area around a building. New open space concepts for housing and large-scale urban and landscape planning emerged at the same time, often in group work with architects, sociologists and economists. From 1978 to 1984 the practice continued in partnership with Paul von Pattay in Kassel and Saarbrücken, and from 1984 first in Kassel and then in Freising, by the two founder partners.

Two projects shed light on the development of an independent approach to landscape: the landscape analysis and planning for the Saar-Hunsrück nature park, and the general development plan for the new University of Marburg on the Lahnberge in the mid seventies. Peter Latz's research, linked with his teaching in Kassel, in the field of alternative building technologies was related to open space concepts in close co-operation with architects, who were often friends.

The practice has traded as "Latz + Partner · Landschaftsarchitekten und Planer" since 1990. Tilman Latz became the third partner in 2001, the congenial designer at the side of Peter Latz.

A team of committed colleagues (mostly former students of Peter Latz) meets the high demands of planning and realizing projects. Some have been associated with the practice for many years: Gunter Bartholmai followed Peter Latz from Kassel to Munich as a teaching colleague in 1984. Wigbert Riehl went free-lance in 1985, has been professor at Kassel University since 2004 and still supports the practice as a realization partner. Christine Rupp-Stoppel has been a colleague for 20 years and has directed numerous projects at home and abroad.